Media Law in Botswana

Media Law in Botswana

Second Edition

Charles Manga Fombad

With Co-Author

Tachilisa Badala Balule

This book was originally published as a monograph in the International Encyclopaedia of Laws/Media Law.

Founding Editor: Roger Blanpain
General Editor: Frank Hendrickx
Volume Editors: Peggy Valcke & Eva Lievens

Wolters Kluwer

Published by:
Kluwer Law International B.V.
PO Box 316
2400 AH Alphen aan den Rijn
The Netherlands
E-mail: international-sales@wolterskluwer.com
Website: lrus.wolterskluwer.com

Sold and distributed in North, Central and South America by:
Wolters Kluwer Legal & Regulatory U.S.
7201 McKinney Circle
Frederick, MD 21704
United States of America
Email: customer.service@wolterskluwer.com

Sold and distributed in all other countries by:
Air Business Subscriptions
Rockwood House
Haywards Heath
West Sussex
RH16 3DH
United Kingdom
Email: international-customerservice@wolterskluwer.com

Printed on acid-free paper

ISBN 978-94-035-0030-0

e-Book: ISBN 978-94-035-0031-7
web-PDF: ISBN 978-94-035-0032-4

Printed in the United Kingdom.

The Author

Born in Nyen-Medig in Cameroon, Professor C.M. Fombad holds a Licence en Droit (University of Yaounde), LLM and PhD (University of London) and a diploma in Conflict Resolution (University of Uppsala, Sweden). He was, from 2003 to 2007, Professor *Honorarius* of the Department of Jurisprudence, School of Law, University of South Africa, South Africa and from 1997 to 2009, a Professor of Law at the Department of Law, University of Botswana, South Africa. He is presently a Professor of Law and Head of the Comparative African Constitutional Law Unit, Institute for International and Comparative Law, Faculty of Law, University of Pretoria, South Africa.

Professor Fombad is the author/editor of ten books and has published more than eighty articles in international refereed journals, more than two dozen book chapters as well as numerous other publications and conference papers. In 2003, Professor Fombad received the Bobbert Association prize for the best first article in the *Journal for Juridical Science*. He was also awarded the Wedderburn prize in 2003 for a paper that appeared in the *Modern Law Review*. He has on three occasions, received a special commendation from the University of Botswana Research Awards Committee for research excellence in 2004, 2005 and again in 2007.

Besides being a member of the international Advisory Board of the *International Encyclopaedia of Laws*, he is also a member of the Editorial Board of the following international journals: *the African Journal of International Affairs*, the International Encyclopaedia of Laws, Belgium, *Fundamina: A Journal of Legal History*, the *City University of Hong Kong Law Review*, the *Journal of Eastern and Central African Studies*, the *Revue Doctrinale du Droit Guinéen*, the *Pretoria Students Law Review*, the *McGill Journal of International Law & Legal Pluralism*, the *Africa Journal of Comparative Constitutional Law*, the *De Jure Law Journal Pretoria Students Law Review* (PSLR), the *Pretoria University Law Press*, and the *Review of Constitutionalism and Constitutional Change*. He is also the founding Editor-in-Chief of the *University of Botswana Law Journal* (UBLJ). He is a member of the following professional

The Author

associations: the Southern African Society of Legal History, the African Network of Constitutional Lawyers (ANCL), the International Association of Constitutional Law, and the Society of Law Teachers of Southern Africa. He holds the following positions in these international professional associations: member of the Advisory Committee of the African Network of Constitutional Lawyers (ANCL), member of the Advisory Committee of Southern African Society of Legal History and Vice President of the International Association of Constitutional Lawyers. He is a member of the Academy of Science of South Africa and an associate member of the International Academy of Comparative Law.

Professor Fombad has taught and written widely on media law, delict (tort), constitutional law, comparative law, legal history, HIV/AIDS and the law, and international law.

Co-Author

Tachilisa Badala Balule holds a Bachelor of Laws (University of Botswana), LLM and PhD (University of Edinburgh). He joined the University of Botswana as a Staff Development Fellow in September 1993, and was appointed a Lecturer in the Department of Law in October 1995. In May 2009, he was promoted to the rank of Senior Lecturer. He is presently an Associate Professor of Law in the Department of Law, University of Botswana, a rank which he was promoted to in December 2015. Professor Balule was the Head of the Department of Law at the University of Botswana from March 2010 to June 2013.

Professor Balule is the author of one book, more than ten articles in refereed international journals, more than a dozen book chapters as well as several other publications and conference papers. Professor Balule has been a member of the University of Botswana Law Journal since 2010 and is currently serving as the Assistant Editor responsible for finances and circulation. He has served on the Board of Trustees of the Press Council of Botswana and is currently a member of the Governing Board of PANOS Institute of Southern Africa. Professor Balule is an admitted Attorney in the higher courts of the Republic of Botswana.

Professor Balule teaches Media Law, the Law of Delict (tort), and Alternative Dispute Resolution.

Table of Contents

Table of Contents

Table of Contents

List of Abbreviations

ACHPR	African Charter on Human and Peoples' Rights
AIPPA	Access to Information and Protection of Privacy Act
ASMS	Automated Spectrum Management System
AU	African Union
BCP	Botswana Congress Party
BDP	Botswana Democratic Party
BHC	Botswana Housing Corporation
BIDPA	Botswana Institute of Development Policy Analysis
BMD	Botswana Movement for Democracy
BNF	Botswana National Front
BOCRA	Botswana Communications Regulatory Authority
BOPA	Botswana Press Agency
BPC	Botswana Press Council
BPP	Botswana People's Party
BTA	Botswana Telecommunications Authority
BTC	Botswana Telecommunications Corporation
Btv	Botswana Television
CKGR	Central Kalahari Game Reserve
DCEC	Directorate on Corruption and Economic Crime
DIB	Department of Information and Broadcasting
DIS	Department of Information Services
DSTV	Digital Satellite Television
FLSS	Frequency Licensing Subsystem
GBC	Gaborone Broadcasting Company
GDP	Gross Domestic Product

List of Abbreviations

HD PVR	High Definition Personal Video Recorder
HRC	Human Rights Committee
ICCPR	International Covenant on Civil and Political Rights
ICT	Information and Communication Technology
IEC	Independent Electoral Commission
ITU	International Telecommunications Union
JA	Acting Judge
JP	Judge President
MIC	Media and Information Commission
MISA	Media Institute of Southern Africa
NBB	National Broadcasting Board
NDB	National Development Bank
NGOs	Non-governmental Organizations
OAU	Organization of African Unity
PEEPA	Public Enterprises Evaluation and Privatization Agency
PSM	Public Service Media
PVR	Personal Video Recorder
RB 1	Radio Botswana 1
RB 2	Radio Botswana 2
SABC	South African Broadcasting Corporation
SADC	Southern African Development Community
UDC	Umbrella for Democratic Change
UDHR	Universal Declaration of Human Rights 1948

General Introduction

§1. The General Background of the Country

I. Political and Legal System of the Country

1. Botswana is one of the few African countries that since its independence in 1966, has maintained a stable and democratic system. In terms of civil and political rights, it can be classified as a free nation that has conformed to the fundamental principles of the rule of law, open and transparent democracy, and respect for human rights.

2. The Botswana Constitution, which became effective at independence in 1966, sets out the principle of separation between the three powers of the state. Executive powers are exercised by the president and his cabinet, legislative powers by the president and the National Assembly, and judicial powers by the courts.

3. The president is both head of state and head of government as well as commander-in-chief of the armed forces. Elections to this office are directly linked to the general election of members of the National Assembly, of which the president is an ex officio member. He holds office for the duration of the Parliament. The president is assisted by a cabinet appointed by him consisting of a vice president, ministers and assistant ministers.

4. Legislative power is exercised by a bicameral parliament, consisting of an elected National Assembly and a consultative *Ntlo ya Dikgosi* (formerly known as the House of Chiefs). The president, acting as ex officio member, and sixty-three elected members of whom fifty-seven are elected directly and six are elected indirectly, make up the National Assembly. The term of the National Assembly is five years. Bills passed by the National Assembly only become law after they have received the president's assent. Where he withholds his assent, the Bill may be presented to him again after six months, and he must either assent to it within twenty-one days or dissolve Parliament.

The forty-member *Ntlo ya Dikgosi* is composed of the chiefs of the eight principal tribes serving ex officio, four members elected by the sub-chiefs from amongst their own number, and three other members elected by the other twelve members of the house. Although the *Ntlo ya Dikgosi* plays an essentially advisory role, the constitution provides that all bills affecting tribal interests and chieftaincy matters must be referred to it.

5. The Constitution allows for a judiciary that interprets and administers the country's laws. The judiciary is independent of both the executive and the legislature. It is headed by the Chief Justice who is also the Chairman of the Judicial Service

Commission, which advises the president on matters relating to the appointment, discipline, and removal of judges.

There are two main streams of courts. The first consists of Customary Courts that administer customary law. There are well over 100 Customary Courts, which are located in both rural and urban areas. The second consists of the more formal modern courts of which the Court of Appeal is the highest and final jurisdiction of appeal in the country. Below it is the High Court which has divisions in Lobatse, Gaborone, and Francistown and several Magistrates' courts. All these courts apply Roman-Dutch law as modified by English law-inspired statutory law. In addition to this, there are a number of special courts and tribunals that have been set up either for special purposes or for special persons. Examples of this include the Juvenile Court, the Industrial Court and the Land Tribunal.

6. Botswana is one of the few African countries that have successfully practised multiparty democracy since independence. However, the political scene has been dominated by one political party – the Botswana Democratic Party (BDP), jointly founded in 1962 by the first President, Seretse Khama and his successor Ketumile Masire. There are at present, four other political parties worth mentioning: the Botswana National Front (BNF), which for a long time has been the official opposition, the Botswana Congress Party (BCP), the Botswana People's Party (BPP) and the Botswana Movement for Democracy (BMD). The latter was formed in 2010 by a group of politicians who split from the BDP over differences with President Ian Khama. The BNF, BPP and BMD contested the 2014 general elections under an umbrella organization, the Umbrella for Democratic Change (UDC), and won twenty seats in the National Assembly.

Starting with the pre-independence elections in 1965, the BDP has won an overwhelming majority of parliamentary seats in all elections. During the 1994 elections, it suffered a setback when the opposition BNF increased its representation from three to thirteen seats, winning all six seats in the urban areas. However, largely because of a split within the BNF, resulting in the creation of the BCP in 1998, the BDP had another landslide victory in the 1999 elections in which it won thirty-three seats as against six for the BNF and one for the BCP. The BDP however suffered another setback in the 2014 general elections when the combined opposition significantly increased their number of seats and for the first time got 47% of the popular vote.

7. Like most African countries, Botswana inherited its legal system from the colonial era, but with the peculiar feature shared by most countries in the Southern African region that it combined elements of two distinct European legal traditions namely, the Roman-Dutch and the English common law. Since the High Commissioners for Botswana during the British colonial rule had their seats at the same place as the seat of the British Cape Colony, most of the legislation enacted in the form of 'Proclamations' and designed for the Cape Colony, were simply extended to Botswana. In fact, by 1895, Botswana was effectively administered from the Cape Colony until 1909 when its administration passed on to the newly created Union of South Africa. On 10 June 1891, the High Commissioner acting under an 1891 British Order in Council, issued the General Administration Proclamation, section 19 of which reads as follows;

8. Subject to the foregoing provisions of this proclamation, in all suits, actions, or proceedings, civil or criminal, the law to be administered shall, as nearly as the circumstances will permit, be the same as the law for the time being in force in the colony of the Cape of Good Hope: provided that no Act passed after this date by the Parliament of the colony of Good Hope shall be deemed to apply to the said territory.

A new section 19 in a Proclamation of 22 December 1909 later replaced this. These two proclamations had several far-reaching consequences, which are still felt today.

First, the term 'Roman-Dutch' law does not feature in the two proclamations, but since this was the common law of the Cape Colony, it automatically became the common law of the then Bechuanaland Protectorate, and has since continued to be so until today. Roman-Dutch law was introduced into the Cape Colony, and in fact, the whole of what eventually became the Union of South Africa, by the Dutch East India Company in the mid-seventeenth century. It was a blend of Roman law, Canon law, the law Merchant and Germanic Civil law as found in Holland.[1] When the British took over the Cape Colony from the Dutch in 1791, they retained the pre-existing Roman-Dutch law as the common law while introducing English law by means of legislation.

Second, the 1909 Proclamation virtually transferred *holus bolus*, subject to certain specified exceptions, most of the statutory enactments made before 1891, from the statute books of the Cape Colony to the statute books of Botswana. The reception formula adopted was 'timeless', unlike that adopted in most former British colonies.[2]

Nevertheless, it must be noted here that the statutes thus received in Botswana were essentially based on or, influenced by English law.

9. The foundations of the Botswana legal system are therefore steeped in the Roman-Dutch law. Nevertheless, the adoption of an English-style judicial structure and system of administration of justice and the progressive introduction, since independence of substantive English law-based legislation in many areas has weakened the Roman-Dutch law legal substratum on which the legal system is built. What has probably enabled English law to penetrate even faster and deeper are some of the inherent weaknesses of the Roman-Dutch legal system. Like its civilian ancestors, it is characterized by a high level of abstraction and generality, which has made it particularly vulnerable to English law.

II. Geography and Population

10. Botswana is a landlocked country in Southern Africa and occupies an area of approximately 582,000 km^2. It is bordered by Zimbabwe, South Africa and Namibia, and touches Zambia at the confluence of the Zambezi and Chobe rivers in the extreme north.

1. *See* A.J.G.M. Sanders, *Legal Dualism in Lesotho, Botswana, Swaziland – A General Survey*, 1 Les. L. J. 51 (1985).
2. *See* A. Allot, *New Essays in African Law* (Butterworths 1970); and J.H. Pain, *The Reception of English and Roman-Dutch law in Africa with Reference to Botswana, Lesotho and Swaziland*, 11 CILSA 163 (1978).

11. With a population of about 2,266,900 according to the to the August 2017 population estimates, its population density of 3.1 persons/km^2 is quite low. The growth rate stands at 1.9%.

According to the 2011 national census, population estimates for its major towns were as follows:

Gaborone (capital)	264,300
Francistown	110,100
Selibe-Phikwe	49,411
Lobatse	32,864,29,900

12. The nomadic Basarwa (also known as the Bushmen) are probably the earliest inhabitants of what is now Botswana. Mainly the Tswana-speaking people later settled upon the area during the seventeenth and eighteenth centuries. By the time Europeans began to venture into the region in the early nineteenth century, Khama III had emerged as the most prominent indigenous leader. It were his appeals to the British for protection from both the Afrikaners in South Africa and the Matabele in the north that led the British to reluctantly establish a protectorate over the territory from 1885. Although a High Commissioner was appointed, his seat was in the Cape Colony. The Bechuanaland Protectorate, as Botswana was then known, was essentially governed from South Africa. Botswana remained a largely neglected territory until it became independent in 1966 under the leadership of President Seretse Khama, the grandson of Khama III.

13. At independence, Botswana was classified amongst the twenty-five poorest countries in the world. Since then however, it has combined an impressive record of dramatic economic growth, due to the discovery of diamonds in 1967, with political stability to become a middle-income country, with an income per head of about BWP 3,250 in 1997. The country's gross domestic product (GDP) recorded an average annual growth rate of 10% between 1981 and 1991, which was exceptional even by global standards. With growth rates of 7% and 6.8% in 1996–1997 and 1997–1998, respectively, the country was still able to enjoy economic growth at a time of generalized crisis.

14. About 90% of the population are Tswana, of Tswana-speaking descent. According to legend, the Tswana are descendants of the sons of Chief Malope who gave their names to the eight main tribes that inhabit the country today, namely: the Bakgatla, the Bakwena, the Bamalete, the Bamangwato, the Batawana, the Bangwaketsi, the Batlokwa, and the Barolong. Most of the rest of the population are Kalanga-speaking in origin, and the remainder are Basarwa and Herero. There is also a substantial non-African population of Westerners, mainly British, Afrikaners, and Asians.

The official language is English, while Setswana, which is widely spoken, has the status of co-official and national language.

III. Social and Cultural Values

15. As will be seen below,[3] the constitution of Botswana and several laws provide for freedom of speech and of the press, and the government generally respects this. While Botswana is not as ethnically and tribally polarized as most other African countries, there have been problems with the few minorities that are in the country. This has been the case with the Basarwa.

16. The Basarwa or San, who inhabit mainly the Central Kalahari Game Reserve (CKGR) in the Kalahari Desert, are the earliest known inhabitants of Botswana until the Bantus arrived in the sixteenth century. Although they are physically, linguistically and culturally distinct from the rest of the population, it is not clear whether they can be classified as a race distinct from the other inhabitants of the country. However, their distinct features have made them the object of discrimination by the rest of Batswana. The estimated 52,000–55,000 Basarwa represent only about 3% of the population and because of their isolation, ignorance of their civil rights, and lack of political representation, they have been marginalized politically and economically.

Traditionally, the Basarwa are hunter-gatherers but the creation of the CKGR by the colonial administration in 1961 has since substantially interfered with their traditional way of life and as a result many of them are now being employed as agricultural workers on farms or at cattle posts belonging to other ethnic groups. The most serious problems facing the Basarwa since independence has been the government's policy of resettling them outside the CKGR in order to preserve wildlife in the reserve for tourism. In fact, the conflict came to a head in 2002 when the government forcibly resettled those Basarwa living in the CKGR from the game reserve to the settlement areas of Kaudwane, New Xade, and Xere.[4] After the longest and most expensive case in Botswana's history,[5] the High Court ruled in favour of the Basarwa but the government has interpreted the judgment in a very restrictive manner as applying only to the 189 actual applicants in the suit and not to the rest of their community.

Because the Basarwa issue has attracted widespread international attention and the protracted and expensive High Court case was sponsored by several national and international non-governmental organizations (NGOs), the government has become extremely sensitive about the matter. As a result, journalists who report on these matters must tread a tightrope for fear of being branded as unpatriotic or trying to damage the international image of the country. In fact, the international NGO, Survival International, which has been the most prominent NGO championing the Basarwa case has been castigated as an enemy of the country because they have campaigned that Botswana's diamonds, the mainstay of the economy, should be boycotted on the grounds that the action taken against the Basarwa was in order to enable the government to open new diamond mines in the area. The effect of government sensitivity on the Basarwa issue is that many journalists and newspapers practise self-censorship and many of the issues affecting this marginalized group are no longer freely ventilated. In fact, in the past,

3. *See* Part I *infra* .
4. Because of the way they have been treated, the numbers of Basarwa are not only rapidly declining but their language, culture and way of life risks extinction with all the consequences that this entail to the country's cultural and ethnic diversity.
5. *See Sesana v. Attorney-General* [2006] 2 BLR 633.

the deputy permanent secretary in the then Ministry of Communications, Science and Technology urged public media editors to ensure that all negative reports on the Basarwa relocation programme produced by the independent media were 'contrasted strongly with freshly sought government statements'.[6]

§2. The Media Landscape

17. Botswana has since its independence shown a strong commitment to freedom of the mass media.[7] It did not clamp down on the media, like most Africans did, on the pretext of national unity and development. It can be argued that it is widely admired clean, transparent, and a democratic system of government has been sustained by its relatively free media. An analysis of two important international surveys which provide an indication of the state of the media in the different countries of the world, namely the annual worldwide press freedom index that has been published since 2002 by Reporters Without Borders, and the Freedom House Press Freedom Rankings, based on a survey conducted since 1980, show that Botswana has generally done reasonably well, especially when compared with the performance of other African countries.[8] But as we shall see later on in this study, there remain a number of challenges which need to be overcome. Notwithstanding this, it is still true to say that the overall regulatory environment is favourable to the growth of a free, diverse, and independent media.

I. Overview of Media Markets and Main Actors

18. With respect to ownership, control and accessibility, the media in Botswana is characterized by and large, by a reasonable degree of diversity, independence and sustainability. There are however important differences in this respect, between the print media on the one hand, and the broadcast media, on the other. Before we look at each of them, it is worthwhile recalling that Botswana is a very large, sparsely populated country (density of 3.1 persons/km^2). This factor poses enormous challenges not only for the distribution of newspapers but also for providing access to the broadcast media to some of the remote areas. Media accessibility has to some extent stifled the growth of the media industry because some in Botswana have relied on print and broadcast media from neighbouring South Africa, and even sometimes on Zimbabwe, on account of their easy accessibility as well as the perception that they are of better standards and quality.[9]

19. Although Botswana has a high literacy rate (84%) and newspapers are generally affordable as the prices are below that of a loaf of bread, an internationally

6. *See* 'Botswana state media "muzzled" in San expulsion affair', www.afrol.com/articles/22207.

7. *See* Part I *infra* .

8. *See* C.M. Fombad, *Media Reform in Southern Africa: Challenges and Prospects*, 5 Openspace 49–52 (2006).

9. *See* Balule, *Enhancing the Media's Democratic Role: A Comparative Study of the Legal Environment of the Media in Botswana and South Africa* 47–48 (Unpublished PhD thesis submitted to the University of Edinburgh 2003).

accepted form of measuring the affordability of newspapers, the print media has generally speaking been small. This is not only due to the small size of the population but also the fact that the widely dispersed nature of the population has made the distribution of newspapers throughout the country costly and problematic. Most newspapers are published in the urban areas or places with high population concentrations. The local private newspapers houses often distribute the newspapers themselves or use other means such as subscriptions, courier and various forms of public transport. This is not very efficient. At present, the government-owned and controlled *Daily News* reaches the widest section of the reading public.[10] Some South African newspapers enjoy a better distribution than local newspapers because they use the well-established and dominant South African-owned retail trading outlets which are found all over the country. The far easier access to print and broadcast media of neighbouring South Africa and until after the late 1990s, Zimbabwe, has to some extent impeded the rapid growth of the Botswana media industry.

Efforts have been made to improve on the distribution of local newspapers throughout the country. The *Daily News* has engaged private couriers and the newspaper is now able to reach many remote areas. Private newspapers are outsourcing distribution services to buses and other forms of transport in order to extend their circulation reach. Many private publications have increasingly become available to those who can afford it through the Internet. Even then, urban areas have better access than rural areas, especially remote areas with no electricity or those not being reached by the national grid. However, the number of villages being reached by electricity has been growing in recent years, especially after the introduction of an accelerated village electrification project.

20. The government-owned *Daily News* is directly under the control of the Media Division of the Office of the President.[11] Although the government has guidelines in place that are designed to promote editorial independence, the journalists who work for this paper are government employees and are vulnerable to political interference. The main source of information is the government-owned Botswana Press Agency (BOPA), which has often made its material available to the private media as well. However, most of the private media now rely on Sita News Agency, an independent agency that was set up in 2005 and Front Page News, a second agency which was set up that specializes in feature stories.[12]

21. The private print media, unlike the government-owned *Daily News* which is distributed free of charge, depends for their sustenance on the sale of the papers and the revenue generated by adverts. The government also competes with the private

---

10. This is the oldest publication in the country and was started by the British Protectorate administration in 1965 as the *Bechuanaland Daily News*. This name was changed after independence to *Daily News*. For a background on its establishment, *see* A.P.N. Thapisa & E. Megwa, *Situation Analysis and Profile of Mass Communications in Botswana* (A Consultancy Report Prepared for the Ministry of Finance and Development Planning 1998).
11. It is actually published by the Department of Information Services (DIS) which is controlled by the Office of the President.
12. *See* MISA & Friedrich Ebert Stiftung, *African Media Barometer. Botswana 2007*, 21.

media for advertising in the print and broadcast media,[13] which does not make for a level playing field, since these public media also depend on the tax payers' money. Besides this, no incentives have been given to the private media, whether by way of tax exemptions or otherwise. Government has sometimes also tried to use the threat of withholding the placement of its advertisements in private newspapers to punish papers that are hostile and too critical of it, and although this policy was declared unlawful in 2001, there is still a feeling that it is still applied in a more subtle manner.[14] Nevertheless, studies have shown that despite the small population, the advertising market is large enough and new titles appear all the time. There thus appears to be enough money to sustain a media industry that is growing all the time.[15] Table 1, from a 2014[16] study on the media scene in Botswana, shows the diversity of newspapers in the country.

Table 1 Media Diversity in Botswana

Newspaper	*Publisher*	*Circulation*		*Frequency*
Botswana Gazette	News Co. Botswana (Pty) Ltd	19,814	National	Weekly
Botswana Guardian	CBET	19,000	National	Weekly
Daily News	Department of Information Services	65,000	National	Daily
Echo	Echo Publishing (Pty) Ltd	10,000	National	Weekly
Midweek Sun	CBET	16,080	National	Weekly
Mmegi	Dikgang Publishing		National	Tuesday–Friday
Monitor	Dikgang Publishing	14,332	National	Weekly
Ngami Times	Ngami Times Printing & Publishing Co. (Pty) Ltd	5,000	National	Weekly
Sunday Standard	Tsodilo Services (Pty) Ltd	17,000	National	Weekly
The Voice	The Francistowner (Pty) Ltd	29,095	National	Weekly
The Telegragh	Tsodilo Services (Pty) Ltd	10,000	National	Weekly

13. This is exacerbated by the fact that the *Daily News* charges lower rates and does not collect its advertising revenue efficiently.
14. *See Media Publishing (Pty) Ltd v. Attorney-General* [2001] 2 BLR 485.
15. *See* MISA & Friedrich Ebert Stiftung, *African Media Barometer. Botswana 2007*, 27.
16. Friedrich Ebert Stiftung, *Botswana Office, Media Ownership in Botswana: Implications for News Coverage and Political Presentation* 7–8 (FES 20140).

Newspaper	*Publisher*	*Circulation*		*Frequency*
The Patriot on Sunday	Inskip Investments (Pty) Ltd	3,700	National	Weekly
Global Post	Global Media Group (Pty) Ltd	2,500	National	Weekly
Business Weekly & Review	Genuispoint Investments (Pty) Ltd	10,000	National	Weekly

22. As regards the broadcast media, the Communications Regulatory Authority Act, 2012 provides for two types of broadcasters, state and commercial. Previously, the Broadcasting Act, 1998, provided for public, private, and community broadcasting services. The Broadcasting Act 1998 was repealed in 2011. Before 1998, the broadcast media in Botswana was dominated by the state-owned *Radio Botswana* (RB), which enjoyed an absolute monopoly until 1998 when two commercial radio broadcasters were granted licences. The absence of a broadcasting policy had impeded the growth of commercial and community broadcasting as well as adversely impacted on the rationalization of the state broadcasting media and its transformation into a genuine public broadcasting service. In fact, a draft broadcasting policy was developed by the National Broadcasting Board (NBB) in a broad public consultation process in 2002, and was tabled before Parliament in 2006. Parliament failed to adopt the policy because of differences on the issue of public service broadcasting and community broadcasting services.

23. As in the case of the print media, the government broadcast media[17] is under the control of the Office of the President. Like the *Daily News*, *RB* started its operations as a pilot project established by the British Protectorate administration in 1965 and was then known as *Radio Bechuanaland.* It became RB after independence and now has two channels *Radio Botswana 1* (RB 1) and *Radio Botswana 2* (RB 2). The former operates as a public service channel and offers educational and informational programming targeted at educational institutions, particularly primary and secondary schools while the latter is a semi-commercial channel primarily aimed at providing entertainment.

24. The first private radio station to be granted a licence to operate in 1999 is *Ya Rona FM*. It broadcasts from Gaborone, the capital city and it initially covered a radius of 50 km. This was followed, later in that year by the licensing of *Gabz FM*, which like *Ya Rona*, is broadcast from Gaborone and covered an 80 km radius from the city. In 2007, the third station, *Duma FM* went on the air. In May 2007, the NBB issued nationwide broadcasting licences to all the three private broadcasters.

In spite of the fact that the Broadcasting Act of 1998 expressly provides for community broadcasting services, the idea of community radios appears to be so politically sensitive that it is one of the main reasons why the draft national broadcasting

17. For a full account on the history of the broadcast media in Botswana, *see* J.J. Zaffiro, *From Police Network to Station of the Nation. A Political History of Broadcasting in Botswana* (Botswana Society 1991).

policy presented to Parliament in 2006 was never adopted. The African Media Barometer for Botswana 2007 Report accurately summarized the problem in these words.

What has emerged from the debate of the policy so far is that there are many misconceptions about community radio and television broadcasting and that the issue has been highly politicized. This has been made worse by the fact that one of the communities wishing to set up a community radio station is the Basarwa from around the Gantsi area in the north of the country. There seems to be a fear in government circles that an international NGO – Survival International – which has been campaigning against the removal of San people from their original home in the CKGR, could use community radios to promote its cause. Some MPs felt that community stations would bring about tribal tensions and even quoted the example of genocide in Rwanda to make their point.

Efforts to demystify community radio and make parliamentarians and government aware of the potential of this sector as a development tool have so far been in vain.[18] And any hopes for community media in the country were dealt a severe blow by the repeal of the Broadcasting Act, 1998.

25. As regards television, Botswana's first national television, the state-owned *Botswana Television* (Btv) went on the air on 31 July 2000. Prior to this, there were two private television channels. One of them was the *Gaborone Broadcasting Company* (GBC), now e-Botswana, which initially started as a closed-circuit service in 1988 showing mainly British and American films and documentaries but later diversified its programmes. It is today the only private, terrestrial, free-to-air television station. The other one was M-Net, a subscription satellite television service that had been in operation since the 1980s. Meanwhile, those who could afford a satellite dish and analogue or digital decoders were able to have access to the South African Broadcasting Corporation (SABC) television channels and in some cases international broadcasters such as BBC World, Sky Television and CNN. Today, only MultiChoice allows access to cable television channels. Mention should also be made of two other television stations that are located in the mining towns of Jwaneng and Orapa, which are operated by DeBeers, the diamond giant. These stations are confined to these two towns. Table 2 shows the different actors in the broadcast sector in Botswana.

Table 2 Stakeholders in the media sector in Botswana

Radio/TV Station	*Owner*	*Classification*	*Coverage*	*Licensed or Unlicensed*
Gabz FM	Your Friend (Pty)	Ltd Private	National	Licensed
Ya Rona FM	Your Friend (Pty) Ltd	Private	National	Licensed
Botswana Television (Btv)	Botswana Government	State	National	Unlicensed

18. MISA & Friedrich Ebert Stiftung, *African Media Barometer, Botswana 2007*, 19–20.

Radio/TV Station	*Owner*	*Classification*	*Coverage*	*Licensed or Unlicensed*
e-Botswana	e-Botswana (Pty) Ltd	Private	50 km radius from Gaborone	Licensed
DSTV	MultiChoice Botswana (Pty) Ltd	Private	Pan-African	Unlicensed
Duma FM	Duma FM (Pty) Ltd	Private	National	Licensed
Radio Botswana 1	Botswana Government	State	National	Licensed
Radio Botswana 2	Botswana Government	State	National	Unlicensed
VOA	Foreign Government	State	International	Unlicensed

26. The media in Botswana can be considered to be quite diversified. However, the inadequacies of the Communications Regulatory Authority Act, 2012, and in particular, its failure to provide for PSB and community broadcasters, coupled with the absence of a national broadcasting policy will continue to create difficulties especially with respect to the status of the state-owned media and the ability of those who work there to operate independently without political interference or fear of persecution. The private media are presently doing fine even in the face of economic challenges such as the shrinking pool of advertising revenue.

II. Broadcasting Infrastructure

27. The broadcasting infrastructure consists of the integration of power, communications medium, terminals, and all the resource management required to meet national needs. This also involves access to networked communications networks. The access to networked communication is determined by a combination of availability and affordability of use of the network itself as well as the hardware and software needed for network interface. The existence of a good and up-to-date broadcasting infrastructure is critical to the existence of a credible, modern, and effective media.

In general, Botswana enjoys a modern infrastructure with high penetration fibre in urban areas. Nevertheless, public access to the different broadcasting media has been affected by several technological challenges which the government is making serious efforts to address. As elsewhere in Africa, there is a challenge of achieving national coverage for the state broadcasting services. Presently, only 80% of the population can receive radio transmissions from the state broadcaster and only 64%

can receive television transmissions. These figures however represent the top-end of transmission coverage for Africa as there are many countries where television is not widely available outside the main cities. Supply of electricity is often a significant limiting factor on television ownership. In 2007, the Government of Botswana embarked on a Transmission Expansion Project, which entailed the installation of forty-two TV transmitters (thirty-eight new and four existing) whose aim was to ensure that both radio and television would reach about 98% of the population.[19] For those with satellite dishes and decoders, television is 100% accessible. Nevertheless, the accessibility to television will remain limited by the fact that there is still a large portion of the population, especially those living in the rural areas who cannot afford a television set. The three private radio stations have also formed a signals distribution company which is tasked with the responsibility to expand the stations' broadcasting transmissions grid across the country.

28. Besides the Btv, the other widely used television service in Botswana is the Digital Satellite Television (DSTV) which is a multichannel DSTV service operated by MultiChoice, a South African company that launched this service in Africa in 1995. Subscribers in Southern Africa require a small dish to receive its transmissions. DSTV has expanded the range of products and services it offers its customers from the Personal Video Recorder (PVR) it introduced in 2005 to products such as the High Definition Personal Video Recorder (HD PVR) and DSTV Easy-View.

III. Technological and Economic Developments on the Media Markets

29. Vision 2016, a national document which was drawn up after elaborate consultations in 1997, presented Botswana's long-term vision by the year 2016 when the country celebrated fifty years of independence. It outlined the plans to achieve this vision as well as the challenges that lie ahead.[20] One of the vision goals was that Botswana will have entered the information age on an equal footing with other nations and will have sought and acquired the best available information technology as well as become a regional leader in the production and dissemination of information.[21] It went further to state that 'Botswana will have developed its communication capacity, particularly in the electronic media, radio and television.'[22] This blueprint also pointed out that 'Botswana must recognize the importance of information and of developing efficient information systems and networks for the support of research, education, development and communication with the rest of the world.'[23]

By 2016, the country had made tremendous strides in improving its broadcasting infrastructure. This was by and large made possible by huge investments in modern technology as well as the adoption of policies which have promoted competition.

19. *See* 'Botswana to up TV and radio coverage to 97+% of population, Namibia may follow', www.afridigital.net/archive/broadcast_023.html and, *Daily News* of 29 Oct. 2007.
20. *See* Presidential Task Group, *Vision 2016. Long Term Vision for Botswana* 5 (Government of Botswana 1997).
21. *Ibid.*
22. *Ibid.*
23. *Ibid.*, 19.

Vision 2016 has lapsed and it has been replaced with Vision 2036.[24] Vision 2036 does not say anything about whether the country has achieved its goal to acquire the best available information technology or whether it has become a regional leader in the production and dissemination of information. The new Vision also does not have any express statements on the electronic media, radio, and television.

30. In terms of the extent of progress towards an information society and the level of development of the information and communication technology (ICT) sector, Botswana ranks fourth after Mauritius, South Africa, and Namibia in ICT infrastructure development in the Southern African Development Community (SADC) region.[25] These ICT infrastructural developments have had tremendous impact on the growth of the media sector.

An example of a development in ICT infrastructure, which has helped the media market, was the acquisition by the Botswana Telecommunications Authority (BTA) of an Automated Spectrum Management System (ASMS), which comprises of a frequency licensing subsystem (FLSS), sixteen remote radio frequency monitoring stations spread throughout the country, and two mobile monitoring stations. The FLSS consists of two servers and workstations which are used for frequency licensing database maintenance and the licensing of radio users.

The BTA developed a broadcasting frequency plan for terrestrial digital broadcasting for both sound and television. The plan was developed through a regional radio communication conference organized by the International Telecommunications Union (ITU). The main task outstanding was to develop a migration plan from analogue television transmission to digital television transmission, known as the 'digital switchover'.[26] The country subsequently opted for the Japanese originated Integrated Services Digital-Terrestrial (ISDB-T) standard. It committed itself to meet the June 2015 deadline for migration of state-owned media, but at the time of writing, the switchover had not been met.

31. Since the adoption of a Privatization Policy in Botswana in 2000, there have been attempts to undertake a privatization exercise.[27] In pursuance of this policy, the government established the Public Enterprises Evaluation and Privatization Agency (PEEPA) as an autonomous agency with a mandate to carry out the twin tasks of effective monitoring and evaluation of public owned enterprises and companies and advising the government on the commercialization and privatization processes. PEEPA carried out a major review of the operations and activities of public enterprises, including an examination of opportunities for private sector participation in the activities

24. Presidential Task Group, *Vision 2036. Long Term Vision for Botswana: Achieving Prosperity for All* (Government of Botswana 2016).
25. *See* S.M. Mutula, *Making Botswana an Information Society: Current Developments*, 22(2) Electronic Lib. 145–147 (2004).
26. In fact a Digital Switchover Reference Group, with the Chairman of the NBB as chair, was established and in 2008, they developed initial recommendations which were submitted to the Minister of Communications, Science and Technology and included the need for a formal Digital Migration Working Group and specific terms of reference for such a group.
27. For a fuller discussion of the process so far, *see* Cornelius Dube, *Privatisation Initiative in Botswana: Any Bearing on Competition?*, *CUTS C-CIER Policy Brief*, No. 1/2008, www.cuts-ccier.org/7up3/pdf/PolicyBrief6.pdf.

of central government departments and authorities. The review culminated in the development and adoption of the Privatization Master Plan of 2005, which outlines strategies and practises to be followed to achieve privatization objectives and regulatory, institutional, and legal changes required to ensure effective implementation of the policy. A competition policy which provides a coherent framework that integrates privatization, deregulation, and liberalization of trade and investment into a strategy for promoting a dynamic market-led economy was adopted in August 2005. This led to the promulgation of the Competition Act, 2009 and establishment of the Competition Authority.

In the telecommunications market, the Telecommunications (Amendment) Act, 1996 had ended the monopoly of the Botswana Telecommunications Corporation's (BTC's) monopoly in the provision of all public services in line with the market liberalization policies that were being pursued. In 2005, a report commissioned by the BTA strongly recommended further liberalization of the telecommunications industry.[28] The consultants who prepared the report argued that full liberalization will *inter alia* help the government to roll-out telecommunications to rural areas more quickly and more cost effectively as well as help it to reach the goals of its ICT policy quickly and cost effectively. They also recommended that the liberalization programme and privatization programme of the BTC should proceed independently and also that, in order to increase investor confidence. There was further liberalization of the telecommunication sector in the form of the award of service-neutral licensing, which in turn led to the merger of the regulators NBB and the BTA.

Although the privatization initiative in the country appears to be well planned and is backed by a general commitment to embrace market-oriented reforms, there is clearly a danger of anticompetitive practices unless and until a sound competition law is finalized and adopted.

32. On the whole, it is fair to conclude that, as compared to most other African countries, the Botswana political and regulatory environment is quite favourable to the growth of a modern, diverse and vibrant media but is constrained by certain factors, such as the size of the population and its dispersed nature, about which nobody can do anything. It certainly has its weaknesses as the subsequent chapters of this monograph will show, but these could be overcome if there is political good will. But in Botswana, as elsewhere in the world, a free and vibrant media is not something that politicians look forward to with relish.

28. *See* Robert Hall & David Lewin, *Recommendations on Further Liberalisation of the Telecommunications Industry of Botswana. A Final Report to the Botswana Telecommunications Authority*, February 2005 www.bta.org.bw/pubs/Liberalisation%20Consult2.pdf. A similar study by the Botswana Institute of Development Policy Analysis (BIDPA) on the possibility of introducing competition policy in Botswana generally, also recommended the adoption of such a policy. S.M. Mutula, *Making Botswana an Information Society: Current Developments*, 22(2) The Electronic Lib. 144–153 (2004).

§3. Sources of Media Law

33. As explained earlier,[29] the Botswana legal system is a hybrid which combines elements of the Roman-Dutch law with elements of English law. Like most other African countries, Botswana is still preoccupied with the challenging task of modernizing its laws not only to reflect the socio-economic and political changes the country is undergoing but also the realities of the emerging digital and globalized world of today. Over and above this, the so-called third wave of democratization that swept through the African continent in the 1990s has left in its wake an acute human rights consciousness which African governments can no longer ignore. The desire to introduce provisions recognizing and protecting fundamental human rights, one of which is the freedom of the media, is one of the reasons that provoked the infectious fever of constitution-making or revisions in Africa in the post-1990 period. Although Botswana is one of the few countries that has until date maintained its independence constitution with only few changes, the 'third-wave' euphoria has nevertheless had an impact on the increased drive towards liberalization and privatization discussed above.[30]

In discussing the sources of media law in Botswana the constitution is inevitably the starting point. Besides the constitution, there are other important sources such as statutory law, and the common law. But because many aspects of the national media law have been influenced by or are based on international laws and treaties, this discussion will be prefaced by a consideration of some of the treaties that have influenced and continue to influence Botswana's national law. The discussion will end with a consideration of ethical codes which generally supplement the legal framework and sometimes even also provide a source for new national legislation.

I. International Influences on National Media Law

34. One of the most striking developments in international law since the end of the Second World War has been the increased concern over the protection of human rights including media rights. This revolutionary development has seen the individual being transformed from an object of international law into one of its subjects, capable of seeking remedies before international bodies for breaches of fundamental human rights. As a result of this, a government's treatment of its nationals has now become a legitimate concern of the international community. Perhaps the most significant aspect of these developments has been in the series of rules adopted to protect the human rights of individuals in the form of declarations, conventions, covenants, protocols, and so forth. Although not all these 'rules' are legally binding, they have played a very important part in promoting media rights at the national level.

In its very first session in 1946, the United Nation's General Assembly adopted Resolution 59(1) which stated:

Freedom of information is a fundamental human right and … the touchstone of all freedoms to which the United Nations is consecrated.

29. *See* para. 2 *supra* .
30. *See* para. 30 *supra* .

On 10 December 1948, what can be considered to be the first comprehensive statement of human rights of universal applicability, the Universal Declaration of Human Rights (UDHR) was adopted. Although not legally binding, the UDHR is regarded as reflecting the common understanding of those rights which its Member States have pledged to observe and respect and laid the foundation for subsequent international and regional instruments. The main international human rights instruments protecting media freedom can be put into two main categories viz., those of a global or universal character and those of a regional character. The main instruments of a global character are the UDHR of 1948[31] and the International Covenant on Civil and Political Rights (ICCPR) 1966.[32] For those of a regional character, the most important ones are the African Charter on Human and Peoples' Rights (ACHPR) 1981[33] which has now been reaffirmed and reinforced by the African Union's Commission on Human and Peoples' Rights' 2002 'Declaration of Principles on Freedom of Expression', or what is usually referred to the Banjul Declaration and the African Charter on Broadcasting. At a subregional level, in 2001, the heads of state of the SADC signed the SADC Protocol on Culture, Information and Sport, section 17 of which, *inter alia*, contains a commitment by the states to the 'promotion, establishment and growth of independent media, as well as free flow of information'.[34] There is also a Windhoek Declaration on Promoting an Independent and Pluralistic Media, which affirms the fact that the establishment and maintenance and fostering of an independent media is essential to the development and maintenance of a democracy. Although Botswana ratified the ICCPR and the ACHPR, as well as the Windhoek Declaration and SADC Protocol, none of these have been incorporated into national law.

35. As Botswana is a dualist state, the non-domestication of the above-mentioned international human rights instruments appears to deprive them of any effect at the national level.[35] Notwithstanding this, there are a number of ways in which these international instruments can and do impact positively on the quality of media rights protection in the country. This is mainly relevant in adjudication before the courts, but is by no means the only way. These instruments are relevant in the following situations:

- as an integral part of the domestic law upon its incorporation into national law;
- as an aid to statutory interpretation;
- as part of the common law of Botswana;
- as a factor to be taken into consideration by administrative bodies in exercising their discretion;
- through the activities of human rights institutions such as NGOs.

These different situations will be discussed below.

36. As regards the first situation, it is to be noted that although Botswana has generally speaking, signed and ratified only a few of the numerous international human

31. *See* Art. 19.
32. *See* Art. 19.
33. *See* Art. 9.
34. Also *see* Art. 20 of this Protocol.
35. *See* C.M. Fombad, *The Protection of Human Rights in Botswana: An Overview of the Regulatory Framework*, in *Essays on the Law of Botswana* 8–15 (C.M. Fombad, Juta & Co. 2007).

rights instruments, these instruments in principle, will only have effect at the national level when the ratified instrument is actually domesticated by an Act of the legislature giving it effect as part of national law. It is a firmly established principle of English constitutional law, received as part of the common law received in Botswana, that an international instrument does not constitute part of the domestic law until it has been incorporated by an Act of Parliament.[36]

37. The second situation is that, an instrument which has been signed, whether or not it has been ratified and domesticated, still has important legal consequences domestically as an aid to statutory interpretation. In dealing with the position where the instrument has been signed but has not been domesticated, Amissah JP in *Attorney-General v. Dow*, cited with approval the following passage from the judge *a quo* in the same case:

I bear in mind that signing the Convention [the Organisation of African Unity (OAU) Convention] does not give it the power of law in Botswana but the effect of the adherence by Botswana to the Convention must show that a construction of the section which does not do violence to the language but is consistent with and in harmony with the Convention must be preferable to a 'narrow construction' which results in a finding that section 15 of the constitution permits discrimination on the basis of sex.[37]

In doing so, the court basically followed the well-established presumption in statutory interpretation that courts will strive to interpret legislation in such manner that it will not conflict with international law. The judge went further to explain this thus:

> Botswana is a member of the community of civilised States which has undertaken to abide by certain standards of conduct, and, unless it is impossible to do otherwise, it would be wrong for its courts to interpret its legislation in a manner which conflicts with the international obligations Botswana has undertaken. This principle, used as an aid to construction as is quite permissible under section 24 of the Interpretation Act….[38]

This well-established common law presumption has therefore only been reinforced by section 24(1) of the Interpretation Act, which allows courts to refer to 'any relevant international treaty, agreement or convention' as an aid to statutory interpretation. Such an approach however must only be adopted when the domestic legislation in question is obscure. This caveat was explained by Diplock LJ in *Saloman v. Commissioners of Custom & Excise*, thus:

> If the terms of the legislation are clear and unambiguous, they must be given effect to whether or not they carry out Her Majesty's treaty obligations, for the sovereign power of the Queen in Parliament extends to breaking treaties, and

36. For a detailed discussion of the domestication of treaties in Botswana, *see* O. Tshosa, *Giving Effect to Treaties in Domestic Law of Botswana: Modern Judicial Practice*, 10 Les. L. J. 205 (1997); and O. Tshosa, *The Status and Role of International Law in the National Law of Botswana*, in *Essays on the Law of Botswana* 229–246 (C.M. Fombad, Juta & Co. 2007).
37. [1992] BLR 119, at 154.
38. *Ibid.*

> any remedy for such a breach of an international obligation lies in a forum other than Her Majesty's own courts. If the terms of the legislation are not clear, however, but are reasonably capable of more than one meaning, the treaty itself becomes relevant, for there is a prima facie presumption that Parliament does not intend to act in breach of international law, including therein specific treaty obligations; and if one of the meanings which can reasonably be ascribed to the legislation is consonant with the treaty obligations and another and others are not, the meaning which is consonant is to be preferred. Thus, in case of lack of clarity in the words used in the legislation, the terms of the treaty are relevant to enable the court to make its choice between the possible meanings of these words by applying this presumption.[39]

Two conclusions are possible here. First, the mere fact that a human rights instrument has not been incorporated through an Act of Parliament does not mean that courts in Botswana should pay no regard to it. Courts must consider them seriously when interpreting statutory language and wherever possible reach a conclusion that is consistent with Botswana's international obligations, unless of course, it is absolutely clear that Parliament wanted to disregard or break these treaty obligations. Second, one could go further to posit that the importance of international human rights instruments is such that courts should not only consider their provisions but should also take account of their philosophy and the practice that has emerged, as the Court of Appeal did in the *Dow* case. Unforeseen situations could thus be resolved in an imaginative and creative manner by the judges without waiting for Parliament to enact implementing legislation and in this manner the courts can reflect the changing perceptions when dealing with an old Constitution like Botswana's.

38. The third situation arises from the failure of the government to sign and ratify many of the core international human rights instruments. This, to a large extent denies its citizens the full benefits of these instruments, especially the right for them to submit complaints to the monitoring bodies charged with responsibility for receiving and considering individual complaints from citizens of contracting states. However, it does not necessarily mean that these particular instruments have no legal force domestically. As 'core international human rights instruments', it is very likely that many of them either do no more than codify well-established principles of customary international law or some of the principles contained in these instruments have been so widely accepted and adopted that they have crystallized into customary international law. Although it is quite clear from the discussion above on the domestication of treaties that Botswana is a dualist state, insofar as customary international law is concerned, the approach adopted is monist in effect. It is submitted that this is still the position, although in *Bojang v. The State*,[40] Gyeke-Dako J expressed doubts about this in these terms:

> Undoubtedly, the embodiment of these laudable principles in the different instruments reflects a universal acceptance of the right to legal representation as an important factor in the concept of fair trial. But even assuming that the right

39. [1966] 3 All ER 875.
40. [1994] BLR 146.

> to legal representation is part of the customary international law, can it be seriously contended that such right to legal representation as embodied in international instruments, automatically forms part of the municipal laws of Botswana without any act of legislative incorporation? I doubt it.[41]

It can be argued that this approach to the reception of customary international law was received as part of the reception of English law during the colonial period. This English law approach, which it is contended applies to Botswana, has been explained as follows by Ian Brownlie:

> The dominant principle, normally characterised as the doctrine of incorporation, is that customary rules are to be considered part of the law of the land and enforced as such, with the qualification that they are incorporated only insofar as is not inconsistent with Acts of Parliament or prior judicial decisions of final authority. This principle is supported by a long line of authority and represents a practical rather than theoretical policy in the courts.[42]

The contrary approach, that is, a procedure which would require the legislature to transform customary international law into municipal law would be impracticable simply because it would require a regular review of all changes of norms and principles of international law, a task which nobody can realistically do.[43] John Dugard has even gone further to state that the rule favouring the direct and immediate incorporation of customary international law is derived from Roman-Dutch law and not English law.[44] Although he was referring specifically to the pre-1994 South African situation, there is no reason why this is not true of Botswana, given the common historical roots of the two legal systems.[45] It can therefore be concluded that once it is shown that a principle contained in an international human rights instrument has crystallized into customary international human rights law, then unless such a principle has been expressly excluded by legislation or judicial precedent, it is considered as part of national law of Botswana, irrespective of whether or not the particular instrument has been signed and ratified. In other words, the courts in Botswana are obliged to take into account and treat as part of national law, any rules of customary international law that have emerged from human rights instruments that Botswana is not a party to.

Although the UDHR 1948, as its name suggests, is not a treaty and thus not binding, it has come to occupy a special status amongst international human rights instruments. Over the years, as a result of the fact that its provisions have now been extensively incorporated into numerous international and regional instruments as well as national constitutions and there have been numerous affirmations of its special status in judicial decisions, there is no longer any doubt that the principles contained in the

41. *Ibid.*, at 157.
42. Ian Brownlie, *Principles of Public International Law* 41 (Oxford University Press 2003).
43. P. Malanczuk, *Akehurt's Modern Introduction to International Law* 69 (Routledge 1997).
44. John Dugard, *International Law. A South African Perspective* 52 (Juta & Co. 2005).
45. The South African situation now has been clarified by s. 232 of the 1996 Constitution which states that, 'Customary International law is law in the Republic unless it is inconsistent with the Constitution or an Act of Parliament'.

UDHR are rules of customary international human rights law.[46] Nihal Jayawickrama cites examples of the innumerable pronouncements made at gatherings of states in which the UDHR has been endorsed as an obligatory standard.[47] The scholar, Sir Humphrey Waldock, is one of the many who have expressed the opinion that 'the constant and widespread recognition of the principles of the Universal Declaration clothes it in the character of customary law'.[48] On several occasions, the judges in the International Court of Justice and even in some national courts have stated unequivocally that most of the principles contained in the UDHR are now part of customary international law. For example, Ammoun J in his separate opinion in the *Legal Consequences for States of the Continued Presence of South Africa in Namibia (South West Africa) Notwithstanding the Security Council Resolution 276* Case opined, that 'although the affirmations of the Declaration are not binding qua international convention ... they can bind the states on the basis of custom ... or because they have acquired the force of custom through a general practice accepted as law ...'.[49] One can therefore argue that a party can rely on most of the provisions of the UDHR as customary international human rights law that are *ipso facto* directly applicable in Botswana as part of national law.

39. As regards the fourth situation, it can be argued that once an international human rights instrument has either been incorporated or its principles progressively become customary international law, these principles have to be considered not only by courts but also when a discretionary power is being exercised. For example, the strength of international human rights instruments in dealing with a situation where a statute gives police discretionary powers to restrict marches and demonstrations is that the police in exercising their discretion must take into account the overriding human rights of the marchers and demonstrators. Should the police exercise their powers unreasonably, their decision could be challenged by means of judicial review and the failure to conform to accepted human rights standards in restricting the marchers and demonstrators will certainly be a factor to be considered in determining whether or not they acted reasonably.[50]

---

46. It is worthwhile noting that since it is not a treaty, the question of signatures or ratifications did not arise.
47. Nihal Jayawickrama, *Hong Kong and the International Protection of Human Rights*, in *Human Rights in Hong Kong* 156–158 (R. Wacks, Oxford University Press 1992).
48. Humphrey Waldock, *Human Rights in Contemporary International Law and the Significance of the European Convention* 11 Intl. Comp. L.Q. 15 (1965).
49. ICJ Reports 1971, 18 at 76. *See also* the dissenting opinion of Judge Guggenheim in the *Nottebhom* Case (Second Phase) ICJ Reports 1955 at 63; Judge Tanaka in his dissenting opinion in the *South West Africa* Case (Second Phase) ICJ Reports 1966 at 293; and the dissenting opinion of Evensen J in the *Application for Review of Judgment No. 333 of the United Nations Administrative Tribunal* Case ICJ Reports 1987, at 173. At the domestic level, an important example is the decision of the United States Federal Court of Appeals in *Filartiga v. Pena-Irala* 630 F.2d 876 (2nd Cir. 1980) and Lord Reid in the English case of *R v. Miah* [1974] 1 WLR 683 at 698.
50. *See further*, A. Clapham, *The European Convention on Human Rights in the British Courts: Problems Associated with the Incorporation of International Human Rights*, in *Promoting Human Rights through Bills of Rights: Comparative Perspectives* 128–129 (P. Alston, Oxford University Press 1999).

Courts in Australia have even gone further than this. In *Minister for Immigration and Ethnic Affairs v. Ah Hin Teoh*,[51] the High Court stated that the executive act of ratification of a treaty (in this case, the Convention on the Rights of the Child) without legislative incorporation of the treaty, created a legitimate expectation that the Commonwealth government would act in accordance with its terms. As the court put it:

> Ratification by Australia of an international convention is not to be dismissed as merely platitudinous or ineffectual act, particularly when the instrument evidences international accepted standards to be applied by courts and administrative authorities in dealing with basic human rights affecting the family and children. Rather, ratification of a convention is a positive statement by the executive government of this country to the world and to the Australian peoples that the executive government and its agencies will act in accordance with the convention.[52]

Although this remains a controversial decision, the fact remains that one does not expect governmental agencies to make administrative decisions in a manner that is contrary to international obligations that the government has voluntarily undertaken.

40. Finally, through the activities of NGOs and other civil society organizations, international human rights instruments, especially those that have not been ratified or domesticated can be made to impact positively on the human rights situation in the country. The activities of NGOs and institutions such as the law commission, the Ombudsman's office, and human rights commission can act as an efficient conduit through which international standards can informally affect the domestic situation. They can exert pressure on government to ratify and domesticate these instruments or suggest ways in which the instruments can be domesticated or even intervene in court cases to draw the court's attention to policy implications of different interpretative options.

II. National Sources of Media Law

41. The main sources of media law in Botswana that will be discussed below are the constitution of 1966 as amended on numerous occasions, statute law, the common law administrative law, and executive action.

A. The Constitution

42. The principal source of law governing the media in Botswana is the 1966 Constitution. Although this is not expressly stated, the constitution establishes a system of constitutional supremacy (as opposed to the British system of parliamentary supremacy) meaning that the constitution is the supreme law of the land. In the famous case of *Attorney-General v. Dow*, Aguda JA put this matter beyond doubt when he stated that, 'the [Botswana] constitution is the supreme law of the land and it is meant

51. [1995] 128 ALR 353.
52. *Ibid.*, per Mason CJ and Deane J at 365.

to serve not only this generation but also generations unborn'.[53] As the supreme law of the country, all the applicable media law that is applied in Botswana today is either expressly or impliedly based on the constitution.

43. The provisions of the constitution that expressly regulate the media are found in the bill of rights in Chapter II of the constitution labelled 'protection of fundamental rights and freedom'. In this chapter of the constitution, the whole of section 12 deals with the 'protection of freedom of expression', while section 16 provides for instances where these rights can be derogated from. The exact scope of this constitutional protection of freedom of expression will be discussed below.[54]

No constitution, however long and comprehensive it may be, can contain all the laws that will regulate the media. It is because of this that the power to make statutes has been conferred on Parliament in section 86 of the constitution which states:

> Subject to the provisions of this constitution, Parliament shall have the power to make laws for the peace, order and good government of Botswana.

It is clear from the wording of this provision that although the constitution has given the Botswana Parliament the 'power to make laws for the peace, order and good government' of the country, these powers are not unlimited. These powers are 'subject to the provisions of the Constitution'. Section 86 in an indirect manner recognizes the supremacy of the constitution as the fundamental law of the land and the effect of this on all Acts of Parliament has been reiterated in several key decisions of the courts. For example, in *Petrus & Another v. The State*, Aguda JA said:

> Under a written Constitution such as we have in the Republic of Botswana, the National Assembly is supreme only in the exercise of legislative powers. It is not supreme in the sense that it can pass any legislation even if it is 'ultra vires' any provision of the Constitution. I believe it is clear, and this point must be clearly made, that every piece of legislation is subject to the scrutiny of the courts at the instance of any citizen, or indeed in an appropriate case at the instance of a non-citizen living in the country, who has the necessary 'locus' to challenge the constitutionality of legislation.[55]

While section 86 of the constitution thereby gives Parliament the powers to enact legislation in various areas, such as the media, it is clear that all such legislation must conform to the constitution. The courts have not hesitated to invalidate legislation that was found to be inconsistent with the constitution. Thus, in *Petrus & Anotherv. The State*,[56] the Court of Appeal declared section 301(3) of the Criminal Procedure and Evidence Act void on the grounds that it infringed section 7(1) of the constitution prohibiting torture, inhuman, or degrading punishment. In *Attorney- General v.* Dow,[57] the Court of Appeal also declared section 4(1) of the Citizenship Act void for violating

53. [1992] BLR 119 at 166.
54. *See* Part I *infra.*
55. [1984] BLR 14 at 33.
56. *Ibid.*
57. *Ibid.*

the constitutional prohibition of discrimination in sections 3 and 15, because it denied citizenship to the offspring of Batswana women married to foreigners, but granted citizenship to the offspring of Batswana men married to foreigners. A third example, this time of subsidiary legislation, is the case of *Students' Representative Council of Molepolole College of Education v. Attorney-General.*[58] The Court of Appeal held that a college regulation, which required pregnant women to leave college for at least one year, was contrary to section 15 of the constitution and therefore void. In fact, section 105 of the constitution vests exclusive jurisdiction on the High Court and the Court of Appeal to entertain any matter involving the constitutional interpretation. Although this gives these courts the power to review all legislation and quash any that infringe any constitutional provisions, it does not give them the power to nullify sections of the constitution itself. Thus, the High Court in *Kamanakao & Another v. Attorney –* General,[59] while expressing sympathy with the plaintiffs' case that sections 77–79 of the constitution discriminated against certain tribes in the country, pointed out that it had no powers to order their amendment.

B. Statutes

44. Most of the law that regulates the media in Botswana is based on statutes enacted by Parliament. The main statutes are:

- Communications Regulatory Authority Act, 2012 Media Practitioners Act, 2008.
- Cinematograph Act, 1970.
- National Security Act, 1986.
- Printed Publications Act, 1968.
- Penal Code, 1964.
- Cybercrime and Computer Related Crimes Act, 2007.
- Intelligence and Security Services Act, 2007.

The Communications Regulatory Authority Act, 2012 is without doubt the main piece of legislation regulating the broadcast media in Botswana today. It establishes the general regulatory framework for broadcasting services. It also provides for the establishment of Botswana Communications Regulatory Authority (BOCRA) as a regulator of the communications sector and sets out a framework for the licensing of television and radio broadcasters.[60]

The Cinematograph Act, 1970, regulates the making and exhibition of films within Botswana and licensing of cinemas. It primarily applies to the film, theatre, and entertainment sectors. The main purpose of the National Security Act, 1986, is to make provision for matters relating to national security, including official state secret information. As regards the media, the Act prohibits the dissemination or use of information that is prejudicial to the national security interests of Botswana. The Printed Publications Act, 1968, provides for the registration of newspapers and thus

58. [1995] BLR 178.
59. [2001] BLR 654.
60. *See* B.T. Balule, *Diversity and Pluralism Compromised: From the Botswana Brodcasting Act 1998 to the Communications Regulatory Authority Act 2012*, 34 Stat. L. Rev. 189 (2013).

applies essentially to the print media. The Media Practitioners Act, 2008 provides for the registration and accreditation of media practitioners and establishes a statutory Media Council. The Penal Code, 1964, which has been amended several times, establishes a Code of criminal law for Botswana. Some of its provisions have an impact on the operation of media practitioners. The Cybercrime and Computer Related Crimes Act, 2007, aims to combat cybercrime and computer-related crimes, repress criminal activities perpetrated through computer systems and facilitate the collection of electronic evidence. Enacted as a result of the recent liberalization of the IT services, this law is expected to provide the public with more access to news outlets. The Intelligence and Security Services Act, 2007 has been described as 'one of the most controversial laws to be passed by Botswana's National Assembly'.[61] This is because of the extensive powers it confers to the president to limit some of the media freedoms that the constitution guarantees in cases of national security.

45. Generally, the bulk of modern Botswana legislation consists of delegated or subsidiary legislation, which is the vast body of law created by subordinate bodies under specific powers delegated to them by Parliament. Section 49 of the Interpretation Act 1984 after stating that 'subsidiary legislation' has the same meaning as 'statutory instrument', defines a statutory instrument as, 'any proclamation, regulation, rule, rule of court, order, bye-law or other instrument made, directly or indirectly, under any enactment and having legislative effect'.

Delegated legislation has become an inevitable feature of modern governments for several reasons. First, because of the complex and protracted nature of the lawmaking process[62] and the pressure on parliamentary time, the legislative machinery will break down if Parliament attempted to enact absolutely every piece of legislation by itself. Second, legislation on certain complex and technical topics necessitates prior consultations with experts and stakeholders. The giving of some legislative powers to ministers and certain other bodies facilitates this consultation. Third, in enacting legislation, Parliament can neither foresee every administrative or other difficulty that may arise, nor is it feasible for there to be recourse to Parliament for amending an Act each time adjustments become necessary. Finally, in times of emergency, the government usually needs to take prompt and effective action outside its usual powers without resorting to Parliament.[63]

Examples of such subsidiary legislation on the media are the Telecommunications Regulations, 1997 (Statutory Instrument 52) made under section 26 of the Telecommunications Act, 1996 and the Broadcasting Regulations, 2004 (Statutory Instrument 97) made under section 23 of the Broadcasting Act, 2001. As discussed earlier,[64] any subsidiary legislation which violates either the constitution or the parent Act will be declared invalid by the courts.[65]

---

61. *See* MISA, *So This Is Democracy?*, 22.
62. For details about the lawmaking process, *see* C.M. Fombad & E.K. Quansah, *The Botswana Legal System* 183–193 (LexisNexis Butterworths 2006).
63. *See* s. 17 of the constitution.
64. *See* para. 42 *supra*.
65. *See further*, *Botswana Motor Vehicle Insurance Fund v. Marobela* [1999] 1 BLR 21 and *Maauwe & Another v. Attorney-General* [1999] 1 BLR 275.

C. Common Law

46. Although as discussed earlier,[66] the main source of Botswana media law is statutory, the common law still provides another vital source. Tebbutt JA in *Silverstone (Pty) Ltd v. Lobatse Clay Works (Pty) Ltd*, stated that the 'common law of Botswana is the Roman-Dutch law'.[67] This is technically correct provided it is understood as being Roman-Dutch law as influenced by English law.[68] Historically, the Roman-Dutch law that was extended to Botswana from South Africa, and which today is the substratum of the legal system was not pure Roman-Dutch law but rather a mixture of Roman-Dutch law and English law as developed in South African courts. In fact, a number of studies have shown that by the time the Roman-Dutch law that was applied in South Africa was extended to Botswana, it had been deeply penetrated by English law.[69] Be that as it may, the common law as a source of media law in Botswana is significant in two main ways:

> First, in those aspects of media law where the Botswana legislature has not made any laws and there are no relevant and applicable pre-independence statutes, then the common law principles will apply. A typical example of an area which is regulated essentially by common law principles because of the absence of detailed legislation is the law of defamation as well as the law of privacy.
>
> Second, even in areas which are regulated either partially or wholly by statutory law, common law principles are incrementally laid down whenever the courts intervene to interpret such statutes. This is based on the well-established English law doctrine of 'stare decisis', which is considered to have been received in Botswana, as part of the general reception of English law. The effect of this doctrine is that all court decisions, especially those interpreting statutes such as those regulating the media create a source of law which can be applied in subsequent cases where the facts are similar.[70]

D. Administrative Law

47. Despite the fact that media law is dominated by statutory law as complemented by subsidiary legislation, the enactments of Parliament and the bodies to which it

---

66. *See* para. 43.
67. [1996] BLR 190 at 194–195.
68. For a detailed discussion of this, *see* Fombad & Quansah, *The Botswana Legal System* 70–72 (LexisNexis Butterworths 2006).
69. *See* for example, R. Zimmermann, *Roman Law in a Mixed Legal System – The South African Experience*, in *The Civil Law Tradition in Scotland* 41–78 (R. Evans-Jones, The Stair Society 1995); and A.B. Edwards, *The History of South African Law. An Outline* 80–83 (Butterworths 1996).
70. *See further*, Fombad & Quansah, *The Botswana Legal System* 72–90 (LexisNexis Butterworths 2006).

sometimes delegates the lawmaking function cannot possibly keep pace with all of today's fast moving and often technical dilemmas. Hence, Parliament sometimes delegates lawmaking powers to some of the administrative agencies that it creates. It usually confers these agencies with the power to adopt and enforce administrative regulations which have the force of law. These are regulations on issues such as licensing which Parliament cannot itself oversee the everyday details of. Two examples will suffice.

The first is the Broadcasting Act, 1998 which provided for the creation of the NBB. According to section 10(1) of the Act, the functions of the NBB were:

(3) to issue broadcasting licences;
(4) to exercise control over and to supervise broadcasting activities, including the relaying of radio and television programmes from places in and out of Botswana to places in and out of Botswana;
(5) to allocate available spectrum resources in such manner as to ensure the widest diversity of programming and optimal utilization of the spectrum resources.

The second is the BTA which was established under the Botswana Telecommunications Act, 1996. Its mandate, under section 17(1) of the Act was to 'supervise and promote the provision of efficient telecommunication services in Botswana'.

Other more specific functions were stated as follows:

> Section 18(1). The authority shall publish, in the Gazette, the principles established by it, applied in the setting of tariffs by telecommunications systems operators and telecommunication service providers.

> Section 19. The authority shall settle any disputes that may arise between licensees and other service providers, and between licensees and members of the general public.

> Section 21(1). The authority may make regulations specifying the types of telecommunication equipment which may be used for providing a telecommunication service, for operating or connecting to a telecommunication systems, or for terminal equipment....

It is clear that the two authorities had powers that would seemingly violate the traditional concept of separation of powers. They could write rules, enforce them and even sometimes try or recommend to the Director of Public Prosecutions that alleged offenders should be tried. These enormous powers to make and enforce administrative regulations play a very important part in the corpus of media law and if not checked, can be abused. The courts, as in the case of subsidiary legislation, will intervene and invalidate any regulations or other actions taken by these bodies which violate the general scope of powers granted to it under the Act or where it is inconsistent with any other piece of legislation. Thus, in *Ntuane v. Your Friends (Pty) Ltd t/a GABS FM*

96.2,[71] it was held that although section 10(1)(b) of the Broadcasting Act gave the NBB the function of exercising control over and of supervising broadcasting activities, such functions should be for the purposes of the Act and not to play an interventionist role in litigation between broadcasters and aggrieved parties. In 2007, the BTA referred two matters relating to directives that it had issued to some operators to implement, to the Director of Public Prosecutions.[72] However, the best example of the supervisory and review powers that the courts exercise over the lawmaking authority conferred to these authorities by Parliament is the case of *MultiChoice (Botswana) Pty v. National Broadcasting Board.*[73] The case arose when the NBB sought to regulate MultiChoice like a television station whereas it is a service provider that receives its content from abroad. Walia J in the High Court ruled that the services provided by MultiChoice do not amount to broadcasting in the context of the Broadcasting Act. Hence, in issuing a broadcasting licence to an entity that was not providing a broadcasting service, the NBB acted *ultra vires*. The judge while pointing out that it is possible that the legislation empowering the NBB to exercise regulatory authority had not kept pace with advances in technology, stated that it was a defect that could not be remedied arbitrarily by the NBB assumed or conferring powers on itself.

E. Executive Action

48. Executive action in the form of presidential directives and other executive orders given by governmental executive officers do also form a source of media law, insofar as these legally compel or restrain a certain course of conduct, with the possibility of some sanctions for non-conformity with the orders or directives. Many of these directives, orders and even instructions are issued daily and often in a casual manner without regard to their legal validity. For example, with no broadcasting policy, mainly due to the disagreements over the issue of the transformation of the present state-owned media into a public service media (PSM), the mandate of the state media is currently based on a number of Information Media Directives, which in the absence of any law operate like the law governing them.[74] In 2007, the deputy permanent secretary in the Ministry of Communications, Science and Technology issued a memorandum which he said should be considered 'both as an instruction and as a guideline', in which he urged public media editors to ensure that all negative reports on the relocation programme of the Basarwa by the independent media were 'contrasted strongly with freshly sought government statements'.[75] It is now clear that questionable directives, instructions or advice from government officers or government departments can be challenged. The important precedent concerning questionable executive directives was laid down in

71. [2003] 1 BLR 49.
72. *See* , 'BTA – Botswana Country Report to CRASA 10th AGM – 2007', www.crasa.org/docs/reports/10AGM-BotswanaCountryReport.pdf.
73. Civil Appeal 022/07 (Unreported).
74. *See* , B.T. Balule, *An Overview of the Regulatory Framework of the Media in Botswana*, in *Essays on the Law of Botswana* 45–46 (C.M.Fombad, Juta & Co. 2007). More recently, *see* 'Government giving editorial directives to state media', www.pambazuka.org/en/category/media/51170.
75. *See* 'Botswana State Media "Muzzled" in San expulsion affair', www.afrol.com/articles/22207.

the 2001 High Court case of *Media Publishing (Pty) Ltd v. Attorney-General*.[76] The court held that a directive which banned government departments from placing advertisements in two private newspapers because they had been critical of the government was unconstitutional as it violated the newspapers' constitutional right to freedom of expression.

III. Ethical Codes

49. The Botswana Press Council (BPC), on 26 June 2004 launched a Media Code of Ethics.[77] The main purpose of the Code is to establish rules of conduct and rules of practice to be applied to all media and enforced by the BPC. Although the Code is expressly stated to 'govern the conduct and practise of all media practitioners, media owners, publishers and media institutions', the content appears to target mainly the print media.[78] The Code is not intended to be either comprehensive or exclusive, hence clause 1.2 states that 'each media sector shall submit its Code of Ethics, which will align to that of the Press Council of Botswana'.

The Code's preamble extols the virtues of freedom of expression and the right to access to information. Under general duties, the Code lays down certain general standards that media practitioners must comply with. These require that media practitioners must:

- maintain the highest professional and ethical standards;
- carry out their functions, which include informing, educating, and entertaining the public professionally and responsibly;
- take reasonable steps to ensure that they disseminate accurate and balanced information, and that their comments upon events are genuine and honest; and
- never publish information that they know to be false or maliciously make unfounded allegations about others that are intended to hurt their reputation.

The general duties section of the Code places a duty on media practitioners to be honest, fair, and courageous in their work and expects them to defend the principles of freedom of the press at all times. A section on good practice requires media practitioners to thoroughly verify the accuracy of their stories before publication; to correct any inaccuracies or distortions; and give any persons or institutions a right of reply where they have been unfairly criticized. The Code includes a number of rules of the profession. It prohibits media owners and practitioners from suppressing or distorting information on account of pressure from advertisers or other private interests. Media practitioners are enjoined from succumbing to cultural, political or economic intimidation. They are required to act in the public interest without undue pressure from any quarters. Media owners, and practitioners are neither prohibited from

76. [2002] 2 BLR 485.
77. This is available on their website, www.presscouncils.org/library/Botswana.doc and is discussed in Konrad Adenauer Foundation, *SADC Media Law: A Handbook for Media Practitioners* 37–43.
78. *See* clause 1.1 of the Media Code of Ethics.

suppressing the publication of information in return for financial or other benefits nor should they pay for information, unless this is demonstrably in the public interest, in which case the fact that such payments have been made must be disclosed. In reporting criminal investigations, media practitioners are not allowed to publish the name of the suspect until formal charges have been laid, unless this is in the public interest. The Code also prohibits the media from reporting on a person's private life unless this is in the public interest. Cases involving personal grief or shock are to be handled with due sensitivity. The Code contains a number of rules concerning the interviewing and photographing of children and generally requires that these be done with at least the consent of the child's parents or a legal guardian/authority. The Code contains a final section with certain editorial rules. The first of this prohibits the media from publications that are intended or are likely going to cause hostility or hatred towards persons on a variety of grounds such as their race, ethnic origins, nationality, gender, religion, and political affiliation. It also prohibits the publication of dehumanizing and degrading pictures of people without their consent. The second one prohibits the publication and broadcast of material prejudicial to the legitimate national security interests of the country but does not prevent information exposing corruption in security, intelligence, and defence agencies. The third rule forbids media practitioners from engaging in plagiarism. The final rule states that when sources are promised confidentiality, unless released by the source, this promise must be honoured.

Although the consequences for violating any of the clauses in this Code are not spelt out, clause 8.2 of the constitution of the BPC authorizes it to establish a Complaints Committee and an Appeals Committee to adjudicate upon and impose sanctions in respect of any complaints made against the media.[79] While the BPC could play a critical role in preventing lawsuits against the media, the Council has not been functional for the past years due to lack of resources and commitment from the media.

79. *See further* Part II, Chapter 6 *infra.*

Part I. Freedom of Speech

§1. Introduction

50. Freedom of speech lies at the very heart of media law. In order to fully appreciate the extent of media freedom in any country, it is necessary to examine the basis on which it operates. Where this base is solid, the scope for media freedom will be broad but where it is weak, this will inevitably impact negatively on the ability of the media to operate freely. This chapter is divided into four sections. The first section will look at the rationales for freedom of speech, the second will examine the constitutional basis of freedom of speech in Botswana, the third section will consider the constitutional limitations within which the exercise of this freedom is allowed and the last will look at some of the laws that limit freedom of expression in the country.

§2. The Rationales for Freedom of Speech

51. Throughout the ages, diverse philosophical arguments have been advanced to justify the need for a fundamental principle recognizing and protecting freedom of speech. A very brief and probably over-simplified glance at some of these classical arguments or theories will be attempted here for a number of reasons.

First, the language of some of the constitutional provisions on freedom of speech is reminiscent of some of these philosophical rationales. Second, some judges have not hesitated to use these rationales to explain and justify their interpretation of the free speech provisions. For example, in the Namibian High Court cases of *Fantasy Enterprises v. Minister of Home Affairs*[80] and *Louise Nasilowski v. Minister of Justice*,[81] the court in interpreting Article 21 of the 1990 Namibian Constitution which, *inter alia*, guarantees freedom of expression, cited with approval, the philosophical justifications for freedom of speech enunciated by Thomas Emerson in his book, *The System of Freedom of Expression.*[82] Gubbay CJ in the Zimbabwean case of *Re Munhumeso*[83] referred to the philosophical rationales as accurately reflecting the broad purposes of freedom of expression. Third, as Tom Campbell points out, these classical theories may, 'enable us to see which legislative or constitutional proposals may be philosophically defensible, which may be realistic ideas in different types of society,

80. Case No. A159/96 (Unreported).
81. Case No. 158/96 (Unreported).
82. (New York: Vintage Books, 1970).
83. [1995] 2 BCLR 125 (ZS).

and what sort of political institutions may be required to implement them'.[84] Some constitutional provisions may reflect a commitment to a particular concept of free speech and can thus best be understood and interpreted in the context of its broader philosophical underpinning rather than merely through the normal conventional techniques. This is however no *carte blanche* for resolving constitutional free speech cases solely on abstract philosophical arguments, especially where there are established legal precedents and textual and structural constraints within the constitution itself.[85]

52. A variety of arguments have over the years been proffered.[86] Three most commonly used rationales are: the argument from truth, the argument from democracy, and the argument from self-determination or self-fulfilment.

53. Historically, the argument from truth is the most durable rationale and has many variations and refinements at the core of which freedom of speech is conceived as the best means of advancing knowledge and identifying and accepting the truth. One of the strongest proponents, J.S. Mills argues that nobody has a monopoly on truth, neither has the majority in society any right to suppress the opinions of the minority however much they dislike them.[87] The theory demands that all discussion be kept open however true or false they might be. In American judicial and extra-judicial writings, this is characterized as the 'market-place of ideas', doctrine through which truth, it is assumed, will ultimately surface.[88] It will suffice to point out here that this argument suffers from at least two major flaws. First, it is too optimistic in assuming that all people are sufficiently educated and enlightened to be able to distinguish truth from falsehood. Yet, history provides too many examples of falsity triumphing over truth.[89] Second, the argument elevates the search for the truth and knowledge to a position of absolute priority over other values when there are, in fact, many instances when a legal system may justifiably prefer to protect other values at the expense of allowing the truth to be exposed.[90] Today, the argument from truth is considered to state no more than an ideal. As Frederick Schauer puts it, whether one adopts a Platonic or Aristotelian position that truth is intrinsically and self-evidently good, or the Millian argument based on the principle of utility or any of the more contemporary arguments for the value of truth, the advantages of truth are almost universally accepted.[91] The search for truth is very important and a highly desirable goal and a society with more knowledge is better than one with less knowledge.

---

84. Tom Campbell, *Rationales for Freedom of Communication*, in *Freedom of Communication* 20 (T. Campbell & W. Sadurski, Dartmouth Publishing Co. 1994).
85. *See* Eric Barendt, *Freedom of Speech* 3–4 (Clarendon Press 1987).
86. For example, Tom Campbell, *Rationales for Freedom of Communication*, 7 identifies seven rationales; Thomas Emerson, *Towards a General Theory of the First Amendment*, 72 Yale L. J. 877–885 discussion 4 (1963) ; and Kent R. Middleton, William E. Lee & Bill F. Chamberlin, *The Law of Public Communications* discussion 5 (Pearson Education Inc. 2003).
87. *See* J.C. Suffolk (ed.), *Areopagitica* (University Tutorial Press 1968); and D. Spitz (ed.), *On Liberty* (W.W. Norton 1975).
88. *See* Holmes J in *Abrams v. US* 250 US 616, 630–631 (1919), Brandeis J in *Whitney v. California* 274 US 357, 375–378 (1927), and Frankfurter J in *Kovacs v. Cooper* 336 US 77, 95–97 (1949).
89. *See* Frederick Schauer, *Free Speech: A Philosophical Enquiry* 26–29 (Cambridge University Press 1982).
90. *See ibid.*, 33; and Barendt, *Freedom of Speech*, 9.
91. Schauer, *Free Speech* 17.

54. The argument from democracy is probably the most attractive and certainly the most popular free speech rationale today. As it is based on the a priori assumption of an acceptance of democratic principles as the proper guidelines for the organization and governance of the state, it is wholly inapplicable to autocracies, oligarchies, and theocracies.[92] The content and scope of this freedom will depend on the nature of the democracy being practised. Freedom of speech according to this argument, serves at least two main purposes. First, it provides the widest possible scope for the exchange of information which voters need to exercise their sovereign rights intelligently. To this extent, it overlaps with the argument from truth in that what is required for a rational choice to be made is an informed consent. Because we cannot vote intelligently without full information, it has been argued that denying access to that information is as serious an infringement of the fundamental tenets of democracy as denying the right to vote.[93] Second, it involves the recognition of the right to criticize and reject all persons holding public office, especially political leaders. Its basic premise is that government is there to serve the wishes of the people and act as their servant. Talk of absolute freedom of speech is strong in the political sphere because it is here that the dangers of the abuse of any legitimate restrictions of freedom of speech are thought to be greatest. As Meiklejohn, one of the main proponents of this theory argues, it would be illogical for the government, as servant of the people, to preselect the information available to the people.[94] This argument is undoubtedly at its strongest in relation to 'speech' which has a clear political content and becomes weaker the more divorced from relevance to the citizen's democratic responsibilities the material becomes. Arguably, the most influential theory of the trio, the value of the argument from democracy in any given situation will depend less on abstract philosophical theories and more on the values and commitments embodied in the particular constitutional document in issue. It is because freedom of speech is a right most likely to be abused by elected politicians and government that it has been argued that it is best protected when put beyond legislative power in the constitution, preferably in the form of a bill of rights.

55. The third rationale in the trio, the argument for self-fulfilment or self-determination is probably the most contentious and weakest as a justification either for a free speech principle or its special recognition and protection in the constitution. In its simplest formulation, freedom of speech is considered to be an inherent aspect of human nature, part of the very essence of humanhood and the crucial means to enable him develop intellectually and fulfil his goals. Man is seen as continually striving for improvement and self-development and the free exchange of ideas is perceived as the means of achieving this objective. In a broad sense, the argument underscores the importance of freedom of speech but fails to offer any particular reasons why this is more valuable than anything else. It offers little guidance as to the scope and weight to be ascribed to such a right especially when it is clear that intellectual self-development could be attained in many other ways, other than merely through the communication of ideas.

92. *See* Schauer, *Free Speech* 35.
93. *Ibid.*, 38.
94. A. Meiklejohn, *Political Freedom: The Constitutional Powers of the People* (Oxford University Press 1965).

56. Despite the differences in the free speech theories, there is some consistency in their support for the recognition and possible constitutional protection of freedom of speech. None of these theories supports this as an absolute right, either generally or for a specified category of speech. It will therefore now be necessary to see how the Botswana constitution recognizes and protects the right to free speech and what restrictions it provides to check against abuse of this rights.

§3. Constitutional Protection of Freedom of Speech

57. Declarations of fundamental rights and freedoms, such as that on freedom of speech, pose serious problems to constitutional experts. It is not easy to find an appropriate formulation of words which would comprehensively but succinctly state the nature and scope of this right in a manner that is entirely satisfactory and realistic. The situation in Botswana is even more complex because there is no constitutional provision that expressly guarantees the freedom of the mass media. Nevertheless, sections 3 and 12(1) of the constitution are generally considered to be the provisions that guarantee freedom of expression in the country. Section 3 states:

> Whereas[95] every person in Botswana is entitled to the fundamental rights and freedom of the individual ... but subject to respect for the rights and freedoms of others and for the public interest to each and all of the following, namely –
>
> ...
>
> (b) freedom of conscience, of expression and of assembly and association;
>
> ...
>
> Subject to such limitations of that protection as are contained in those provisions, being limitations designed to ensure that the enjoyment of the said rights and

95. Although s. 3 appears in the substantive part of the constitution, in *Attorney-General v. Dow* [1992] BLR 119, at 165, it was argued that the use of the words 'whereas', at the beginning was indicative of the Legislature's intention that the provision should not be read as creating any binding obligation. The Court of Appeal in rejecting this argument held that since a contravention of s. 3 gives rise to enforcement by legal action, this was not only indicative of it being a substantive provision but also of the fact that it was a key or umbrella provision under which all rights and freedoms protected under that chapter of the constitution could be subsumed. In the Zimbabwean cases of *Re Munhumeso* [1995] 2 BCLR 125 at 125 (ZS) and *Rattigan v. Chief Immigration Officer, Zimbabwe* [1994] 1 ILR 243, the Supreme Court also held that a similarly worded section, although cast in the form of a preamble, conferred substantive rights on individuals and was not merely a guide to the framer's intentions.

> freedoms by an individual does not prejudice the rights and freedoms of others or the public interests.

The scope of this right is defined in section 12(1) as follows:

> Except with his own consent, no person shall be hindered in the enjoyment of his freedom of expression, that is to say, freedom to hold opinions without interference, freedom to receive ideas and information without interference, freedom to communicate ideas and information without interference (whether the communication be to the public generally or to any person or class of persons) and freedom from interference with his correspondence.

It is worth noting that the Botswana constitution uses the formulation 'freedom of expression'. Some constitutions use other formulations such as 'freedom of communication', 'freedom of speech', and 'freedom of the press' either exclusively or in combination with others. Besides, some writers have expressed doubts whether freedom of the mass media is necessarily covered by the phrase 'freedom of expression'.[96] Some of these difficulties can be traced, partly to the American First Amendment, which in a rather confusing manner refers to both 'freedom of the press' and 'freedom of speech'. Much ink has been spilt in debating the issue whether both expressions refer to two different phenomena or are synonymous rendering their joint use a redundancy.[97] The widely accepted view today is that 'freedom of the press' refers to 'written' communication, while 'freedom of speech' refers to 'oral' communication. It is however a dichotomy which also owes its origins partly to the fast disappearing distinction in the US legal system at least, between slander and libel, and is probably of little practical importance.[98] For all practical purposes, the expressions 'freedom of speech' and 'freedom of expression' can be considered as synonymous and are sufficiently broad in scope to cover 'freedom of the press'. The High Court in *Media Publishing (Pty) Ltd v. Attorney-General*,[99] was right to opine albeit *obiter*, that media freedom is an aspect of the freedom of expression provided for in the constitution. Support for this conclusion can be seen in the jurisprudence of the European Court of Human Rights which has held that the principles of freedom of expression are of particular importance as far as the press and other media are concerned.[100]

The *Media Publishing (Pty) Ltd v. Attorney-General*[101] case provides an illuminating example of judicial protection of the right of freedom of speech guaranteed under section 12 of the constitution. Because the applicant's two newspapers had published a number of articles critical of certain leaders, including the president and vice president, the government issued a directive to 'all Government ministries/Departments, parastatals and private companies in which the government is a shareholder' instructing them to

96. *See* J.P. Sangwa, *Zambia*, 7 Media L. & Prac. S. Afr. 8–15 (1998).
97. *See* F.S. Haiman, *Speech and Law in a Free Society* 10–12 (University of Chicago Press 1981); and Schauer, *Free Speech* 106–113.
98. Haiman, *Speech and Law in a Free Society* 10.
99. [2001] 2 BLR 485.
100. *Sunday Times (No. 1) v. United Kingdom* (1979) 2 EHRR 245.
101. [2001] 2 BLR 485.

cease advertising in the two newspapers. The applicants challenged the directive as unconstitutional on the grounds *inter alia*, that it violated their right to freedom of expression under section 12(1) of the constitution. The respondent argued *inter alia* that inasmuch as the government voluntarily decided to advertise in the applicant's papers, it was entitled without assigning a reason to withdraw from advertising in the papers. After coming to the conclusion that the clear reason for the directive was to punish the applicants for being too critical of the government, the court in granting the application for an interim interdict said:

> 'Government is not a consumer like any other consumer. It carries a lot of responsibilities vis-à-vis the individual. It carries the duty to protect the individual and to ensure that the rights and freedoms granted upon the individual by the constitution are not infringed....'
>
> The message implicit in the directive is that an individual being a beneficiary to governmental patronage, who in the exercise of its freedom of expression goes beyond what the government is comfortable with, faces the possible unpleasant consequence of losing certain benefits which it would otherwise have received. This hinders the freedom to express oneself freely.

58. Although in the case of *Media Publishing (Pty) Ltd v. Attorney-General* and other subsequent cases the higher courts in the country have held that the freedom of expression guaranteed under the constitution extends to the media, what still remains is a pronouncement on the scope of the media freedom guaranteed. Traditionally, fundamental rights have a negative character, they do not impose positive obligations on the government. There is however a view that the negative character of media freedom in itself is not sufficient to ensure the full enjoyment of the right.[102] There is emerging consensus in the United Nations, European and African human rights instruments that the protection of media freedom does impose positive obligations on the government to ensure the full enjoyment of the right, for example, in promoting diversity and pluralism in the media.[103] A generous and purposive interpretation of the provision guaranteeing media freedom demands that such interpretation should reflect the deeper inspiration and aspiration of the basic concepts of fundamental rights and freedoms of the individual as reflected in international human rights instruments. The guarantee of media freedom under the constitution of Botswana should be construed

102. A. Coltay, *The Concept of Media Freedom Today: New Media, New Editors and the Traditional Approach of the Law* 7 J. Media L. 36, 41 (2015).
103. *See* United Nations Human Rights Committee, General Comment No. 34: Article 19: Freedoms of opinion and expression, CCPR/C/GC/34 (adopted at 102nd session, Geneva, 11–29 Jul. 20110) para. 14; African Commission on Human and Peoples' Rights, Declaration of Principles on Freedom of Expression in Africa (adopted by the African Commission on Human and Peoples' Rights, meeting held at its 32nd Ordinary Session, in Banjul, The Gambia, from 17–23 Oct. 2002) Principle III; and *Case of Centro Europa 7 S.R.L and Di Stefano v. Italy*, Application no. 38433/09 (judgment of 7 Jun. 2012) para. 129.

as imposing both negative and positive obligations on the government to ensure to the full enjoyment of the right.

§4. CONSTITUTIONAL LIMITATIONS TO FREEDOM OF SPEECH

59. Freedom of speech has never been an absolute right in any society. The challenge is usually to find a formulation of words that will balance the right to freedom of speech with the protection of other legitimate interests that can be damaged by the abuse of the exercise of the right of freedom of speech. The limitations on the exercise of freedom of speech are provided in section 12(2) of the constitution which states as follows:

> Nothing contained in or done under the authority of any laws shall be held to be inconsistent with or in contravention of this section to the extent that the law in question makes provision –

(a) that is reasonably required in the interests of defence, public safety, public order, public morality or public health; or
(b) that is reasonably required for the purpose of protecting the reputations, rights and freedoms of other persons or the private lives of persons concerned in legal proceedings, preventing the disclosure of information received in confidence, maintaining the authority and independence of the courts, regulating educational institutions in the interests of persons receiving instruction therein, or regulating the technical administration or the technical operation of telephony, telegraphy, posts, wireless, broadcasting or television; or
(c) that imposes restrictions upon public officers, employees of local government bodies, or teachers,and except so far as that provision or, as the case may be, the thing done under the authority thereof is shown not to be reasonably justifiable in a democratic society.

This provision appears to incorporate a three-point test similar to that found in many international legal instruments on human rights in the determination of the legitimacy of restrictions on media freedom.[104]

First, a restriction must protect one or more of the interests enumerated in subsection 2. However, the list of permissible restrictions under the constitution is much broader than the permissible restrictions under international instruments.

Second, any restrictions must be done 'under the authority of law'. The phrase 'under the authority of any law', although worded differently from the equivalent phrases such as 'provided by law', 'prescribed by law', or 'in terms of the law', used in other constitutional and international human rights instruments, carries substantially the same meaning.[105] To satisfy this test, 'done under the authority of law', the law

104. These are discussed in B.T. Balule, K. Kandjii & R. Louw, *Undue Restriction. Laws Impacting on Media Freedom in the SADC* 18–19 (MISA 2004).

105. *See* the decision of the Zimbabwean Supreme Court in *Chavunduka & Another v. Minister of Home Affairs* [2000] 4 SA 1.

must be adequately accessible and formulated with sufficient precision to enable a person regulate his conduct accordingly.[106] In addition, the law must not confer unfettered discretion for the restriction of freedom of expression on those charged with its execution.[107]

Finally, any restriction must also be shown to be reasonably justifiable in a democratic society. What exactly is meant by 'reasonably required' or 'reasonably justifiable in a democratic society', has not been defined by the constitution. In Zimbabwe which has a similar constitutional provision, the Supreme Court in one case observed:

> What is reasonably justifiable in a democratic society is an illusive concept – one which cannot be precisely defined by the courts. There is no yardstick save that the quality of reasonableness of the provision under challenge is to be judged according to whether it arbitrarily or excessively invades the enjoyment of a constitutionally guaranteed right.[108]

Ultimately, the determination of whether a restriction is or is not reasonably justifiable in a democratic society involves a balancing exercise. The balancing exercise involves the application of the principle of proportionality: a restriction must be appropriate to achieve its protective function; must be the least intrusive amongst those which might achieve their protective function; and must be proportionate to the interest to be protected.[109] The decision revolves around the issue whether the benefits to a democratic society resulting from the specific restriction demonstrably outweigh the detriment caused to a democratic society by the restriction.

60. One of the consequences of the broad grounds for limiting freedom of speech is that laws which undermine this freedom are presumed to be constitutional unless declared otherwise by the courts. The right to challenge any violations of section 12 or the constitutionality of any legislation that violates this provision is provided for in section 18(1) and (2) of the constitution which states as follows:

> (1) Subject to the provisions of subsection (5) of this section, if any person alleges that any of the provisions of sections 3 to 16 (inclusive) of this Constitution has been, is being or is likely to be contravened in relation to him, then, without prejudice to any other action with respect to the same matter which is lawfully available, that person may apply to the High Court for redress.
> (2) The High Court shall have original jurisdiction –

106. *Ibid.*, and *Sunday Times (No. I) v. United Kingdom, supra* .
107. United Nations Human Rights Committee, General Comment No. 34: Article 19: Freedoms of opinion and expression, para. 25.
108. *In Re Munhumeso* [1994] 1 ZLR 49 (S). The European Court of Human Rights in *Handyside v. United Kingdom* [1976] 1 EHRR 737, has held that to satisfy the test whether a restriction is 'reasonably justifiable in a democratic society', it must be proved that there is a pressing social need for the restriction.
109. United Nations Human Rights Committee, General Comment No. 34: Article 19: Freedoms of opinion and expression, para. 34.

(a) to hear and determine any application made by any person in pursuance of subsection (1) of this section; or

(b) to determine any question arising in the case of any person which is referred to it in pursuance of subsection (3) of this section, and may make such orders, issue such writs and give such direction as it may consider appropriate for the purpose of enforcing or securing the enforcement of any of the provisions of sections 3 to 16 (inclusive) of this Constitution.

Section 18(3) even allows subordinate courts before whom any question concerning the violation of section 12 arises to stay the proceedings and refer the matter to the High Court, unless the subordinate court comes to the conclusion that the question is merely frivolous or vexatious.

§5. Statutory Limitations to Freedom of Speech

61. The problems of freedom of speech in Botswana, as in Africa as a whole, have been caused less by their non-recognition in the constitution, than by the manner in which the constitutional provisions are enforced in practice. As we noted above, although the Botswana constitution does not explicitly say so, the reference to 'freedom of expression' includes media freedom. In spite of this, and the fact that the media in Botswana as compared to that in most African countries is reasonably free and vibrant,[110] there are currently in force in the country a number of laws whose constitutionality is doubtful. Many of these laws are either couched in language that is too vague and obscure or give the government too much discretionary powers thereby creating uncertainty on the exact scope of freedom of speech that obtains in the country.

Some of those laws that unduly restrict media freedom will now be discussed.[111]

I. Printed Publications Act

62. This Act makes provision for registration of newspapers printed and published in Botswana. Section 5 makes registration with the Registrar of Newspapers compulsory.[112] This provision contains a long list of items, such as the title of the newspaper, its business address, and details of the publisher which the publisher is required to lodge with the registrar. Failure to comply with these registration requirements constitutes a criminal offence. The requirement of prior registration is an interference with a newspaper's right to freedom of expression and must comply with the limitation clause to the freedom in the constitution. The information that is required to be submitted to the Registrar of Newspapers could easily be published in the newspaper itself, which raises the question whether the registration requirements can be said to be reasonably justifiable in a democracy.

110. *See* Fombad, *Media Reform in Southern Africa* 49–52.

111. This section is based entirely on the study by Balule et al., *Undue Restriction. Laws Impacting on Media Freedom in the SADC* 21–32 (MISA 2004).

112. Cap. 20:01.

II. Anthropological Research Act

63. The Anthropological Act regulates the conduct of anthropological research. Section 3 requires that a researcher obtains permission from the minister.[113] The Act gives the minister very wide powers to refuse applications for permission to carry out anthropological research on the grounds that:

- the applicant is not fit and proper to conduct the research;
- the applicant does not have qualification to enable him to conduct the research adequately;
- the research may disrupt the life of the community or any inhabitants who are the subject of the research;
- the applicant is ill-equipped to conduct the research; and
- the safety of the applicant is at stake.

The Act effectively gives the minister excessive discretionary powers which can easily be abused in a manner that will hinder the scientific research and the dissemination of information resulting from it.

III. Cinematograph Act

64. The objective of the Act is to, *inter alia*, regulate the making and exhibition of cinematograph films and the licensing of cinemas.[114] The permission of the minister must be obtained before any filming is done and the film must be made in accordance with the terms and conditions of the permit. Failure to comply with the conditions of the permit exposes the producer, proprietor, promoter, photographer or any other person engaged in the making of the film to criminal sanctions.

The Act gives the minister the power to appoint a Board of Censors which is supposed to issue certificates of approval before films can be shown publicly. The Board has the powers to prohibit the showing of any film. The minister may also prohibit both public and private exhibitions.

The Cinematograph Act unreasonably interferes with the constitutionally guaranteed freedom of speech in its broadest sense and can have a negative impact on the development of an independent, indigenous, professional, and creative film industry. The Act effectively gives the minister powers that can cause him to pre-empt the editorial and creative roles and responsibilities of the film producer and director. The scope of liability is too wide because everyone involved in the production of a film which is considered to contravene the Act, such as writer, photographer, sound recorder, and actor run the risk of a fine or an imprisonment. All these restrictions combined with the bureaucratic processes that the Act imposes make film production a tedious and an expensive enterprise.

113. Cap. 59:02.
114. Cap. 60:02.

IV. National Assembly (Powers and Privileges) Act

65. In order to protect the dignity of the Botswana Parliament, section 19(h) of the National Assembly (Powers and Privileges) Act makes it an offence for any person to utter or publish any false or scandalous slander or libel 'on the Assembly or upon any member in his capacity as such'.[115] An identical stipulation is found in section 19(h) of the *Ntlo Ya Dikgosi* (House of Chiefs).[116] The terms 'false' and 'scandalous' are not defined in these two acts. These manifestly subjective concepts can be used to stifle legitimate criticism in the Assembly. Besides the fact that an honest error is not a defence, these provisions expose the publisher to double jeopardy because the criminal sanctions do not bar the aggrieved party from suing for defamation under the common law.

V. Botswana Housing Corporation (Amendment) Act, 1994

66. Section 10 of this Act makes it obligatory for every member of the Board and officers, employees and auditors of the corporation to take an oath or declaration of secrecy not to reveal any matter or thing that has come to their knowledge in the performance of their duties. What makes this provision a threat to freedom of expression is the fact that it is couched in unreasonably broad language. It does not allow for those instances where disclosure of information is in the public interest, for example, disclosure of information about improprieties or maladministration in such a public body.

VI. Public Service Act

67. Both section 21 dealing with publications, interviews and use of official information and section 38 dealing with improper disclosure extensively restrict the right of public officers to disclose information that comes to them in the course of their duties.[117] While it is certainly desirable to protect information whose disclosure may adversely affect the public policy, defence, military or economic interests or resources of Botswana, such a blanket gag is a clear threat to freedom of expression. It does not provide an exception to cover information that is in the public interest to disclose. It does not allow public officers to blow the whistle on any abuses or improprieties within the public service. This in many ways makes the work of the media very difficult since they can only rely on official information which may not always be accurate.

115. Cap. 02:03.
116. Cap. 02:05.
117. Cap. 26:01.

VII. Penal Code

68. The Penal Code is perhaps the piece of legislation with the most far-reaching restrictions on freedom of speech on account not only of the variety of offences it provides for but also for the severity of the penalties contemplated.[118] Some of the most significant and problematic ones will be briefly discussed below.

69. Section 37 of the Penal Code deals with treasonable offences. It provides that any person who forms an intention to effect any of the following purposes, that is to say:

(a) prepares or endeavours to procure by unlawful means any alteration of the law or the policies of the government;
(b) prepares or endeavours to carry out by unlawful means any enterprise which usurps the executive powers of the state in any matter of both a public and general nature;
(c) threatens the security of Botswana; or
(d) prepares or endeavours to give assistance to any person who threatens the security of Botswana, and manifests such intention by an overt act, or by publishing and printing or writing, is guilty of an offence and is liable to imprisonment for not less than fifteen years nor more than twenty-five years.

There is certainly a legitimate interest in ensuring that the media does not indulge in publications that threaten the security of the state. However, the provision is couched in such vague and broad language that it can easily be used to silence genuine criticism against a government or a political party in power.

70. Section 91 of the Penal Code deals with the offence of insults relating to Botswana. It punishes any person who does any act or utters any words or publishes any writing with intent to insult or to bring into contempt or ridicule the arms or ensigns armorial of Botswana, the national flag, the standards of the president and the national anthem. Because of the lack of a precise definition for the word 'insult' it would be difficult to determine the existence of an intention to insult. The obscurity of this offence may therefore cause uncertainty which is not healthy for freedom of expression.

71. Another serious threat to freedom of speech is posed by the offence dealing with prohibited publications provided for in section 47 of the Penal Code. Subsection 1 provides as follows:

> (1) If the President is of the opinion that there is in any publication or series of publications published within or without Botswana by any person or association of persons matter which is contrary to the public interest, he may, in his absolute discretion, by order published in the Gazette and in such local newspapers as he may consider necessary, declare that that particular publication or series of publications, or all publications of any class of publication specified in the order published by that person or association of persons, shall be a prohibited publication or prohibited publications, as the case may be.

118. Cap. 08:01.

Although section 47(8) defines 'public interest' to mean 'the interests of defence, public safety, public order, public morality or public health', this does little to diminish the sweeping powers that this provision gives the President to ban any publication that he does not like.

72. The offence of seditious intention in respect of an act, speech or publication is punished in section 50(1) of the Penal Code where there is an intention:

(a) to bring into hatred or contempt or to excite disaffection against the person of the President or the Government of Botswana as established by law;
(b) to excite the inhabitants of Botswana to attempt to procure the alteration, otherwise than by lawful means, of any other matter in Botswana as established by law;
(c) to bring into hatred or contempt or to excite disaffection against the administration of justice in Botswana;
(d) to raise discontent or disaffection amongst the inhabitants of Botswana; or
(e) to promote feelings of ill will and hostility between different classes of the population of Botswana.

Although a proviso to this provision qualifies this, the language used is still sufficiently vague to cause caution in publishing information. This is particularly so because section 50(2) makes it clear that 'in determining whether the intention with which any act was done, any words were spoken, or any document was published, was not seditious, every person shall be deemed to intend the consequences which would naturally follow from his conduct at the time and under the circumstances which he so conducted himself'. An attempt to challenge the constitutionality of section 50(1) on the ground that the provision is vague failed in the High Court in the case of *Outsa Mokone v. Attorney-General and Others.*[119] The High Court however failed to interrogate the provision to satisfy itself whether or not it is crafted with sufficient clarity. In reaching its decision, the court seem to have been persuaded by the applicant's admission that the publication of the story in question was false and defamatory and hence qualified to be classified as falling under section 12(2) of the constitution. It is contended that the court misdirected itself because the constitutional issue was whether section 50(1) is crafted with sufficient clarity and not whether the statement in question was false.[120]

73. Section 59 of the Penal Code punishes as alarming publications, 'any person who publishes any false statement, rumour or report which is likely to cause fear and alarm to the public or to disturb the public peace is guilty of an offence'. In spite of the fact that it is a defence 'if the accused proves that, prior to publication, he took such measures to verify the accuracy of such statement, rumour or report as to lead him reasonably to believe that it was true', this may not help. The offence is not committed by actually causing 'fear and alarm', which in any case are all very subjective factors, because what may cause fear to one person or a group of person may not do so to others. Rather the mere likelihood to do so is sufficient. It makes it very difficult to distinguish as a matter of law, what false statements are punishable because they

119. UAHGB-000153-14 (delivered on 26 Aug. 2016, unreported).
120. At the time of writing, an appeal against the decision of the High Court was still pending before the Court of Appeal.

are 'likely to cause fear and alarm', and which ones may not lead to this result and thus do not qualify to be punished.

The very notion of 'false statement' is extremely problematic. In a valuable and forward-looking judgment, Mclachlin J (as she then was) in the Canadian case of *R v. Zundel* said:

> (The) guarantee of freedom of expression serves to protect the right of the minority to express its view, however unpopular it may be; adapted to this context, it serves to preclude the majority's perception of 'truth' or 'public interest' from smothering the minority's perception. The view of the majority has no need of constitutional protection; it is tolerated in any event. Viewed thus, a law which forbids expression of a minority or 'false' view on pain of criminal prosecution and imprisonment on its face, offends the purpose of the guarantee of free expression.
>
> ...
>
> Before we put a person beyond the pale of the constitution, before we deny a person the protection which the most fundamental law of this land on its face accords to the person, we should, in my belief, be entirely certain that there can be no justification for offering protection. 'The criterion of falsity falls short of this certainty, given that false statements can sometimes have value and given the difficulty of conclusively determining total falsity. Applying the broad purposive interpretation of the freedom of expression guaranteed by s 2(b) hitherto adhered to by this court, I cannot accede to the argument that those who deliberately publish falsehoods are for that reason alone precluded from claiming the benefit of constitutional guarantees of free speech' (emphasis added).[121]

74. In order to protect the public morals, section 178(1)(e) punishes anybody who publicly exhibits any indecent show or performance or any show or performance tending to corrupt morals. There is no generally agreed definition of the vague concept of morality and the Penal Code itself does not provide any. Morality varies from place to place and from time to time. It is therefore unsatisfactory for the law to be couched in language which leaves everyone in doubt as to what particular manifestation of speech violates public morals.

75. One of the greatest threats to freedom of speech in Africa generally is the offence of criminal defamation. Its potency in Botswana, like in many places, lies less in its use than in the chilling effect it has on the media just by being there. The relevant sections of the Penal Code are as follows:

121. [1992] 10 CRR (2d) 193 (Can SC) 206, 209.

A. Definition of Criminal Defamation

76. Any person who, by print, writing, painting, effigy, or by any means otherwise than solely by gestures, spoken words, or other sounds, unlawfully publishes any defamatory matter concerning another person, with intent to defame that other person, is guilty of the offence termed criminal defamation.

B. Definition of Defamatory Matter

77. Defamatory matter is matter likely to injure the reputation of any person by exposing him to hatred, contempt or ridicule, or likely to damage any person in his profession or trade by an injury to his reputation.

C. Definition of Publication

78.

(1) A person publishes defamatory matter if he causes the print, writing, painting, effigy or other means by which the defamatory matter is conveyed to be so dealt with, either by exhibition, reading, recitation, description, delivery, or otherwise, that the defamatory meaning thereof becomes known or is likely to become known to either the person defamed or any other person.

(2) It is not necessary for criminal defamation that a defamatory meaning should be directly or completely expressed; and it suffices if such meaning and its application to the person alleged to be defamed can be collected either from the alleged defamation itself or from any extrinsic circumstances, or partly by the one and partly by the other means.

The difficulty with criminal defamation is that it deals essentially with a matter that is sufficiently dealt with by the law of delict which enables the victim to obtain damages for any wrong suffered and thus needlessly exposes the wrongdoer to double jeopardy. In many modern legal systems, the criminal defamation laws have either been repealed or fallen into disuse. In other countries, prosecutions under the criminal defamation laws are rare or have been discouraged by the courts. There is also section 60 of the Penal Code which punishes defamation of 'foreign princes'.

79. The above examples are merely some of the numerous instances where the Penal Code punishes certain manifestations of the right of freedom of speech in a manner that is likely to restrict the exercise of this right. Some of the offences, such as criminal defamation and various forms of sedition are clearly irreconcilable with modern concepts of freedom of speech, while other offences are couched in vague and obscure language that certainly has a chilling effect especially on the mass media.

VIII. National Security Act

80. This Act was enacted to counter the destabilizing violence directed against Botswana from South Africa during the apartheid era.[122] This law was introduced for

122. Cap. 23:01.

the worthy purpose of preventing acts – likely to be prejudicial to the safety and interests of the country – from being committed. Section 4 of the Act in rather general terms makes it unlawful for any person who has obtained any official information as a result of his position as a public servant or government contractor to reveal that information without authorization. It is a strict liability offence and penalizes the disclosure of official information however trivial and irrespective of the harm likely to be caused by the disclosure. A public servant charged under this section cannot raise a plea that the disclosure of the information was in the public interest. Section 4(3) of the Act deals with secondary disclosure of official information; it makes receipt and retention of information obtained in contravention of the Act an offence punishable by imprisonment of up to thirty years imprisonment.

81. The very concept of national security is not defined anywhere in the Act. Not only does this Act make it illegal for any public servant to blow the whistle on any governmental improprieties that they are aware of but also it makes it almost impossible to obtain any information about the government without going through lengthy and time-consuming bureaucracy. Public servants have used this law as an excuse for refusing to answer questions from the media. The obscure and broad nature of the law has regularly been used by the government to suppress the dissemination of embarrassing or inconvenient information to the public.

In 1992, the *Mmegi* newspaper was charged under this Act for passing information contained in a confidential report outlining government policy on workers' demands made during a general strike.[123] The charges were subsequently dismissed by the High Court in 1996 on the grounds that the Attorney-General's consent to prosecute had not been obtained. It was also reported in 1996 that a journalist who had obtained a transcript in which a parent had confessed to having participated in the murder of his daughter was threatened with charges under the National Security Act.[124]

IX. Corruption and Economic Crime Act, 1994

82. Section 44 of this Act makes it an offence for anyone to disclose information relating to an ongoing investigation or to the identity of a person being investigated for corruption or the commission of an economic crime. Media practitioners in the country have regularly complained that the prohibition of publication of issues under investigation makes it almost impossible for them to report on and expose corrupt practices in the country.[125]

X. Criminal Procedure and Evidence Act

83. Court proceedings in Botswana are generally conducted in public save for those exceptional circumstances where the law provides for hearings in camera in

123. MISA, *So This Is Democracy?* 5.
124. *Ibid.*
125. *See* 'Panelists Slam DCEC Act', *Mmegi*, 1 Dec. 2003.

order to protect the rights of the parties involved in certain situations.[126] Examples of these are cases involving indecent assault or rape of girls under the age of 16 years and boys under the age of 14 years.[127] Similarly, sections 23(3) and 24(2) of the Children's Act 1981, also restricts those who can sit in during the proceedings of the Juvenile court. In all these cases, there is restriction on the publication of any information concerning the parties or what happened in court. While these restrictions are understandable, it is difficult to justify the restrictions imposed under sections 70(5) and 179(1) which provide that the proceedings of preparatory examination or a trial on a charge relating to indecent assault or extortion cannot be published without the consent of the presiding judicial officer. It is difficult to understand why the media is being prohibited from publishing information disclosed during court proceedings which are held in public.

XI. Education Act

84. Section 23 of the Education Act gives the minister of education the power to declare any publication unsuitable for use in schools.[128] The rationale behind this is to protect school children from what the minister considers as not being in their best interest. While the objective of this legislation may be legitimate and commendable, the language used is too broad because it gives the minister wide discretionary powers that could easily be abused. Thus, this provision can be used by the minister to prevent school children from reading a publication that is critical of the government.

XII. Immigration Act

85. If the Penal Code, on account of the number of offences that punish diverse forms of the expression of freedom of speech can be said to have a chilling effect generally, the Immigration Act contains provision that potentially place all immigrants in Botswana permanently *in terrorem*.[129] The Act gives the president sweeping powers to order the expulsion of any immigrant in section 7 which reads as follows:

> Subject to this Act, the following persons shall be prohibited immigrants and their entry into or presence within Botswana is unlawful-.
>
> …

126. Cap. 08:02.
127. Section 2 of the Act.
128. Cap. 58:01.
129. Cap. 25:02.

(f) any person who, in consequence of information received from any source deemed by the President to be reliable, is declared by the President to be an undesirable inhabitant of or visitor to Botswana.

The actual bite in the exorbitant powers conferred on the President to declare any immigrant a prohibited immigrant lies in sections 11(6) and 36(1) and (2) which read as follows:

> 11(6) No appeal shall lie under subsection (2) against any notice that a person is a prohibited immigrant by reason of any declaration by the President under section 7(f) and no court shall question the adequacy of the grounds for any such declaration.

> 36(1) No person shall have the right to be heard before or after a decision is made by the President in relation to that person under this Act.

> 36(2) No person affected by any such decision shall have the right to demand any information as to the grounds of such decision nor shall any such information be disclosed in any court.

Over the years, this law has been extensively used to deport foreign journalists who have been considered too outspoken.[130] The law has been used against others including an academic at the University of Botswana, apparently to stop him from giving a public lecture on the system of presidential succession in the country.[131] The matter came before the Court of Appeal in *Good v. Attorney-General*.[132] Professor Good, an Australian national who was employed at the University of Botswana and had worked there for more than ten years, was in February 2005 declared an undesirable inhabitant or visitor to Botswana by the president acting under section 7(f) of the Immigration Act and given three days to leave the country. He appealed against the decision of the High Court dismissing his application to have the decision set aside. He argued *inter alia*, that sections 11(6) and 36 of the Act were *ultra vires* the constitution and therefore invalid. The court, without making any attempt to address the specific issue of the constitutionality of the provisions challenged was content to hold that the president had been entrusted by Parliament with responsibility to make the necessary decision. It was thus an executive function and it was not a matter on which the courts could second-guess him in his decision. And again, without any clear and convincing

130. *See further*, S.T. Sechele, *Deepening Democracy or Creeping Authoritarian Rule?: Media/ Government Relations in Botswana in Historical Perspective* 128–130 (University of Botswana 2000).

131. Kenneth Good & Ian Taylor, *Presidential Succession in Botswana: No Model for Africa*. Scheduled to have been delivered on 23 Feb. 2005.

132. [2005] 2 BLR 337. For a commentary on this case, *see* B.T. Balule, *Good v. The Attorney-General (2): Some Reflections on the National Security Dilemma in Botswana*, 7 U. Bots. L. J. 153–172 (2008).

explanation for this conclusion, the court held that Parliament in giving the president these powers had not acted *ultra vires*. It may well be that the court did not dwell too long on this issue because the appellant did not pursue this argument with much conviction during the proceedings. It is not clear how the court would have dealt with the matter had the appellant made this the main focus of its case. The African Commission on Human and Peoples' Rights subsequently found section 36(1) incompatible with Article 9(1) of the ACHPR. The Commission opined that the right to receive information, especially that which is relevant in a trial for the vindication of a right, cannot be withheld for any reason.[133]

XIII. Others

86. There are a host of other pieces of legislation which contain provisions which potentially limit the scope of freedom of expression guaranteed under the constitution. Examples of these are the Defence Force Act,[134] the National Security Act,[135] the Botswana Housing Cooperation (Amendment) Act,[136] and the Electoral Act.[137] Perhaps the most controversial piece of legislation in recent times is the Intelligence and Security Services Act of 2007, the introduction of which strained the media-government relationship. The media waged an unsuccessful campaign to prevent this legislation ever seeing the statute book. The main criticism against the legislation is that it does not contain any accountability mechanisms, a situation aggravated by the absence of an access to information legislation. The law vests enormous discretionary powers on the president which can be used to restrain the media and freedom of speech generally, under the pretext of national security.

87. All the above laws certainly address issues of legitimate national interest. However, the difficulty is that the language used is often too broad and they often confer wide discretionary powers on government officials thus allowing too much scope for the restriction of the freedom of expression provided for under the constitution. It is doubtful if many of these limitations can successfully pass the three-part or three-point test alluded to above.[138] This is especially so where the restrictions on freedom of speech create an offence of strict liability. The last limb of the three part test requires a balancing of competing interest. Strict liability offences do not give the courts any discretion to balance the competing interest involved and therefore raise doubts about the constitutionality of such legislation.[139] As in the *Media Publishing* and *Good*

133. Communication 313/05: *Kenneth Good/Republic of Botswana* at para. 193.
134. Cap. 21:05, and *see* s. 9(1) of this Act.
135. Cap. 23:01, and *see* s. 4 of this Act.
136. Act No. 5 of 1994. *See* s. 10 of this Act.
137. Cap. 02:07, and *see* s. 9 of this Act.
138. *See* para. 59 *supra*.
139. In fact, in Zimbabwe, the Supreme Court in a number of cases has held that provisions that impose strict criminal liability on journalist are bound to be too broad and unlikely to be able to satisfy the three-part test and hence unconstitutional. *See S v. Chogugudza* [1996] 1 ZLR 28; *Tsvangirayi v. The State* SC-91-2001; and *Association of Independent Journalists & Others v. The Minister of State for Information and Publicity & Others* S.C. 136/02.

cases,[140] although the issue of the constitutionality of some of these laws have been raised before the courts, the latter have usually preferred to decide the cases on other grounds without dealing with the constitutionality issue.[141] It is clearly a matter that the courts will have to deal with some day.

140. *See* para 56 *supra.*
141. *See further*, Balule et al., *Undue Restriction. Laws Impacting on Media Freedom in the SADC* 32.

Part II. Regulation of Print Media

88. For a long time, the main piece of regulation which regulated the print media in Botswana was the Printed Publications Act.[142] In December 2008 Parliament adopted what became law on 31 December 2008 as the Media Practitioners Act, 2008. This Act is mainly designed to introduce a new statutory Media Council, which once operational, should replace the present Press Council. It was publicly criticized though by one member of the ruling BDP who broke rank and described the Act as an 'assault' on the 'fundamentals' and 'undermining' a free and independent media.[143] It is however necessary to point out that this Act is a considerable improvement on what the government had initially intended to introduce.

In 1997, the government had proposed a Mass Media Communication Bill to regulate the media in the country. After it was introduced in Parliament, the opposition to the law from the media houses, journalists, and human rights organizations was so fierce that the government shelved it. In 2001, the bill was once again revived and although there was still strong opposition to it, the government decided to try to convince the media through a series of consultations that took place between 2001 and 2003. In August 2003, the Press Council of Botswana was established by the media industry to counter a similar body that the government had proposed in its Mass Media Communications bill. There were numerous problems that the media freedom activists had with the bill. One was the fact that it provided for absolute control of newspapers by the Minister of Communications who will have the powers to determine which papers will operate and which will not. The minister was given the powers to nominate a registrar who will be responsible for press matters in the country. The registrar may decline to register a newspaper if it fails to meet certain specified requirements such as failure to disclose its financial status, ownership, and the name and place of residence of the proprietor, publisher, and printer. Under the bill, a police officer of the rank of inspector and above may seize any publication or newspaper if the officer reasonably suspects that such newspaper has been published in contravention of the law. Police officers were also given the power to enter and search newspaper premises and seize whatever they suspect to have been published in contravention of the law. Furthermore, the bill proposed that all journalists, including foreign correspondents must be registered and issued with press cards before they can be allowed to operate in the country. If this bill had succeeded to become law, it would certainly have seriously eroded many of the media freedoms that made Botswana to be respected as one of the few countries in Africa which encourages the existence of a free and vibrant media. The Media Practitioners Act, 2008 now deals with some of the issues that the Mass Media Communications bill attempted to address and although it is far from perfect, it is

142. Cap. 20:01.

143. *See* 'Botswana: Media Laws Stir Dissent within Ruling Party', www.bizcommunity.com/29/15.html.

nevertheless an improvement on the latter. Many of the draconian measures that the government had intended to introduce in order to rein in on the media have now been abandoned. This Act deals with a number of important issues concerning the journalists' profession.

89. The Media Practitioners Act, 2008 is now the main piece of legislation that regulates the media as well as the journalists' profession. The Act uses the term 'media practitioner' instead of journalist. In section 2, it states:

> 'Media practitioner' means a person engaged in the writing, editing or transmitting of news and information to the public, and includes a broadcaster under the Broadcasting Act, a journalist, editor or publisher of a publication and the manager or proprietor of a publication or broadcasting station.

A journalist is therefore just one of the media practitioners covered by the Act. As the Act quite rightly makes clear, a journalist like the other media practitioners is involved in the business of collecting, analysing, and communicating information to the public.

90. Until 2009, there were no legal restrictions on becoming or working as a journalist in Botswana. One of the important matters that the Media Practitioners Act addresses is the issue of registration. One of the most contentious issues in the draft Mass Media Communications bill had been a proposal to introduce a system of compulsory registration of journalists. This appears to have found its way into the Media Practitioners Act. Section 4(i) and (j) of the Act confers on the newly created statutory Media Council, *inter alia*, the duties to 'register and accredit resident media practitioners' and 'to issue accredited resident media practitioners with identity cards'. According to section 6(1), 'a resident media practitioner shall be registered and accredited by the Executive Committee' in accordance with regulations that this Committee will draw up. The exact nature of these regulations and whether or not they will be restrictive remains uncertain. Section 7(1) provides that the 'membership of the Council shall consist of all publishers of news and information, whether or not in the private or public sector'. However, membership is not automatic on application because section 7(2) states that 'subject to the provisions of subsection (1), a publisher of news and information shall apply to the Executive Committee for membership of the Council'. The only exception to this compulsory registration is a person who only has what section 7(3) describes as 'a legitimate interest in the development of the local media industry' who 'may' apply to the Executive Council for associate membership only. The sting in this process is provided by section 7(5) which states that any person who contravenes any of the provisions in section 7 is liable to 'a fine not exceeding P5,000 or imprisonment for a term not exceeding three years, or both'. A person's application for membership and termination of membership of the Council will depend on regulations made by the Executive Committee.[144]

91. The subject of prerequisite licences in order to practice journalism is a contentious matter. Some of the arguments that are raised to justify the registration and accreditation of media practitioners include that:

- compulsory registration is the normal way to organize the practice of professions;

144. Section 8(2) of the Media Practitioners Act.

- licensing and accreditation seeks to achieve goals linked with professional ethics and responsibility; and
- licensing is a means of guaranteeing the independence of journalists in relation to their employers.[145]

92. The arguments advanced to justify the registration of journalists are said to be aimed at the preservation of public order. Public order in this regard, has been defined as implying conditions that ensure the normal and harmonious functioning of institutions based on an agreed system of values and principles.[146] The African Commission on Human and Peoples Rights (ACHPR) has opined that registration and accreditation procedures for media practitioners are not in themselves a violation of the right to freedom of expression, provided they are purely technical and administrative in nature and do not impose onerous conditions.[147] In the ACHPR's view, it must be ascertained what the rationale for registration and accreditation is. The question here will be whether the registration and accreditation are to control or regulate the media profession. The Commission concluded that registration will be acceptable where it aims at the identification of journalists, the maintenance of ethical standards, competence, and the betterment of the welfare of journalists.[148] The ACHPR further held that there should be no official involvement in the registration of journalists as such may create considerable scope for politically motivated actions by the authorities. The regulation of the media should be a matter for self-regulation by journalists themselves through their professional associations, the Commission added.[149] The ACHPR also observed that the freedom of expression of journalists is not absolute, and that it can be restricted by legislation that aims to protect the public or individuals against practice of journalism that deviates from certain norms and legitimate interests in a democratic society.[150]

The Human Rights Committee (HRC) has held that accreditation schemes for journalists are permissible only where they are necessary to provide journalists with privileged access to certain places or events.[151] The HRC further cautioned that accreditation schemes have to be applied in a manner that is non-discriminatory and compatible with Article 19 of the ICCPR. The criteria for accreditation must be fair and reasonable and its application transparent for it to comply with the ICCPR.

93. Opponents of registration and accreditation of journalists argue that these requirements constitute a violation of the right to freedom of expression. The Inter-American Court of Human Rights has held that the guarantee of freedom of expression has two facets. First, that it encompasses the individual dimension which recognizes

145. *See* M.E. Price & P. Krug, *The Enabling Environment for Free and Independent Media* 30 (Programme in Comparative Media Law & Policy, Wolfsen College 2000); and *Compulsory Membership in an Association Prescribed by Law for the Practice of Journalism, Advisory Opinion* OC-5/85 of November 13, 1985, paras 59–62.
146. Communication 287/2005: Scanlen & Hoderness/Zimbabwe, adopted during the 6th Ordinary Session of the ACHPR, Banjul, The Gambia, April, 2009, at para. 109.
147. *Ibid*, para. 90.
148. *Ibid*, para. 97.
149. *Ibid*, para. 90.
150. *Ibid*, para. 107.
151. *See* Communication No. 1985/2010, CCPR/C/111/D/1985/2010 (26 Aug. 2014).

the individual's right to speak or to write. And second, the right to use whatever medium is deemed appropriate to impart ideas and to have them reach as wide an audience as possible.[152] In terms of this view, the two dimensions of freedom of expression are indivisible. Thus any registration or accreditation requirements as a pre-condition to the practice of journalism will be a restriction on the right to freedom of expression because any person who is not registered or accredited will be denied the opportunity to use the mass media to impart his/her ideas. It must be noted that the decision of the Inter-American Court was based on its interpretation of Article 13(2) of the American Convention of Human Rights. This article specifically prohibits any prior censorship on the exercise of freedom of expression.

94. In determining the constitutionality of the requirements of registration and accreditation under section 6(1) of the Media Practitioners Act, 2008, it is submitted that the ACHPR's approach would be the appropriate one. The Constitution of Botswana, like the African Charter on Human and Peoples Right does not prohibit any prior censorship on the exercise of freedom of expression like the American Convention of Human Rights.

In assessing whether, section 6(1) of the Media Practitioners Act, 2008 is or is not a justifiable restriction on the right to freedom of expression, the rationale for registration and accreditation under the provision must be ascertained. In Communication 297/2005, the ACHPR was called upon to rule upon the compatibility of sections 79 and 80 of the Zimbabwean Access to Information and Protection of Privacy Act (AIPPA) with the journalists' right to freedom of expression.[153] Section 79 of the AIPPA required that before a journalist could practise his/her profession in Zimbabwe, he/she should apply for and obtain a certificate of accreditation from the Media and Information Commission (MIC). The MIC was managed by a Board appointed by a government minister and its regulations were drawn up by government. Section 80 of the AIPPA provided that any person who practised as a journalist without a certificate of accreditation was deemed to have abused his/her journalist privileges and was liable, upon conviction, to a fine or imprisonment for a period not exceeding two years. The ACHPR had to determine whether sections 79 and 80 of the AIPPA were aimed at facilitating or controlling the practise of journalists. The Commission found that the registration and accreditation conditions in the said provisions were onerous and were aimed at controlling journalists through the exercise of prior censorship. It held that the two provisions were incompatible with the guarantee of freedom of expression of the individual under Article 9(2) of the African Charter on Human and Peoples Rights.

95. Section 6(1) of the Media Practitioners Act, 2008 requires all resident media practitioners to be registered and accredited by the Media Council's Executive Committee. The Act does not prescribe any penalties for not complying with the provision. The regulations for registration and accreditation under the Media Practitioners Act, 2008 are determined by the media practitioners themselves through the Media Council's Executive Committee. The position under the Media Practitioners Act, 2008 can be distinguished from the position under the Zimbabwean AIPPA where registration requirements were determined by the state. It is submitted that the position under the

152. *Compulsory Membership in an Association Prescribed by Law for the Practice of Journalism*, *supra* no. 145. para. 31.

153. Chapter 10:27 of the Laws of the Republic of Zimbabwe.

MPA is consistent with the ACHPR's ruling that regulation by journalists should be a matter for self-regulation through associations. It is further submitted that since the Media Practitioners Act, 2008, unlike the AIPPA, does not prescribe any penalties for failure to get registration and accreditation before practising journalism, one can conclude that registration and accreditation requirements under the former are not intended to be a means of control, rather, they are aimed at facilitating the enjoyment of the freedom of expression of media practitioners.

The registration and accreditation requirements under section 6(1) of the Media Practitioners Act, 2008 cannot be said to be unconstitutional as they are consistent with both section 12(2) of the Constitution of Botswana and Article 9(2) of the African Charter on Human and Peoples Rights. In terms of the conditions that any restriction on freedom of expression must comply with set out in the Constitution of Botswana, section 6(1) of the Media Practitioners Act, 2008 is clearly crafted and is unambiguous and therefore satisfies the first condition of 'done under the authority of any law'. The provision serves a legitimate purpose, the public order, in that registration and accreditation can serve to identify media practitioners and contribute towards the maintenance ethical standards in the profession. Finally, while registration and accreditation, on the face of it, restrict an individual's right to freedom of expression, such limitation would be justified in a democratic society if it is for purposes of the betterment of the profession rather than its control.

Chapter 2. Journalists' Rights

96. In considering some aspects of journalists' rights, this section will concentrate on four issues: the role of journalists as watchdogs of society, journalists' independence, protection of journalistic sources, and access to judicial proceedings.

§1. Role of Journalists as Watchdogs of Society

97. The term 'watchdog journalism' has been defined in many ways. For example, Lance Bennett and William Serrin define it as:

> (i) independent scrutiny by the press of the activities of government, business, and other public institutions, with an aim toward (ii) documenting, questioning, and investigating those activities, in order to (iii) provide publics [sic] and officials with timely information on issues of public concern.[154]

The watchdog role of journalism may thus involve simply documenting the activities of government, business and other public institutions in ways that expose little-publicized or hidden activities to public scrutiny. Another defining element of watchdog journalism involves clarifying the significance of documented activities by asking probing questions of public officials and authorities.[155] It also involves enterprise or investigative reporting aimed at finding hidden evidence of social ills, official deception, and institutional corruption. Some instances of investigative journalism may lead to constructive reforms, or alert and mobilize the public to take action on pressing problems such as environmental hazards or health care abuses. Whatever form watchdog journalism takes, the ultimate objective of independent journalistic scrutiny of social, economic, and governmental institutions is commonly regarded as fundamental for keeping authorities in line with the values and norms of the rule of law and good governance. In fact, it is said that a democratic society cannot function without journalism acting as a watchdog.[156]

98. A number of studies have shown that one of the keys to Botswana's strong and commendable democratic credentials is the watchdog role that the media has played. Thus, Sechele points out that since its establishment in the early 1980s, the independent media in Botswana has provided a necessary alternative voice in a set-up generally dominated by the government. He points out that the media through journalists asserting their watchdog role have operated like a power bloc by influencing the formulation of public policy and by acting as an independent mirror of Botswana

154. Lance Bennett & William Serrin, *The Watchdog Role*, in *The Press* 169 (Geneva Overholser & Kathleen Jamieson, Oxford University Press 2005). Another definition refers to it as forms of activist journalism aimed at holding accountable public personalities and institutions whose functions impact social and political life. The term lapdog journalism sometimes used as a conceptual opposite to watchdog journalism. http://en.wikipedia.org/wiki/Watchdog_journalism.
155. Bennett & Serrin, *The Watchdog Role* 170.
156. *Ibid.*, 172.

society.[157] This watchdog role has been manifested in diverse ways that have positively influenced social, legal, economic, and political developments in the country. Through playing this role, journalists have provided a much-needed forum for public debate, especially during elections. Because of a weak civil society in the country, the media has taken a central role in shaping political debate. This was particularly effective in the 1990s when the media carried a series of stories detailing corruption in government and parastatal organizations such as the Botswana Housing Corporation (BHC); mismanagement in the National Development Bank (NDB) and the Botswana Building Society, human rights abuses, especially of the minorities such as the Basarwa and women in general, and other cases of maladministration and miscarriage of justice. The scandals led to the appointment of several presidential commissions.[158] The first such commission was appointed to carry out an enquiry into the award under highly dubious circumstances of a lucrative contract to supply teaching materials for the country's primary schools to an inexperienced company. As a result of several gross errors for which the commission held certain senior civil servants responsible, BWP 27 million was dissipated. Another presidential commission appointed in 1991, looked into illegal land transactions in peri-urban villages near Gaborone, found evidence of the misuse by certain parliamentarians and ministers of their official position for personal gain. The Vice President and Minister of Local Government and the Minister of Agriculture, who were also National Chairman and Secretary General respectively of the ruling BDP were specifically named and criticized in the Commission's report. They were forced to resign from government three months later. A third presidential commission which investigated the activities of the BHC, revealed that millions of Pula had been lost in various questionable projects to construct a headquarters for the corporation and to put up several high-cost houses in Lobatse. It reported that ministers and senior civil servants had used the opportunity to enrich themselves and many irresponsible decisions had been taken. Besides these three examples, there were several other instances in which state funds were plundered. There was for example the case of the NDB, where leading politicians of the ruling party including ministers were responsible for the decline and downfall of the bank by obtaining loans for which they did not qualify and failing to repay this. Three things are particularly significant about all this. First, unlike what obtains in most other African countries, immediately the media exposed all these irregularities, presidential commissions were appointed to probe into the matter and their findings were made public. Second, again, unlike in many other countries, senior politicians and civil servants who are found to have abused their official positions are not only required to resign but have often been prosecuted. But perhaps the most significant impact of the journalist acting as watchdogs is that the law has usually been changed to address the abuses exposed. Hence, as a result of the scandals in the 1990s, the Corruption and Economic Crime Act 1994 under which an anti-corruption agency, the Directorate on Corruption and Economic Crime (DCEC) was established and this was followed by the Ombudsman Act 1995,

157. S.T. Sechele, *The Role of the Press in Independent Botswana*, in *Botswana Politics and Society* 415 (W.A. Edge & M.H. Lekorwe, J.L. van Schaik 1998); and *id.*, *Deepening Democracy or Creeping Authoritarian Rule?*, Ch. 6.

158. For a detailed account of this, *see* Kenneth Good, *Corruption and Mismanagement in Botswana: A Best-Case Example?*, 32(3) J. Modern Afr. Stud. 499–521 (1994).

under which the Office of the Ombudsman was established to deal with issues of maladministration.[159]

Since the 1990s in spite of the chilling effect of many media unfriendly laws discussed above,[160] journalists in Botswana, mainly those in the private media, have continued to play their watchdog role. The private media have also covered, with lively discussion and analysis, the apparent differences in opinion between the Director of Public Prosecutions and the Attorney-General, over the prosecution of Mr Louis Nchindo, former Managing Director of the Debswana mining giant and an influential member of the ruling BDP party. Mr Nchindo was accused along with two former managers of Debswana of fraudulently acquiring state land.[161] Another high profile case of corruption involved a BWP 80 million water project corruption scandal at the Department of Water Affairs widely reported in the newspapers which led to the prosecution of the principal water engineer, Epharim Kelaeng over allegations of irregularities against the latter, the supervising engineering firm and the contractor.[162]

99. The role of journalists as watchdog has been underscored by the judiciary as well. Thus in *Media Publishing (Pty) Ltd v. Attorney-General* case, Lesetedi J made this point very clear when he said:

> Freedom of expression is one of the fundamental cornerstones of every democratic society. Freedom of the media is but one aspect of that freedom. In a democratic society the media plays a very important role. It is normally the media that forms a vehicle for communication between the governed and those that govern. It is usually the press, as part of the media, that acts as a watchdog against abuse of power and corruption where it may occur in society. It is through the media that members of the society communicate their ideas and feelings about the way they are governed. It plays the very important role in civil society of informing the public of many matters including the way the organs of state operate and by giving general information. It is the press which in many occasions has been in the forefront in the fight against abuse of power, corruption, dictatorship and other ills like blatant disregard of the rule of law committed by those that govern in many a number of countries. As was succinctly pointed out by Hefer A.J.A. in National Media Ltd and Others v Bogoshi 1998 (4) SA 1196 (SCA) at 1209I-J:

159. These are discussed in Charles Manga Fombad, *Curbing Corruption in Africa: Some Lessons from Botswana's Experience*, 160 Intl. Soc. Sci. J. 241–254 (1999); Charles Manga Fombad, *The Enhancement of Good Governance in Botswana: A Critical Assessment of the Ombudsman Act 1995*, 27 J. S. Afr. Stud. 57–77 (2001); Andrew Bricoe & H.C.L. Hermans, *Combating Corruption in Botswana: A Review of the Relevant Policies, Law and Institutional Capacity to Combat Corruption in Botswana* (Friedrich-Ebert-Stiftung 2001); and Charles Manga Fombad & David Sebudubu, *The Framework for Curbing Corruption, Enhancing Accountability and Promoting Good Governance in Botswana*, in *Essays on the Law of Botswana* 82–126 (Charles Manga Fombad, Juta & Co. Ltd 2007).

160. *See* paras 61-86 *supra.*

161. 'Oh Yes, We Are There in Nchindo Case, Says AG', *Mmegi*, Friday, 13 Mar. 2009: 1&3.

162. 'P 80m Corruption Case Set for April', *Mmegi*, Friday 13 Mar. 2009: 12.

> [I]t is the right, and indeed a vital function, of the press to make available to the community information and criticism about every aspect of public, political, social and economic activity and thus to contribute to the formation of public opinion (Prof JC van der Walt in Gedenkbundel: HL Swanepoel at 68). The press and the rest of the media provide the means by which useful, and sometimes vital, information about the daily affairs of the nation is conveyed to its citizens – from the highest to the lowest ranks (Strauss, Strydom and Van der Walt Mediareg 4th ed. at 43). Conversely, the press often becomes the voice of the people – their means to convey their concerns to their fellow citizens, to officialdom and to government.

The views of the media may not always be palatable to those that govern. The relationship between a free media and government can at times be described as akin to opposing poles of a magnet with the government preferring less and less criticism from the media, getting more irritated by vibrant criticism, for such criticism may at times be strident, while the media on the other side seeks to widen the latitude of its criticism. Indeed because of the important role it plays in a democratic society, freedom of expression is jealously guarded by courts of law.[163]

§2. Journalists' Independence

100. Freedom of speech to the journalists and other media practitioners means some sort of insulation from any pressure or influence that might compromise the presumably 'pure' judgments that they can and should make when disseminating information. To Lee Bollinger, the 'model of journalistic autonomy' confers on the journalist an unfettered 'freedom to make mistakes', and an unconditional 'power to err', and promotes 'a posture to the world that says, in effect, no one will tell you what to do'.[164] Journalistic independence simply requires conditions in which a journalist can live and operate without the entanglements they and others might view as real or potential conflicts of interests. It entails being able to operate free from partisan interests, free from the commercial interests of the mercantile press, and free from the interests of advertisers.[165]

101. Journalistic independence, as was noted earlier, is a feature which is true of the private but not the government-owned media. The latter is under the direct control of the government, who often interferes directly or indirectly with both the government-owned print and broadcast media.[166]

In the private media, ownership can also impact the freedom of expression of journalists when owners use their economic power to restrict journalistic freedoms. In free market economies, owners have the freedom to decide on the direction of their companies and exploit available commercial opportunities to remain competitive and

163. [2001] 2 BLR 485 at 494–495.
164. Cited in Theodore Glasser & Marc Gunther, *The Legacy of Autonomy in American Journalism*, in *The Press* 388 (Geneva Overholser & Kathleen Jamieson, Oxford University Press 2005).
165. *Ibid.*, 389.
166. *See* para. 19 *supra*.

profit-making.[167] Whilst this may be so, we cannot forget that the constitutional value of the media goes beyond the financial interest of the owners. A delicate balance needs to be struck between an owner's proprietary rights and the media's democratic mandate. It is generally considered that media freedom is better safeguarded when ownership and editorial content are kept separate.[168] This ideal can be achieved through a law stipulating mechanisms that the media must develop to ensure editorial independence, or it could be left to self-regulatory mechanisms in the form of editorial agreements between owners and editors.[169]

There is no law in Botswana, like in almost all countries around the world that addresses editorial independence of editors from publishers or owners. This is a matter that is regulated through self-regulatory mechanisms in individual media outlets. At a general level, there appears to be a consensus amongst editors and station managers in the country that media owners recognize the principle that editors ought to have the power to decide on editorial matters free from interference from the owners.[170] The practices on how editorial independence is guaranteed in each media house, however, differ. There are those media houses where editorial independence is formalized through editorial charters or policies. In some of these media outlets, the independence is further reinforced by the existence of editorial committees, which are subcommittees of their respective boards of directors, which oversee editorial matters and advise the respective boards on editorial issues. The strength of these editorial committees lies in that the majority of the members are not shareholders, but persons who have experience in the media and others are drawn from civil society. These committees provide the much-needed insulation to the editorial teams of the respective media outlets from any undue pressure by the owners.

Editorial independence in other media outlets is governed by what one may call 'a gentlemen's agreement' based on an understanding that editors ought to enjoy editorial freedom. While this may arguably be working in practice, the arrangement faces some challenges:

(a) In some media outlets, the owners are also the editors, which means there is no separation between ownership and editorial matters.
(b) In others, editorial content is directly supervised by the Board of Directors which are mainly composed of owners. In such cases, the editorial content is not sufficiently protected against any undue interference by the owners as failure to

167. V. Vike-Freiberga, et al., *A Free and Pluralistic Media to Sustain European Democracy, The Report of the High Level Group on Media Freedom and Pluralism* 13 (European Commission 2013).

168. Council of Europe Committee of Ministers, Recommendation No. R (99) 1 of the Committee of Ministers to Member States on Measures to Promote Media Pluralism, adopted by the Committee of Ministers' on 19 Jan. 1999, at the 656th meeting of the Ministers' Deputies, para. 32.

169. *Ibid*., para. 34. *See also*, African Commission on Human and Peoples' Rights, Declaration of Principles on Freedom of Expression in Africa, n 24 above, Principle VIII.

170. This observation is based on interviews that the writer had with several editors and station managers while conducting a study on 'Media Ownership in Botswana: Implications for News Coverage and Political Presentation' for the Friedrich Ebert Stiftung – Botswana Office (unreported, February 2014).

> agree with the owners may have catastrophic consequences. The undesirability of the direct involvement of owners in the supervision of a media outlet's editorial content manifested itself in an incident at Duma FM, one of the three private national radio stations in the country. A sports commentator who was also a parliamentary candidate for the main opposition party in the 2014 general election was dismissed from his employment. Although the station refused to disclose reasons for his dismissal, it is believed that he paid the price for politically contesting against a candidate who was a close associate of the station's owners.[171]

In spite of the relative independence of journalists in the private media, self-censorship amongst journalists and editors is common. Because of the small size of the country and the fact that people know each other intimately, this has led to a tendency for people not to report things about each other for fear of being ostracized.[172] There are cultural factors too that come into play; the desire not to write anything that will hurt the elders or traditional leaders. Editors sometimes practise self-censorship and refuse to publish some stories that could damage or hurt actual or potential advertisers or high profile personalities. In *Media Publishing v. Attorney-General*[173] although the court ruled that it is illegal for the government to withdraw advertising from newspapers that were critical of it, the court could not compel the government to place adverts in any particular newspaper. Government advertising was to some degree reinstated after that decision, but there is still evidence that the papers that are too critical do not attract much government advertising. The desire to attract government advertising has thus led many papers to be very cautious when reporting stories concerning the government and senior officials.

§3. Protection of Journalistic Sources

102. The question whether journalists should be allowed to conceal their sources is one of the most difficult and complex issues in media law. The obligation to answer a question either from the police or produce a document in court can create a moral and ethical dilemma for journalists where this would involve revealing the identity of a source of information. This is usually the case where the journalist has received information in confidence from a source and given the source an undertaking that his identity will not be revealed. For example, a journalist may publish information based on a document leaked by a source which shows that there is a corruption racket operating within the Ministry of Education and implicating the minister and certain senior officials. The prosecutors may only be able to gather enough evidence to prosecute if they identify and speak to this well-placed source.

On the contrary, the journalist may fear that facilitating this process by disclosing the identity of the informant and lead to the latter being fired and ostracized by his peers. It may also be the case that those against whom the allegations have been made will need to know the source and exactly what information was disclosed in order to

171. *See* 'Rakgare sacked for challenging Masimolole' *The Voice*, Friday 7 Feb. 2014, p. 6.
172. MISA & Friedrich Ebert Stiftung, *African Media Barometer* 42 (Botswana 2007).
173. [2001] 2 BLR 485.

prepare a case for defamation against the newspaper. A further complicating factor may be that the journalist may resist disclosure of the leaked documents on which the story is based under the principle that a person is not obliged to provide information which might implicate him in a crime.[174]

The protection of journalists' sources of information is not accorded any specific protection in Botswana, either in the 1966 constitution or any other statutory instrument. The Press Council of Botswana's Media Code of Ethics in its clause 20 on the 'protection of sources' states that, 'when sources are promised confidentiality, that promise shall be honoured, unless released by the source'. It is however recognized under both the jurisprudence of the African Commission on Human and Peoples' Rights and the European Court of Human Rights that the right of journalists to protect their sources is part of media freedom guaranteed in the respective international treaties.[175] The constitutional guarantee of media freedom under the constitution of Botswana is modelled on Article 10 of the European Convention on Human Rights. A generous and purposive interpretation of the provision would embrace the protection of journalistic sources.

In common law jurisdictions, there appears to be slight differences with respect to the judicial attitude towards journalistic sources. The slight differences depend on whether the protection of journalistic sources is based on common law principles or based on statutory law.

103. In those jurisdictions where the courts rely on the common law to provide some limited protection to journalistic sources the exact scope of the applicable principles are uncertain. What is absolutely clear is that journalists, unlike lawyers, do not have an unqualified right to keep quiet about their client's affairs in the face of judicial interrogation. The right of journalists to keep quiet about their sources depends on who is asking the questions and why.

104. Insofar as legal proceedings are concerned, the position seems to be that a journalist when faced with a perceived conflict between his duty under the law to answer relevant questions and his duty to abide by an undertaking to the informant to maintain silence, he must discharge his duty to the law for the public interest in having all relevant evidence placed before the court outweighs any interest in the journalist maintaining confidences.[176] The principle that has emerged in many common law decisions appears to be that no obligation of honour, secrecy or confidence or private

174. This will be an arguable defence if, for instance, the circumstances of the media defendant's obtaining the document could make it an accessory to theft or the commission of some other crime. This defence is a two-edged sword because to admit to participating in a possible criminal behaviour undermines any public interest claim which might be made in the same proceedings. Besides, the privilege against self-incrimination is not an absolute rule.

175. African Commission on Human and Peoples' Rights, Declaration of Principles on Freedom of Expression in Africa, Principle XV and *Case of Sanoma Uitgevers B.V. v. The Netherlands*, Application No. 38224/03 (judgment of 14 Sept. 2010) at para. 50.

176. Des Butler & Sharon Rodrick, *Australian Media Law* 322–323 (Lawbook Co. 2004).

undertaking arising from the nature of a journalist's pursuit or calling can stand in the way of the imperative necessity of revealing the truth in the witness box.[177]

105. Most of the courts in the Commonwealth have differed on the cogency of the rationale advanced to support the existence of a journalistic/source privilege. In *McGuinness v. Attorney-General (Vic)*,[178] Rich J dismissed it as founded on a paradox in that the media claim that without a guarantee of confidentiality newspapers will not be able to discover the truth and publish it, and yet when courts seek to discover the truth from the media, they claim a privilege to withhold it.

In the present state of the law, it is reasonable to assume that potential sources of information must be aware or made aware of the fact that any undertaking given by a journalist must yield to the paramount requirements of either the law or the interests of justice. It is only with respect to the latter that judges have any discretion. The effect of judicial discretion is the recognition of the fact that it is desirable in certain circumstances to permit non-disclosure of the identity of a source. However, differences of opinion exist as to the circumstances in which this discretion will be exercised to favour non-disclosure of information. In the Zimbabwean case of *Nathan Shamuyarira v. Zimbabwe Newspapers (1980) Ltd t/a The Chronicle and Geoffrey Nyarota*,[179] the court attempted to lay down certain principles that have to be considered in weighing whether a journalist might be required to disclose his sources under certain circumstances. The case itself involved a newspaper investigation into rumours of official corruption in the distribution of motor vehicles which were being assembled in a plant in Willowvale, in Harare. An employee of the plant provided the journalist with information that showed that those involved included the plaintiff, who at that time was the Foreign Minister of Zimbabwe. A police officer also showed the journalist a police list with suspects including the plaintiff. The journalist gave his sources an undertaking that he would not reveal their identity to anyone. After President Mugabe appointed a judicial commission to investigate the allegations, the plaintiff sued the defendant claiming damages for defamation and applied for an order compelling the editor to reveal his sources. He refused on the basis of the undertaking he had given. In deciding the matter, the court in balancing the conflicting interests in the case, outlined the number of interests which weighed in favour of compelling the editor to disclose his sources as well as a number of interests compelling him not to do so. The court came to the conclusion that it had been in the public interest for the editor to expose the corruption taking place in high government circles and that he had been justified in giving his sources personal guarantees that their identities would not be revealed if they furnished him with the information. The court also found that it was in the public interest that it should bend over backwards to protect a journalists' sources, where the journalist had publicly uncovered corruption or some form of iniquity on the part of those in office. However, the court found in favour of the plaintiff on the main issue of defamation.

177. *See* , *McGuiness v. Attorney-General (Vic)* [1940] 63 CLR 73, 102–103 per Dixon; *Attorney-General v. Mulholland* [1963] 2 QB 477, 491, 492; *Re an Inquiry under the Company Securities (Insider Dealing) Act* 1985 [1988] 1 AC 660, 681; *Independent Commission against Corruption v. Cornwall* [1985] 38 NSWLR 207; and *R v. Parry* [1997] 92 ACrimR 295.

178. [1940] 63 CLR 73, 87.

179. [1994] 1 ZLR 445 (H).

106. Although the courts have refused to recognize an evidentiary privilege regarding journalists and their sources, there appear to be two situations where journalists are not generally required to disclose the identity of their sources: at the interlocutory stage of a defamation action and during pretrial discovery procedures.[180]

In a civil action, the general rule is that a party must make available for inspection all relevant documents and answer all questions relevant to the matter at the interlocutory stage of the proceedings. The purpose of this is to clarify the issues to be tried in the action and enable each party to assess the strength of the other party's case. In the defamation action, like the *Nathan Shamuyarira* case above, a plaintiff may seek to use this process to ascertain the identity of the source of the allegedly defamatory material. This may be for the legitimate purpose of demonstrating that in publishing the material, the defendant was motivated by malice, lack of good faith or unreasonableness which could defeat certain defences that may be raised. There is however a rule of practice in certain jurisdictions that except in special circumstances, newspaper defendants in defamation actions will not be forced to reveal the identity of their sources at the interlocutory stage. However, once the trial begins, the newspaper defendant becomes subject to the general obligation to answer all relevant questions.[181] The rule covers journalists, editors, and others in the print as well as the electronic media. This rule is not absolute and will not apply where the defamation is considered to be of a very serious nature or where the making of the order to disclose the information at the interlocutory stage is necessary in the interest of justice. The purpose of this rule is certainly to protect newspapers because of the special role they play in facilitating the free flow of information to the public and the fact that disclosure of the identity of the source at the interlocutory stage is unnecessary if the newspaper accepts responsibility for what it publishes.

The equitable procedure of discovery can be used in an attempt to identify the source of information leaked to the media in order that legal action may be commenced against this source. In the absence of legislation prescribing other relevant considerations, a court will exercise its discretion to compel the disclosure of the identity of the source, where such disclosure is necessary in the interests of justice.[182] To prevent the applicant using the information, for example, simply to dismiss the source from employment, the courts would require the applicant to state the purposes for which the disclosure will be used and will restrict the applicant to use the material only for those purposes.[183] If the applicant has other effective remedies against other persons other than the source, then the court will refuse to compel the newspaper to disclose the source. For example, an applicant will have an effective remedy if the liability of the newspaper is coextensive with that of the source. In other words, there will be an effective remedy if the applicant has the same opportunity to recover adequate monetary compensation from the newspaper as he would have from the source. But if the newspaper has a defence

180. For full discussion of this, *see* Des Butler & Sharon Rodrick, *Australian Media Law* 325–330 (Lawbook Co. 2004).
181. *Wran v. Australian Broadcasting Commission* [1984] 3 NSWLR 241, 250; *John Fairfax & Sons Ltd v. Cojuangco* [1988] 165 CLR 346, 356; *Lew v. Herald & Weekly Times Ltd* [1999] 1 VR 313, 319–320.
182. *British Steel Corporation v. Granada Television Ltd* [1981] AC 1096.
183. *Ashworth Security Hospital v. MGN Ltd* [2002] UKHL 29, 60.

which will not be available to the source, then the order for discovery is likely to be made in the interests of justice.[184]

The difference between the two rules, especially in relation to actions for defamation is that the first rule cannot be used as a basis for refusing to grant an order for pretrial discovery as the respondent to such an application is not a defendant in a defamation action and the application is not an interlocutory proceeding. In fact, there is no subsisting action. Nevertheless, some of the policy considerations that influence the application of the first rule may be considered in deciding whether or not to make an order for preliminary discovery.

107. An excellent example of a country where the anonymity of journalistic sources is protected by statute is England. This is contained in section 10 of the Contempt of Court Act which provides:

> No court may require a person to disclose, nor is any person guilty of contempt of court for refusing to disclose, the source of information contained in a publication for which he is responsible, unless it be established to the satisfaction of the court that disclosure is necessary in the interests of justice or national security or for the prevention of disorder or crime.

The wording of this provision makes it therefore clear that the journalist has no absolute right to keep his source secret. Thus in *Secretary of State for Defence v. Guardian Newspapers*,[185] the House of Lords decided that the Secretary of State for Defence could require the editor of the *Guardian* to return official documents discussing how the government might handle any controversy which might arise on news of the arrival of cruise missiles in Britain. It felt that the disclosure was necessary in the interests of national security, since it was reasonable to fear that a civil servant prepared to leak these documents might on a future occasion supply the press with information, the publication of which would seriously imperil national security.

Three conclusions can be drawn from this approach.[186] First, that English courts do not consider the right not to disclose sources as an aspect of freedom of speech which should be protected unless the applicant makes a persuasive case for this. Second, the right is not confined to journalists alone but applies to just anybody responsible for any publication whether in a national newspaper or in a private leaflet. Third, the courts have to balance the right of freedom of the media on one hand and the interests which militate in favour of disclosure on the other hand. The courts are more concerned with the character of the speech made possible by the confidentiality of the source than any a priori right to secrecy of journalistic sources of information.

108. As noted above, neither the constitution nor statutory law specifically protects journalistic sources. Instead, journalists like ordinary citizens or sometimes, even more than ordinary citizens, are under an obligation under certain statutes to disclose information and thus their sources of information.

---

184. *Application of Cojuangco (No 2)* (Unreported), New South Wales Supreme Court, 6 Jan. 1989; *Cojuangco v. John Fairfax & Sons Ltd* (1991) Aust Torts Reports 81-068.

185. [1985] AC 339.

186. *See* Barendt, *Freedom of Speech* 437.

For a start, insofar as police inquiries are concerned, journalists are in the same position as anyone else. They are under no duty to provide answers. Although this may make the police investigation more difficult, the obdurate interviewee is not committing the offence of obstructing the police in the course of their duties. However, the police sometimes have exceptional powers to insist on answers to their questions in certain circumstances. For example, under section 13 of the National Security Act, which states with regards to the duty to give information as to the commission of offences as follows:

(1) Where the Director of Public Prosecutions is satisfied that there is reasonable ground for suspecting that an offence under this Act has been or is about to be committed and for believing that some person is able to furnish information with regard thereto, he may by writing under his hand authorize a named police officer to require that person to give any information in his possession relating to such suspected offence or anticipated offence and, if so required, to attend at such reasonable time and place as may be specified by such police officer.

(2) Any person who, having been required in terms of subsection (1) to give information or to attend at a specified time and place, wilfully fails to comply with such requirement or knowingly gives false information shall be guilty of an offence.[187]

Journalists may face questions from a court or tribunal. They, like anyone else can be compelled by a court order (a subpoena) to attend and give evidence. As section 114 of the Criminal Procedure and Evidence Act makes it clear, 'every person not expressly excluded by this Act from giving evidence shall be competent and compellable to give evidence in a criminal case in any court in Botswana or before a magistrate on a preparatory examination'.[188] With respect to the subpoena of witnesses, section 65 of the Criminal Procedure and Evidence Act states:

(1) A public prosecutor who has decided to institute or has instituted a preparatory examination, or an accused against whom a preparatory examination is being or is to be held (or the latter's representative), may compel the attendance of any person at such preparatory examination to give evidence, or to produce any book or document, by means of a subpoena, issued at the instance of the public prosecutor or accused, as the case may be, by the clerk of the court of the district in which the preparatory examination is being or is to be held.

(2) If a magistrate holding a preparatory examination believes that any person may be able to give evidence or to produce any book or document which is relevant to the subject of the examination, he may direct the clerk of the court to issue, in the manner aforesaid, a subpoena requiring such person to appear before him at a time and place mentioned therein to give evidence or to produce any book or document.

Under section 66(1) any person subpoenaed or warned to attend a preparatory examination who fails 'without reasonable excuse to obey the subpoena or warning', may be arrested and brought before the magistrate. The South African case of *S v. Matisonn*,[189] based on an analogous piece of legislation is instructive on the interpretation of these provisions. In it, a journalist working with the *Sunday Express* newspaper was subpoenaed in terms of section 205(1) of the Criminal Procedure Act 51 of 1977.

187. Cap. 23:01, Act 14 of 2005.
188. Cap. 08:02.
189. [1981] 3 SA 302 (A).

The nature of the evidence required of the journalist was the disclosure of the identity of the informant or source of the information relating to an article that appeared in the paper. He refused to disclose the information and was sentenced to fourteen-day imprisonment.

109. Although it is now quite clear that journalists' sources should be protected in order to enable them exercise their watchdog role more effectively, little has been done in Botswana to do this. Instead, there are a number of statutes which prohibit the disclosure of information or publication of certain kinds of information.[190] If publication or disclosure does occur in contravention of these statutes, journalists render themselves liable to arrest and punishment. A number of examples will suffice. In September 1995, the *Botswana Guardian* settled out of court in a criminal defamation case brought by Quill Hermans, the then Governor of the Bank of Botswana, which accused him of mismanagement. The paper preferred to pay the huge sum of BWP 250,000 to disclosing the source of its information. In March 1996, the Criminal Investigations Department of the Police Services threatened to charge a journalist working for the *Botswana Guardian* under the National Security Act which carries a twenty-five year imprisonment sentence, because of its refusal to disclose the source of information for an article concerning ritual murder.

110. The right to protect sources is acknowledged by the United Nations (UN). In 2000, the UN Special Rapporteur on the promotion and protection of freedom of opinion and expression wrote that he considers 'the protection of journalists' confidential sources indispensable for maintaining a free flow of information to journalists and therefore safeguarding the public's right to know', and further that 'a journalist should not be used as a source for investigating authorities to obtain evidence from'.[191] The African Commission in Chapter XV of its Banjul Declaration on Freedom of Expression protects the right to non-disclosure of sources. It lists a number of exemptions as follows:

> Media practitioners shall not be required to reveal confidential sources of information or to disclose other material held for journalistic purposes except in accordance with the following principles:

- the identity of the source is necessary for the investigation or prosecution of a serious crime, or the defence of a person accused of a criminal offence;
- the information or similar information leading to the same result cannot be obtained elsewhere;
- the public interest in disclosure outweighs the harm to freedom of expression; and
- disclosure has been ordered by a court, after a full hearing.

190. *See* paras 61—86 *supra* .
191. *See* Report of the Special Rapporteur, UN Economic and Social Council Doc. No. E/CN. 4/20000/63/Add.3 of 11 Feb. 2000.

While this is not ideal, they nevertheless represent minimum standards on which national legislation can be built upon.[192]

§4. ACCESS TO LEGAL PROCEEDINGS

111. There is a special connection between the principle of open justice and media coverage of court proceedings. The open justice principle requires that in general, courts of law must conduct their business publicly unless this would result in injustice.[193] The principle serves two functions:

(1) It is a safeguard against judicial bias, unfairness, and incompetence, by ensuring that judges are accountable in the performance of their duties.
(2) It maintains public confidence in the impartial administration of justice by ensuring that judicial hearings are subject to public scrutiny.[194]

The essence of the open justice principle is that it allows the public as well as the parties to a case to be present during judicial proceedings. It is an embodiment of the values of openness, accountability, and the rule of law in the administration of justice in a democracy. The principle therefore promotes transparency and the integrity of the judicial process by guarding against any potential abuse of the process.

The constitution of Botswana guarantees the principle of open justice under section 10(10), which provides that:

> Except with the agreement of all the parties thereto, all proceedings of every court and proceedings for the determination of the existence or extent of any civil right or obligation before any other adjudicating authority, including the announcement of the decision of the court or other authority, shall be held in public.

The Court of Appeal in case of *Your Friend (Pty) Ltd t/a Gabz FM v. Law Society of Botswana and Others* has observed that in the light of the above provision, the right of the public and the media to access judicial proceedings is not in any doubt.[195] Furthermore, in *Collins Newman & Co and Others v. Genuispoint Investment (Pty) Ltd and Others,*[196] the High Court of Botswana acknowledged that open justice envisages reporting of court proceedings by the media. The court opined that media reporting of judicial proceedings is a corollary to the right of access to the court by members of

192. C. Bussiek & H. Bussiek, *The Media: Making Democracy Work* 43–44 (Friedrich-Ebert-Stiftung 2004).
193. *The Queen on the Application of Guardian News and Media Limited v. City of Westminster Magistrates' Court* [2012] EWCA Civ 420 at para. 2.
194. *Ibid.*
195. CACGB-130-15 (unreported, delivered on 4 Jul. 2016), at para. 22.
196. UAHGB-000085-16 (unreported, delivered on 12 May 2016).

the public, a hallmark of the principle of open justice.[197] Since the rationale of open justice is that justice should be open to public scrutiny, the media are the conduit through which most members of the public receive information about court proceedings.[198] Open justice is thus inextricably linked to the freedom of the media to report judicial proceedings. The principle demands that courts of law should not discourage fair and accurate reports of their proceedings.[199]

112. The media in Botswana play a critical role in opening the administration of justice to the public. The broadcast media, in particular, has potential to promote transparency of the administration of justice because it is the most accessible due to its ability to overcome barriers of illiteracy. While the courts of law have acknowledged the importance of the media in covering legal proceedings, in practice, there is a double standard whereby while the print media is generally allowed to cover court proceedings, the broadcast cast media is denied the same privilege.

Although the media plays an important role in promoting open justice, there may be instances where opening the judicial process to the public through the media may conflict with other equally important constitutional values such as the right to a fair trial and the privacy of participants in the judicial process. When such cases do occur, a fair balance must be struck between the competing interests. In many countries around the world, it would appear that whenever there is a clash between the freedom of expression of the media to cover legal proceedings, especially the broadcast media, and other rights, the former is often sacrificed.

The value of publicity in judicial proceedings, coupled with the public's right of access to court proceedings, present a compelling argument that media coverage of legal proceedings, especially through broadcasting should ordinarily be permitted. The broadcast media today is an important source of news and information for the general public. The medium has one special value in the dissemination of news and information; it 'provides the audience with a personal experience of current events instead of a second-hand reported version'.[200] The potential of the broadcast media in promoting transparency of judicial proceedings and its accessibility to the public has been acknowledged by the Court of Appeal of Botswana. The court has observed that audio and visual recording of judicial proceedings may compensate for the sometimes imperfect reports of court proceedings that are conveyed through the print media.[201]

There is a strong argument that the default position should be, unless there are demonstrable fundamental rights and other interests that are properly substantiated which outweigh the interests of justice, judicial proceedings should be broadcast. However, the reality on the ground seems to be that there is general reluctance by courts worldwide to permit the broadcasting of judicial proceedings. In Botswana, this attitude is reflected in the High Court's decision in the case of *Your Friend (Pty) Ltd*

197. *Collins Newman & Co and Others v. Genuispoint Investment (Pty) Ltd and Others* n 8 above at para. 92.
198. *A (Respondent) v. British Broadcasting Corporation (Appellant) (Scotland)* [2014] UKSC 25 at para. 26.
199. *See Attorney-General v. Leveller Magazine [*1978] AC 440 at 450.
200. M. Dockray, *Courts on Television*, 51 Modern L. Rev. 593–604 (1988).
201. *Your Friend (Pty) Ltd t/a Gabz FM v. Law Society of Botswana and Others* (*supra*) at paras. 47-48.

t/a Gabz FM v. The Law Society of Botswana and Others, In re: The Law Society of Botswana and Another v. The President of Botswana and Others.[202] The applicant in this case, a private radio station, had brought an application for permission to be allowed to bring into the courtroom its equipment and to broadcast live proceedings in a matter that was before the court. The matter concerned an application in which the Law Society of Botswana and another were challenging the powers of the president in the appointment of judges of the High Court. In rejecting the application, the court held that the practicalities on the ground did not permit the broadcasting of the proceedings. The court noted that the inclusion of the broadcast media would take up the limited space in the courtroom leading to over-crowding. It is curious that the decision was taken even though the court had not inquired about the size of the equipment or number of people that the applicant would bring into the court if granted permission. The proceedings which the applicant wished to cover were in no doubt of public importance. Allowing the broadcasting of the court proceedings would have opened the proceedings of the court to the public on an issue of national importance thereby not only serving the principle of open justice, but also giving due regard to the broadcaster's freedom of expression. The court did not consider these important issues in its judgment.

113. Several arguments are advanced to justify the reluctance by courts to allow the live broadcast of the judicial proceeding, but there are arguably two main ones. First, it is said that the broadcasting may infringe upon the privacy of litigants and witnesses.[203] Second, that broadcasting may interfere with the proper administration of justice.[204] There are two facets to the second argument:

(1) That the presence of recording equipment in the courtroom may compromise the right to a fair trial. It is argued that the presence of broadcasting equipment would put stress on witnesses, lawyers, and judges inhibiting interaction thereby creating a material risk that justice may be impaired.[205] Another argument is that the knowledge by potential witnesses that their testimony will receive extensive radio and television broadcasting may deter witnesses from testifying.[206]

(2) The second facet of the argument is concerned with avoiding physical disruption of judicial proceedings and maintaining the dignity and decorum of the court.[207] Opponents of the live broadcast of judicial proceedings contend that cameras and broadcasting equipment may cause physical disruption, for example, that the lighting equipment may be intrusive. Furthermore, that the presence of the

202. MAHGB-000562-15 (unreported, delivered on 15 Oct. 2015).

203. *See South African Broadcasting Corporation Limited v. Mark Thatcher and Others* [2005] 4 ALL SA 353.

204. E. Thompson, *Does the Open Justice Principle Require Cameras to be Permitted in the Courtroom and the Broadcasting of Legal Proceedings?*, 3(2) J. Media L. 211–236 (2011).

205. *See* amongst others, M. Dockray, 'Courts on Television' (1988) 51 Modern Law Review 593-640, *and South African Broadcasting Corporation Limited v. National Director of Public Prosecutions and Others* 2007 (1) 523 at 532.

206. *Ibid.*

207. E. Thompson, *Does the Open Justice Principle Require Cameras to be Permitted in the Courtroom and the Broadcasting of Legal Proceedings?*.

equipment could also have a distracting effect on the participants thereby interfering with a court's primary role in administering justice.[208]

Restrictions on the public's right of access and the broadcasting of legal proceedings constitute limitations on both the open justice principle and the broadcast media's freedom of expression. These two values are not only internationally recognized rights, but are also entrenched in the Constitution of Botswana. Any limitations on the two rights under both international law and Botswana law are required to satisfy both the conditions of necessity and proportionality. These are designed to ensure that derogations from these rights are narrowly and strictly interpreted. The reasons advanced to justify limitations on the right of broadcasters to cover judicial proceedings pursue legitimate aims – protection of privacy and the right to a fair trial. However, a general approach where courts consider the exclusion of broadcasters from covering legal proceedings as the rule and not an exception fails the requirement of proportionality. The principle of proportionality would require that the exclusion of the broadcast media from judicial proceedings must be strictly required and assessed on a case-by-case basis. A court will be called upon to assess all the competing legal interests in a particular case before excluding the broadcast media from covering judicial proceedings. Where there are constitutional rights that clash, it is the responsibility of the court to reconcile them.

208. *Ibid.*

Chapter 3. Journalists' Liability

§1. General Information on the Liability System

114. There is no special liability regime that applies exclusively to journalists. We have however seen a number of statutes which contain restrictions generally on the exercise of freedom of speech which apply to all media practitioners.[209] Most of these statutes provide sanctions for any violations of these restrictions. In addition to the liability that could arise under these statutes, there are also common law limitations on the exercise of freedom of speech, the main ones being right to reputation and privacy, which are discussed below.

§2. Defamation

I. Definition and Nature of Defamation

115. Under the influence of English law, the old delict of *injuria* has split up into different delicts, each with its own name, leaving a residue to bear the ancient title. One of these is the modern law of defamation which now protects reputation not merely as an interest of personality but also as an asset or species of property.[210]

There is no exhaustive and entirely satisfactory definition of defamation. The most widely cited definition that appears is that given by Aguda CJ (as he then was) in *Karim v. Weterings*, where he said:

A defamatory statement is one calculated to lower the plaintiff in the estimation of right-thinking men or cause him to be shunned or avoided, or to expose him to hatred, contempt or ridicule, or to convey an imputation on him disparaging him or injurious to him in his office, profession, calling or trade.[211]

It is a wrong that can be committed not only by words, written or spoken, but also by acts or gestures. To succeed in an action for defamation, the plaintiff must prove that the statement:

- was defamatory;
- that it referred to him; and
- that it was published; that is, communicated to at least one person other than the plaintiff.

In this way, the law of defamation attempts to reconcile and protect two of the most highly valued but often conflicting interests in modern society – the individual's right

209. *See* paras 61-86 *supra.*
210. R.J. Mckerron, *The Law of Delict* 170 (7th edn, Juta & Co. 1971).
211. [1974] 2 BLR 34, 39.

to an unimpaired reputation on one hand, and the free flow of information on the other. It is an antithesis which is particularly acute when the matter at issue is one of public or general interest.[212] The following analysis of the requirements of liability and the defences available to the defendant reflect the law's continuous attempt to come to terms with this difficult dilemma.

II. Requirements of Liability

A. Proof of Defamatory Words or Conduct

116. The plaintiff in an action for defamation must set out and plead the actual words used or the conduct displayed and not merely describe their substance, purpose or effect, and show that this is defamatory in the sense that it tends to lower his reputation in the estimation of right-thinking persons in society generally or tends to cause him to be shunned or avoided.[213] Common examples of statements which have given rise to actions for defamation are:

(1) statements reflecting on the moral character of the plaintiff, for example, by attributing to him the commission of a crime or imputing untruthfulness, dishonesty, immorality or any kind of dishonourable or improper conduct;[214]
(2) the imputation of a contagious or infectious disease like AIDS which is likely to prevent people from associating with the plaintiff;
(3) the imputation of unfitness or incompetence in any office, profession, calling or business.[215]

Spoken words that are merely abusive and thus injure the plaintiff's self-esteem (i.e., dignity) are not actionable as defamation, which is concerned with, and protects only the esteem in which others hold the plaintiff. For instance, in *Muir v. January*, where the plaintiff alleged that the defendant had referred to her as 'you fucking dog', Livesey Luke CJ clearly brought out the difference between statements which are defamatory and those that are merely abusive when he said:

212. *See* J.G. Fleming, *The Law of Torts* 500 (7th edn, The Law Book Co. Ltd 1987).
213. *Karim v. Weterings* [1974] 2 BLR 34; *Muir v. January* C T 860/88 in Otlhogile, *A Casebook on Defamation*, 13.
214. *Masieman v. Maswabi* [1976–1978] BLR 92 (allegation that the plaintiff is a thief who steals government drugs and sells them in private and is a drug addict); *Mulwa v. Mosienyane* 1984 BLR 138 (imputation that the plaintiff was a womanizer and an abortionist); *A-G v. Ghanzi Hotel* [1986] BLR 178 (allegation that the respondents practised racial discrimination); *Monyamane v. Anderson* [1987] BLR 270 (allegation of corruption on the respondent's part); *Masipa v. Leshope* [1991] BLR 133 (allegation of the commission of acts of indecency, immorality and adultery); *Kgafela v. Maoto* [1992] BLR 256 (imputation of immorality); *Gobudilwe & another v. Shaobuye & another* [1993] BLR 56 (allegation that plaintiffs were witches).
215. *Mosieman v. Maswabi*, *infra* no. 262; *Mulwa v. Mosienyane*, *supra* no. 234; *Masipa v. Leshope*, *supra* no. 215.

> The question then is whether the words 'you fucking dog' have a defamatory imputation. In my opinion to call a person a 'dog' may be offensive and insulting, but it does not per se convey a defamatory meaning. And to qualify the 'dog' by using the vulgar adjective 'fucking', does not thereby make the words defamatory; it merely makes the abuse more vulgar. In my judgment therefore the words alleged to have been used by the defendant were not defamatory per se but were mere vulgar abuse.[216]

117. The words or conduct of the defendant may be either:

(1) defamatory per se, that is, defamatory in their natural and ordinary meaning; or
(2) in addition to being defamatory per se, or are only defamatory in the light of an innuendo or a secondary meaning.

1. Where the Words or Conduct are Defamatory Per Se

118. Where the plaintiff relies on the ordinary or natural meaning of the words, he must prove that the circumstances under which they were published were such that an ordinary reasonable man would understand them in a defamatory sense. The ordinary and natural meanings of words are not necessarily their dictionary meaning. The general context and the surrounding circumstances must be examined. In *Kgafela v. Maoto*,[217] Schreiner cited with approval Diddcott J who had said in *Demmers v. Wyllie and Others*,[218] concerning the readers of newspapers:

> One must try not to approach this task [linguistic interpretation of the statement] like a lawyer poring over a contract, a will, or a statute. A 'coldly logical cast of mind'... would not be a recommended tool, even if one had it. The standard is that of the ordinary reader instead, who has no legal training or other special discipline.... The ordinary reader of an organ like that [The Sunday Tribune] does not study its contents critically, analyse than astutely, dissect them minutely, or search them for nuances and subtle implications. He tends rather to take them at their face value, without much discernment.... He seldom notices ambiguities or contradictions which are not blatant. When they are present, the most obvious meaning is all that strikes him as a rule.[219]

Thus, the ordinary and natural meanings of words are judged by the standards of the ordinary reasonable reader, viewer or listener. This excludes the cynics who would think none the worst of a person regardless of what was imputed to him and persons with censorious minds who regard every accusation, however trivial, as lowering a person's reputation.[220]

216. *Muir v. January* C T 860/88 in Otlhogile, *A Casebook on Defamation*, 15.
217. [1992] BLR 257.
218. [1978] 4 SA 619 (A).
219. [1992] BLR 257, 264.
220. *See* W.V.H. Rogers, *Winfield & Jolowicz on Tort* 398 (15th edn, Sweet & Maxwell 1998).

As the court pointed out in *Mulwa v. Mosienyane*,[221] the issue is not whether those who read or heard the words believed them but rather whether they were defamatory. A person can be defamed even though most persons who heard or read the words did not believe them. Where the words are ambiguous and have more than one meaning, then, if on a preponderance of probabilities it is found that ordinary readers would attribute a defamatory meaning to them, then, subject to any defences that the defendant may rely on, the plaintiff will succeed, even though there is room for a non-defamatory meaning.[222]

2. Where the Words or the Conduct Have a Secondary Meaning : Innuendo

119. Where the words or conduct appear so innocent that they are not defamatory per se or even where they are defamatory per se but the plaintiff wishes to rely upon an additional defamatory meaning to highlight the sting in the imputation, he must expressly and clearly plead an innuendo. An innuendo or secondary meaning has been described as an unusual meaning which could only be attributed to the words by a hearer having knowledge of special circumstances.[223] The onus is on the plaintiff to prove the special circumstances which support the defamatory meaning which he attributes to the words.

There are several situations where words may appear per se innocent but become defamatory because of special facts known to those to whom they were addressed. Thus, to publish a story in a newspaper alleging that a Minister regularly visits 'Liberty house' is per se innocent. This becomes defamatory to those who know that 'liberty house' is a brothel. In *Morrison v. Ritchie*,[224] a newspaper inadvertently announced that the plaintiff had given birth to twins. This innocuous announcement became defamatory when it turned out that the plaintiff was married only four weeks before the report. Generally, it is prudent for the plaintiff to plead an innuendo alternatively to the natural and ordinary meaning of the words so that should he fail to prove the innuendo, he will still be able to fall back and rely on the natural and ordinary meaning of the words.

B. Proof of Reference to the Plaintiff

120. A defamatory statement is not actionable unless the plaintiff can prove that it is published 'of and concerning' him and not some other person. The test for identification is the same as that for the defamatory meaning: would a reasonable sensible reader identify the plaintiff as the person defamed?

Where the statement does not on the face of it refers to the plaintiff as an identified or identifiable person, he must plead the special facts and circumstances which support the allegation that the statement refers to him. Three questions have generated a lot

221. [1984] BLR 138.

222. *Demmers v. Wylie* [1980] 1 SA 835 (A).

223. *See* J.A. Schreiner, *National Union of Distributive Workers v. Cleghorn and Harris*, [1946] AD 984, 997.

224. [1902] 4 F 645; *see also*, *Cassidy v. Daily Mirror Newspapers Ltd* [1929] 2 KB 331.

of debate: whether there can be defamation of a class or group; whether there can be defamation of a corporation; and whether there can be defamation of a deceased person?

Where the defamatory statement is made against a class or a group, for example, lawyers, members of a Medical Council, or University Professors, the position appears to be that only members of that class or group who can show that the circumstances were such that any reasonable person acquainted with them was likely to understand the statement as referring to them as individuals stands a chance of succeeding in an action for defamation. Although the actual identification of the plaintiff is not necessary, a reference to his office or some other identifiable characteristic or feature would suffice. However, if the statement either refers to a more restricted and probably easily identifiable class or group or is couched in such terms that it can reasonably be interpreted to refer to each member of that class or group, then each of them is free to sue. In *Neumann CC v. Beauty Without Cruelty International*,[225] a poster read, *inter alia*, 'It takes up to 40 dumb animals to make a fur coat. But only one to wear it' and 'if you don't want millions of animals tortured in leg-hold traps, don't buy a fur coat'. It was held that these words were not reasonably capable of referring to the plaintiff, a seller of furs. And in *Sauls v. Hendrickse*,[226] where the alleged defamatory article had referred to 'office bearers' of a registered trade union not to *all* or *the* office bearers, it was held that this could not be reasonably be considered as referring to the plaintiff in particular.

As regards the defamation of a deceased person, although recognized under Roman and Roman-Dutch law, the modern position is that since reputation is a strictly personal asset, no one should sue in respect of a defamatory statement published concerning another person, whether deceased or alive. Nevertheless, living heirs or relatives can sue where they can prove that the statement was also defamatory of them.

The controversy over the right of juristic or artificial persons such as corporations, trade unions and even the government to sue for defamation has raged over the years. Hannah J in the High Court, and Kentridge J in the Court of Appeal reviewed most of the recent authorities on the subject in *A-G v. Ghanzi Hotel (Pty) Ltd*.[227] This case conclusively settles the law insofar as trading corporations are concerned by holding that, as juristic persons distinct from their members, they have a reputation of their own to maintain and therefore can sue for any defamatory statement that affects their trade or business. At some stage, there were doubts whether a non-trading corporation, such as the university or a political party can also sue for defamation. This can now be regarded as settled since the judgment in *Argus Printing and Publishing Co. Ltd v. Inkatha Freedom Party*.[228] It was strenuously argued in this case that all political parties should be denied the right to sue for defamation on the basis that his would be in keeping with the need to foster freedom of political debate. The court rejected the argument and affirmed the principle laid down in the earlier case of *Dhlomo NO v. Natal Newspapers (Pty) Ltd*[229] that there was no overriding reason of principle or policy to exclude the right of certain categories of juristic persons to sue for defamation,

225. [1986] 4 SA 675 (C).
226. [1992] 3 SA 912 (A).
227. [1985] BLR 607.
228. [1992] 3 SA 579 (A).
229. [1989] 1 SA 945 (A).

although it stressed that each case must be decided on its own merits. However, since *Die Spoorbond v. SAR*,[230] the law is now firmly settled that the government cannot sue for defamation. This does not prevent an individual official, government minister or even a judge from suing for defamation in a private capacity. As the Zimbabwe Supreme Court recently pointed out in *Posts and Telecommunication Corporation v. Modus Publications (Private) Ltd*[231] the prohibition applies not only to government but also extends to artificial persons who are 'part of the governance of the country' such as parastatals. It is felt that it would be improper and even dangerous to allow the state's wealth, derived partly from taxpayers to be used in this way because it could result in freedom of expression being eroded and criticism of government being suppressed.

C. Proof of Publication

121. Publication is the communication of the defamatory matter to at least one person other than the person defamed. There is however no publication if the person to whom the words were addressed is deaf or could not understand the language used. While a communication to the plaintiff's spouse is sufficient publication, a communication between spouses is not.

In many cases, publication of the defamatory matter will be presumed without the plaintiff actually proving this, as for instance, where the matter is contained in a book or newspaper. Similarly, the contents of a postcard which has been posted, or a telegram which has been dispatched, will be presumed to have been published.[232] In *Huth v. Huth*,[233] the defamatory matter was in an unsealed letter sent through the post and the letter was opened by a butler acting out of curiosity and in breach of his duties. As it was not part of his duties to open mails, it was held that there was no publication for which the defendant was responsible.

Everyone who takes an active part in producing or publishing defamatory matter is prima facie liable. For a newspaper article, this includes not only the writer but also the editor, printer, publisher, and proprietor, all of who are presumed to have been acquainted with the material. Mere distributors, such as booksellers, vendors, and other persons who play only a subordinate part in disseminating the material, although prima facie liable, will have a good defence if they show that they were ignorant of the fact that the work being distributed contained defamatory matter and that they acted without negligence, and there were no circumstances which should have put them on their guard or inquiry. It must be noted that one of the few differences that existed between delict and the law of tort,[234] the rule imposing strict liability on the mass media (the press, radio and television) which was applied in *Ghanzi Hotel (Pty) Ltd v. A-G (No. 2)*,[235] has now been altered in the landmark decision of the South

230. [1946] AD 999.
231. *See* 3 *Southern African Media Law*, No. 3 (August), 1998, 3–4.
232. *Patrick Motlhwa v. The State* CR APP 175/82, *see* Otlhogile, *A Casebook on Defamation*, 97.
233. [1915] 3 KB 32.
234. Another difference is that, unlike English law, the law applied in Botswana does not distinguish between spoken defamation (slander) and written defamation (libel). *See* Aguda CJ, in *Karim v. Weterings* [1974] 2 BLR 34.
235. [1985] BLR 452.

African Supreme Court in *National Media Ltd & others v. Bogashi.*[236] The court rejected the doctrine of strict liability of media defendants and held that the defence of absence of fault was available to them as it was to others.

Every repetition of defamatory matter is a fresh publication and creates a fresh cause of action. As the Court of Appeal pointed out in *Kgafela v. Maoto*,[237] the person who first published the defamatory matter will only be liable for its further republication in three exceptional circumstances:

(1) where he authorized or intended that there should be republication;
(2) where republication is the natural and probable result of the original publication; and
(3) where the person to whom the publication was made was under a moral duty to pass on the information to another person and the defendant was aware of the existence of the moral duty to republish the matter.[238]

III. Defences

122. There are several defences that the defendant may invoke to justify his act or to exonerate himself from liability. The three main ones are: justification, privilege, and fair comment. There are other possible defences, such as, consent, mistake, provocation, and probably the absence of *animus injuriandi*, which need to be briefly discussed.

A. Justification

123. While in the law of tort, truth in itself is a good defence, in delict, it is well settled that truth or justification without proof of public benefit, is not a complete defence, and may only be pleaded in mitigation of damages. Thus, the full defence consists of truth and public benefit.

1. Truth

124. Once the defendant pleads justification, the plaintiff does not need to prove the falsity of the statement, for the law presumes this in his favour. The onus is, however, on the defendant to prove the truth of the statement. As Hannah J pointed out in *Ghanzi Hotel (Pty) Ltd v. A-G*,[239] the defendant does not necessarily have to prove that the alleged defamatory statements are true in every minute detail; it is sufficient if he shows that the statement is substantially true. The fact that there is some exaggeration in the language used will not defeat the defence, unless the exaggeration is such that it is calculated to convey a wrong impression to the detriment of the plaintiff's reputation.

236. [1998] 4 SA 1196 (SCA).
237. [1992] BLR 356.
238. *Ibid.*, 268.
239. [1985] BLR 607.

Thus, an allegation that a person is a drunkard cannot be justified by proof that he got drunk on one occasion.

Where the statement contains specific charges, the defendant must prove that each of them is true in substance and fact. And where this consists of comments as well as allegations of fact, both must be proved true.

2. Public Benefit

125. In addition to showing that the statement was true, the defendant must also show that it was published for the public's benefit. In fact, the courts have used both the terms 'public benefit' and 'public interest' to describe this aspect of the defence. Whichever of the two terms is used does not matter, provided the proper emphasis is made; which is whether the information conveyed by the statement will provide some advantage or benefit to the public at large. The publication of information concerning the integrity or competence of public officials or the management of public institutions is clearly in the public interest. In *Mulwa v. Mosienyane*,[240] Hannah J. in holding that the public had no interest in imputations that a medical practitioner was a womanizer and an abortionist who had performed an abortion on a girl he was supposed to have made pregnant many years earlier, cited with approval the dicta of Wessels J, who had pointed out in *Patterson v. Engelenburg and Wallach's Ltd* that 'a scandal cannot be raked up unless it is done for the public benefit: and this depends largely on the time, the manner and the occasion of the publication'.[241] The learned judge also relied on the classic statement of the law contained in the judgment of De Villiers CJ, in *Graham v. Ker*:

> As a general principle, I take it to be for the public benefit that the truth as to the character of individuals should be known. But the worst characters sometimes reform, and some of the inducements to reformation would be removed if stories as to past transgressions could with impunity be raked up after a long lapse of time. Public interest, as I conceive it, would suffer rather than benefit from any unnecessary reviving of forgotten scandals.[242]

Thus, the revelation that a happily married woman was once a prostitute can hardly be considered to serve any public interest other than that of promoting gossip. In the final analysis, before deciding whether a particular statement was in the public's interest, the courts would have regard to all the surrounding circumstances particularly the subject matter of the statement, the time, manner, and occasion of its publication.

B. Fair Comment

126. This defence is based on the fundamental principle that honest and fair criticism is indispensable to the efficient working of any public institution or office

240. [1984] BLR 138.
241. [1917] TPD 350, 361.
242. [1892] 9 SC 185, 187.

and also salutary for those private individuals who make themselves or their work the object of public interest.[243] It is an integral part of the right of free speech.

There are four essentials for the defence to succeed, namely:

(1) the comment must refer to a matter of public interest;
(2) the comment must be an opinion not an assertion of fact;
(3) the comment must be fair; and
(4) the comment must not be malicious.

127. As regards the first requirement, there is no exact definition of what constitutes a matter of public interest. It clearly covers areas of public concern such as the conduct of public officials, the administration of justice, parliamentary proceedings, and the management of public and parapublic institutions. It also includes private matters that have been brought into the public domain and as such may attract comments and criticisms, such as criticisms of a public speech, a book, an article or an arts exhibition.

As a second requirement of the defence, the statement in issue must be one of opinion. Where it consists of assertions of facts, the defendant may only be able to rely on the defence of justification. Although it is not always easy to distinguish statements of facts from opinions, the test is not the intentions of the speaker or writer but rather the effect of the statement on a reasonable hearer or reader. Every statement must be examined in the context in which it was made.

To satisfy the third requirement that the comment should be fair, the statement must be based on true facts in existence when the comment was made. Comments about a person can hardly be fair if the underlying facts on which they are based are false. It is therefore necessary to state all the facts or sufficient facts which justify the comments. The mere violence in criticism or the fact that the criticisms are extravagant, exaggerated or prejudiced will not necessarily render the resulting comments unfair. Nevertheless, the courts will not sanction the use of criticism as a cloak for violent abuse or invectives having no bearing to the facts stated.

Finally, the defence of fair comment will be defeated by proof that the defendant was actuated by malice. Malice means evil motive or spite and is usually inferred from the surrounding circumstances, such as; where the words used are totally disproportionate to the facts; the previous relationship between the parties; and the wider dissemination of the statement than was reasonably necessary.

C. Privilege

128. On certain occasions, the law recognizes that freedom of communication without the fear of an action for defamation is more important than the protection of a man's reputation. Although such communication is generally referred to as privileged communication, it is the occasion that is privileged while the communication is protected. There are two such privileged occasions: the first, absolute privilege is limited in scope but the defamed person has no legal redress however outrageous the untrue statement and however malicious the motive of the maker. The second, qualified

243. W.V.H. Rogers, *Winfield & Jolowicz on Tort* 421 (15th edn, Sweet & Maxwell 1998).

privilege, is much wider in scope but protects the maker of the statement only if he acted honestly and without malice.

1. Absolute Privilege

129. It would seem that the concept of absolute privilege was unknown to Roman and Roman-Dutch law and is essentially of English law origin. In Botswana, the scope of absolute privilege appears to be limited to members of Parliament and members of the House of Chiefs. In this respect, section 3 of the National Assembly (Powers and Privileges) Act, 1980 states:

> No civil or criminal proceedings may be instituted against any member for words spoken before, or written in a report to, the Assembly or to a committee, or by reason of any matter or thing so brought by him by petition, Bill, motion or otherwise.

Section 3 of the House of Chiefs (Powers and Privileges) Act, 1980 states:

> No civil or criminal proceedings may be instituted against any member for words spoken before the house, or by reason of any matter or thing brought by him by motion or otherwise before the house.

According to the respective section 13 of the above acts, the defence of absolute privilege also protects any persons who have been authorized by either House to publish 'any minutes, reports, decisions or messages'.

The effect of these provisions is to protect members of Parliament and the House of Chiefs from being sued for damages or being criminally prosecuted in a court for words spoken or written in the course of parliamentary or House of Chiefs proceedings. It has been repeatedly reiterated in dicta that the privilege, at least, insofar as Parliament is concerned, rests upon two bases: first, that Parliament must have complete control over its own proceedings and its own members and that accordingly, matters arising in this sphere should be examined, discussed and adjudged in Parliament and not elsewhere. Second, that a member must have a complete right of free speech in Parliament without any fear that his motives or intentions or reasoning will be questioned or held against him thereafter.[244] However, not every act done or word uttered in Parliament or in the House of Chiefs is covered by the privilege. A defamatory statement made by one member to another in the course of a private conversation in the precincts of Parliament or contained in a letter posted by a member of the public to a member of Parliament in the precincts of Parliament, is not protected by the absolute privilege that attaches to proceedings in Parliament.[245] In *Poovalingam v. Rajbansi*[246] the respondent, a Member of Parliament is alleged to have arranged for a letter which he

244. *See Church of Scientology of California v. Johnson-Smith* [1972] 1 ALL ER 378; *Rost v. Edwards and others* [1990] 2 QB 460; *In the Matter of Parliamentary Privilege Act*, 1770 [1958] 2 ALL ER 329.
245. S.A. de Smith, cited by Corbett CJ in *Poovalingham v. Rajbansi* [1992] 1 SA 283.
246. [1992] 1 SA 283.

had written, and which the appellant, also a member of Parliament claimed, defamed him, to be distributed to all members of Parliament. The letter was hand-delivered to all the members of Parliament at their seats in Parliament. The respondent contended that the letter, even if defamatory was covered by parliamentary privilege. Corbett CJ, after carefully reviewing the English authorities held that since the letter was neither a 'petition nor a bill, nor a resolution nor a motion' and had nothing to do with the parliamentary business of that day, it was not covered by the privilege. The effect of this decision is that the privilege is limited to what is said and done by a member in the exercise of his functions as a member of Parliament or the House of Chiefs and the transaction of the houses' business.

2. Qualified Privilege

130. Qualified privilege (sometimes also referred to as provisional privilege), unlike absolute privilege, is defeated by proof that the defendant was actuated by malice. The main instances when this privilege applies are:

- statements made in discharge of a duty;
- statements made in the furtherance of or protection of an interest;
- statements made in the course of judicial and quasi-judicial proceedings; and
- reports of parliamentary, judicial, and other public proceedings.

a. Statements Made in Discharge of a Duty

131. This defence applies where both the maker of the statement and the receiver are under a reciprocal legal, moral or social duty to make or receive the statement. This raises two distinct questions; first, whether the occasion was privileged and second, whether the statement made came within the privilege warranted by the occasion.

There is usually no problem where the defendant relies on a legal duty to make the statement. The difficulties arise with regards to arguments based on the existence of a moral or social duty. The most satisfactory test followed by English and South African courts is whether the circumstances are such that any reasonable person in the position of the defendant would have considered it his duty to speak.[247] It is an objective test which clearly does not depend on the state of mind of the defendant. The most common instance where there usually arises a reciprocal duty to make and to receive a statement is where there exists a special relationship between the parties. Thus, qualified privilege attaches to communications between family members concerning, for instance, the suitability of a suitor, and between one public servant and another in the performance of their duties.[248] This is, however, not limited to such special relationships, and no comprehensive catalogue can be given. However, the defence

247. *See* Lindley LJ in *Stuart v. Bell* [1891] 2 QB 341, 350; and Watermeyer A.J.A. in *De Waal v. Ziervogel* 1938 AD 112, 122.

248. *Ngope v. O'Brien Quinn* [1987] BLR 398, [1988] BLR 121; *Masipa v. Leshope* [1991] BLR 133.

of qualified privilege should apply to a confidential reference or testimonial given by a former employer in response to inquiries from a prospective employer. The defence could also cover statements voluntarily made, provided the volunteer felt himself bound to speak. This should protect persons such as police informants.

However, the privilege will be forfeited if the privileged occasion was abused either by the communication of a totally irrelevant and extraneous matter or some evidence that the defendant was prompted by spite or ill will. Two recent cases illustrate the application of these principles in Botswana. In *Masipa v. Lishope*,[249] the defendant, an employee of the Gaborone City Council, in a minute addressed to the Town clerk and copied to the Town Engineer of the Council made the following allegations about the plaintiff, a fellow employee: (a) that the plaintiff abused his position and authority by contravening regulations and not acting in the Council's interest; (b) that on several occasions the plaintiff used an official vehicle for his personal business; (c) that the plaintiff unlawfully borrowed Council stores; and (d) that the plaintiff made love with ladies in Council offices. The defendant pleaded, *inter alia*, qualified privilege. It was held that although the minute was published on a privileged occasion, because the defendant as an employee had a duty to communicate any matters detrimental to the Council, the defence was forfeited because he had been actuated by an improper motive. This was inferred from the fact that he had made the allegations knowing them to be false or recklessly, not caring whether they were true or false. In *Kgafela v. Maoto*,[250] the plaintiff brought an action against the headmaster of a school based on a letter the latter had written to two senior officials in the Ministry of Education. Although the letter purported to be a report of a Board of Governors' meeting which the plaintiff although not a member had instigated, it contained some vague insinuations of misconduct on the plaintiff's part. It was held that although the defamatory words were published to the two officials on a privileged occasion, the defence failed because what the defendant wrote fell outside the scope of the protection afforded. The court felt that since the plaintiff had no official connection with the school, insinuations about his private life were of no interest to the two officials. While the principle applied in this case is valid, the court appears to have taken a rather narrow view of the ambit of protection afforded by the defence. Certainly, the officials must have an interest in the private affairs of a prominent local elite like the plaintiff, whose activities were affecting the proper functioning of the school.

b. *Statements Made in the Furtherance of or Protection of an Interest*

132. The underlying principles here are the same as those that relate to statements made in discharge of a duty. Both the maker of the statement and the person receiving it must have a legitimate interest or a duty to make or receive the statement. Similarly, the communication made must be within the privilege and go no further than is necessary to protect the legitimate interests of the parties. The defence certainly does not apply to idle talk, rumour and gossip. In *Toogood v. Spyring*,[251] it was held that a tenant is entitled to make a complaint to his landlord regarding the conduct of a person engaged

249. [1992] BLR 256.
250. [1992] BLR 356.
251. P1834 1 Cr. M & R 181.

by the landlord to execute repairs on the premises. In the majority of cases, the interest is a business or financial one, although any other legitimate interest worthy of protection by the law will do, provided the matter affects the defendant personally and is not merely something that concerns the community at large. Another illustration of this defence, this time made by a defendant acting in defence of his property is *Force v. Warren*.[252] A shopkeeper who suspected a woman of stealing a piece of meat from his shop was held to be privileged in asking a customer who was present when the theft was supposed to have happened the question, 'Did you not see her take it?'

c. Statements Made in the Course of Judicial and Quasi-judicial Proceedings

133. As a general rule, the statements made by judges, magistrates, witnesses, litigants, and attorneys in the course of judicial proceedings benefit from qualified privilege. A similar privilege is accorded statements made in the course of quasi-judicial proceedings, such as the proceedings of a commission of inquiry. However, the privilege will be defeated if there is proof either that the statement made was totally irrelevant to the proceedings or that the maker of the statement was actuated by some improper motive or spite.

d. Reports of Parliamentary, Judicial and Other Public Proceedings

134. Qualified privilege attaches to fair and accurate reports of the public proceedings of Parliament, courts and public bodies. The basis of the privilege is that it is in the interests of the public that it should be informed of what is said or done in these public institutions.

According to section 24 of the National Assembly (Powers and Privileges) Act, this privilege covers persons who publish, 'any reports, papers, minutes, votes and proceedings' under the authority of the National Assembly. Section 25 defines the extent of the protection in these terms:

> In any civil proceedings instituted for publishing any report or summary of or any extract or abstract of any report, paper, minutes, votes and proceedings of the Assembly, if the court is satisfied that such report, summary, extract or abstract was published in good faith and without malice, judgment shall be entered for the defendant.[253]

Thus, this defence cannot cover a garbled report, which omits things that ought to have been included or introduces things that did not take place.

The protection of fair and accurate reports of public judicial proceedings in Botswana is governed by the general principles of the common law. To this must be added section 23(1) of the High Court Act 1976, which states:

> No judge shall be liable to be sued in any court for any act done or ordered to be done by him in the discharge of his judicial duty whether or not done within

252. [1864] 15 CB (NS) 806.
253. *See* the corresponding provisions in the House of Chiefs (Power and Privileges) Act.

> the limits of his jurisdiction, nor shall any order for costs be made against him, provided that he at the time in good faith believed himself to have the jurisdiction to do or order the act complained of.

The interpretation and application of this provision was one of the issues which arose in the famous case of *Ngope v. O'Brien Quinn*,[254] in which a former clerk of the magistrate's court sued the defendant, then, the Chief Justice of Botswana, for defamation on the basis of certain statements the latter had made to the plaintiff's boss, an Acting Chief Magistrate. The Court of Appeal affirmed the lower court's decision that the statements were published on a privileged occasion and were within the privilege.[255]

Generally, the benefit of qualified privilege attaches to all publications relating to the proceedings of all public authorities or bodies entrusted with the carrying out of any public duties. It is however doubtful if this extends to the publication of defamatory statements made in the report of the proceedings of an ordinary or private meeting of an association, even if it relates to matters of public interest.[256]

D. Consent

135. A person who consents to his reputation being injured cannot claim damages for defamation. A person will not be considered as consenting where it is clearly established that the defendant misled him into consenting. It would also seem that a person 'challenging' or 'inviting' another person, for example, a Member of Parliament, to repeat certain allegations outside Parliament, does not thereby forfeit his right to claim damages for defamation.[257]

E. Mistake

136. Mistake per se is generally no defence to an action for defamation. However, since the consciousness of wrongfulness is an essential element of this delict, mistake in the sense that the defendant was unaware of the wrongfulness of the defamatory publication or that he bona fide believed that his conduct was lawful may be a good defence. This will only succeed if it is clearly shown that the mistake is not attributable to the negligence of the defendant.

F. Provocation (Rixa or Anger)

137. The defendant may plead that the words complained about were spoken under provocation in the course of a quarrel (*rixa*) between the parties. This defence may even be pleaded as an alternative to justification. As McKerron points out, provocation or *rixa* as a defence will only succeed if the defendant can prove that:

---

254. [1987] BLR 398; [1988] BLR 121.
255. *See* a detailed commentary of this case by B. Otlhogile, *Defamation by a Judge: A Note on Idah Ngope v. James Aiden O'Brien-Quinn*, 7(1) Les. L. J. 107–133 (1991).
256. *Carbonel v. Robinson & Co. (Pty) Ltd* [1965] 1 SA 134 (D); *Philpott v. Whittal* [1906] 23 SC 310.
257. *See* J. Burchell, *The Law of Defamation in South Africa* 262 (Juta & Co. Ltd 1985).

- the words were spoken in immediate retaliation for what the plaintiff himself had said;
- they were moderate and proportionate to the injury inflicted and;
- were not subsequently persisted in.[258]

It must be quite obvious from the surrounding circumstances that the words were uttered in anger and meant as merely meaningless abuse and not serious assertion of facts. Where a person makes a definite charge of crime or a charge of dishonest conduct against another, giving such facts as time and the circumstances such as to lead those who were present to believe that the charge was made seriously, the chances of the judge accepting that this could have merely been spoken in anger and nothing more, are very slim.[259] The defence will also be unavailing where the words were heard by persons who were unaware of the provocation under which they were uttered. In *Mosieman v. Maswabi*,[260] the defendant had uttered the following against the plaintiff; 'I am going to expose you. Yes, I will expose you. You thief. You steal government drugs and you sell them in private. You are also a drug addict. I will expose you.' Although the defendant apologized, this apology was tardy and it expressed no regret or penitence. In holding the defendant liable, the court pointed out that the defence of *rixa* was inapplicable because the words complained of were not moderate and proportionate to the injury inflicted and must have been heard by people who were not part of their group who would have taken the defendant seriously.

G. Absence of Animus Injuriandi

138. The publication of a defamatory statement usually raises an inference of unlawfulness and *animus injuriandi*. There has been a protracted debate over whether proof of the absence of *animus injuriandi* can on its own be a defence.[261]

The absence of *animus injuriandi* is clearly at the root of some defences. The weight of authorities generally, and the two Botswana cases where this issue was raised suggest that a defendant can only rebut the presumption of *animus injuriandi* which arises from the publication of defamatory material by relying on any of the recognized defences.[262]

H. Reasonable publication

139. The law of defamation not only protects a person's reputation from unjustified attacks but also plays a balancing role between the protection of reputation and media freedom. The traditional common law of defamation however does not provide adequate

258. McKerron, *The Law of Delict* 204.
259. *See* Lord Maclaren in *Christie v. Robertson* [1899] 1 Fraser 1155, 1157.
260. [1976–1978] BLR 92.
261. *See generally*, Burchell, *The Law of Defamation in South Africa* 183–184; McKerron, *The Law of Delict* 205–206; J. Neethling, J.M. Potgieter & P.J. Visser, *Law of Delict* 347–349 (3rd edn, Butterworths 1999).
262. *Mosieman v. Maswabi* [1976–1978] BLR 92, 93; *Ngope v. O'Brien Quinn* (No. 2) BLR 398, 405.

protection to media freedom. A publisher who diligently tries to verify a story on a matter of public interest before publication may still be held liable for defamation if they fail to prove to the court that the gist of the story was true or bring it within one of the privileged categories exempted from the need to prove truth. A defamatory statement not provably true cannot be published to the public simply because it concerns a matter of public interest under the traditional common law of defamation.[263] The defence of fair comment in a defamatory suit also demands that a defendant show the factual basis of the comment to be true. And the defence of qualified privilege, while not dependent on proof of truth, does not recognize a general media privilege based on information on a matter of public interest.[264] The traditional common law of defamation thus denies protection for dissemination of information on matters of public interest that is honest, albeit erroneous. A free media that is able to comment on public issues without censorship or restraint constitutes one of the cornerstones of a democratic society. The important role played by the media in democratic societies requires that they be given allowance for factual error if their role is not to be unduly inhibited. The last two decades have thus witnessed developments in many common law jurisdictions that have resulted in the law of defamation giving more protection to the media. These changes have generally resulted in the protection of communication by the media to the public that is in the public interest provided the defendant is not at fault.[265] Each legal system however approaches this issue in the light of its constitution, constitutional tradition and its own culture and law. Botswana, like many other common law jurisdictions has developed her law of defamation by adopting a defence of reasonable publication to protect the media from liability for disseminating false information in circumstances where it was reasonable to do so.[266]

140. The defence of reasonable publication essentially absolves the media from liability for defamation where they have published false or untrue defamatory matter in circumstances where such publication was reasonable in the circumstances of the case.[267] The defence has two elements: first, it must be shown that the publication was in the public interest; and second, that there was responsible journalism in the publication of the matter. The determination of whether the publication was in the public interest is a question of law decided by the judge who must look at the published material as a whole without isolating the defamatory statement.[268] The judge must also decide whether the publication was reasonable. A test of responsible journalism was formulated by the English House of Lords in the case of *Reynolds v. Times Newspapers Ltd*[269] to assist in the determination of this issue. The House of Lords in *Reynolds* case provided

263. K. Williams, *Defaming Politicians: The Not So Common Law*, 748 Modern L. Rev. 748 (2000).
264. *Ibid.*
265. C. Forsyth, *The Protection of Political Discourse: Pragmatism or Incoherence?*, in *Freedom of Expression and Freedom of Information: Essays in Honour of Sir David Williams* 87, 99 (J. Beatson & Y. Cripps eds., Oxford University Press 2000).
266. B.T. Balule, *Striking a Balance Between Media Freedom and Protection of Reputation: The Defence of Reasonable Publication in Botswana*, 46 Comp. & Intl. L. J. S. Afr. 1–19 (2013).
267. *Tsodilo Services (Pty) Ltd t/a Sunday Standard and others v. Tibone* [2011] 2 BLR 494.
268. *Jameel and others v. Wall Street Journal Europe* [2006] UKHL 44, per Lord Hoffman at paras 48–49.
269. [1999] 4 ALL ER 609.

a list of factors that a court must take into account in assessing whether a publisher was responsible in publishing a defamatory matter. These factors are:

(1) The seriousness of the allegation. The more serious the charge, the more the public is misinformed and the individual harmed.
(2) The nature of the information, and the extent to which the subject matter is of a matter of public concern.
(3) The source of the information. Some informants have no direct knowledge of the events. Some have their own axes to grind, or are being paid for their stories.
(4) The steps taken to verify the information.
(5) The status of the information. The allegation may have already been the subject of an investigation which commands respect.
(6) The urgency of the matter. News is often a perishable commodity.
(7) Whether comment was sought from the plaintiff. He may have information others do not possess or have not disclosed. An approach to the plaintiff will always not be necessary.
(8) Whether the article contained the gist of the plaintiff's side of the story.
(9) The tone of the article. A newspaper can raise queries or call for an investigation. It need not adopt allegations as statements of fact.
(10) The circumstances of the publication, including the timing.[270]

The test for assessing responsible journalism was refined by the House of Lords in *Jameel* case. The court held that the *Reynolds* factors should not be applied as series of hurdles to be negotiated by a publisher, but as an illustrative guide as to what might constitute responsible journalism on the facts of a given case.[271] The court went further to caution that the assessment of responsible journalism is not an invitation for courts to micromanage the editorial practices of media organizations. A degree of deference should be shown to the editorial judgment of professional editors and journalists.[272] The fact that a judge, with the advantage of leisure and hindsight, might have made a different editorial decision should not destroy the defence. Journalistic ethics and relevant codes of practice should also play an important role in assisting the court in determining whether it was responsible for a media defendant to publish defamatory matter in a given case.

IV. Remedies and the Measure of Damages

A. Remedies

141. Two main remedies are available to a person to protect his reputation:

270. *Reynolds v. Times Newspapers Ltd* (*supra*) at 626.
271. *Ibid.*, per Lord Bingham at para. 33.
272. *Ibid.*, per Lord Hoffman at para. 51.

(1) he can apply for an interdict to restrain or prohibit the publication or further publication of defamatory matter;[273] or
(2) claim damages for the impairment of his reputation.

The plaintiff is entitled to general damages once the defamation is proved. Where he claims that he has suffered or is likely to suffer special damages, for instance, an injury to his business or professional reputation, this must be specially pleaded and proved.

142. In assessing the amount of damages to be awarded, the courts usually take into account several factors, such as the status of the plaintiff, the nature and extent of the publication, and the general conduct of the defendant. For example, in *Masipa v. Leshope*, Livesy Luke CJ, said:

> In awarding damages, I take into consideration the serious nature of the allegations made in the minute, the responsible position held by the plaintiff in the Council, the fact that the plaintiff is a married man, and the fact that he is a Minister of a religion.[274]

In *Monyena v. Gambule*,[275] the plaintiff instituted action against the defendant for damages for defamation arising out of a letter written by the defendant to the Director of Vocational Education and Training. The defendant was the chairperson of the Board of Trustees of a trust and the plaintiff was the coordinator of the trust. The plaintiff alleged that the letter was defamatory of him as it imputed dishonesty and untrustworthiness to him. The court found that the letter could have caused the plaintiff serious difficulties with his effective seniors and that the letter was defamatory. As to the question of damages, it was held that at the letter would have been seen by a small number of people whose minds would not easily be influenced by unsubstantiated allegations, the injury to the plaintiff's reputation was minimal and damages of BWP 5,000 would be adequate having regard to all the circumstances of the case.

Courts however require that damages for defamation must reflect a delicate balance between the promotion of freedom of expression and the protection of reputation. In particular, care must be taken not to award large sums of damages too readily as doing so may inhibit freedom of expression or encourage intolerance to it and thereby opening floodgates to litigation.[276]

B. Mitigation of Damages

143. A number of factors may be taken into account either in mitigation or aggravation of damages.[277] The main mitigating factors are; apology, the character of the plaintiff and partial justification.

---

273. *See Construction Machinery Botswana (Pty) Ltd v. Charles Tsuro*, 1992; and *Tshekedi Khama v. Keaboka Kgamane*, 1951, in Otlhogile, 'Defamation by a Judge', at 246–256.
274. [1991] BLR 133,145.
275. [2004] 1 BLR 102.
276. *Tsodilo Services (Pty) Ltd t/a Sunday Standard and others v. Tibone (supra* no. 267*)*.
277. *See generally*, McKerron, *The Law of Delict* 207–209.

For an apology to constitute a mitigating factor, it must be made as soon as is reasonably possible, be unequivocal and unconditional, and contain an unqualified withdrawal of all the imputations made against the plaintiff. In *Mosieman v. Maswabi*, Edwards J said:

The defendant through his attorney has apologized to the plaintiff, but the apology was very tardy. It was not sent until after the defendant had received a letter of demand. And it was not a personal apology. And in the letter of apology no penitence, no regret, was expressed. In this regard I note that six weeks after the incident when plaintiff met and spoke to the defendant, the latter showed no penitence.[278]

On the basis of this, the learned judge declined to consider the apology in his assessment of the damages awarded against the defendant.

Since the plaintiff is basically complaining that his reputation and good character has been damaged, it is but fair to allow the defendant to show that the plaintiff's character was previously tainted or that he really had little character or reputation to lose. This rule, based on the *obiter* of Cave J in *Scott v. Sampson*[279] provides that only general evidence of the plaintiff's bad reputation, provided it is relevant to the aspect of the plaintiff's character in issue is admissible, not evidence of specific discreditable misconduct.[280] This rule is strictly applied although in *Goody v. Odhams Press Ltd*[281] it was held that previous convictions stand in a class by themselves and evidence of them is admissible, provided they relate to the nature of the allegations complained of.

Finally, the defendant may plead partial justification in mitigation, where his defence of justification fails because although he proved the truth of the allegation, he was unable to establish that the publication was for the public benefit.

C. Aggravation of Damages

144. The following factors have generally been considered as aggravating circumstances that may cause the court to award higher or even exemplary damages not only to compensate the plaintiff but also to punish the defendant and show the court's disapproval of his conduct:

(1) persistence in pleading justification for an unfounded allegation;
(2) the presence of malice;
(3) repetition of the offending statement; and
(4) any evidence that the defendant had intended to make a windfall from the publication.

In *Mulwa v. Mosienyane*,[282] the defendant had written letters to the plaintiff, a medical practitioner, his wife, and his bosses – the Permanent Secretary of the Ministry of Health, the Matron of the Princess Marina Hospital, and the Director of Nursing

278. [1976–1978] BLR 92, 95–96.
279. [1882] 8 QBD 491.
280. *See A-G v. Ghanzi Hotel* [1985] BLR 452, 459; [1986] BLR 178.
281. [1967] 1 QB 333.
282. [1984] BLR 138.

Services, in which he accused the plaintiff of being a womanizer, abortionist and of professional misconduct, and corruption and abuse of the medical profession. In assessing the amount of damages to be awarded, the court decided to take account of the respective standings of the plaintiff and the defendant in the community, the extent of the publication and the type of persons who received it and the fact that the defendant was actuated by malice. Perhaps the most interesting case that illustrates aggravating circumstances is *Dibotelo v. Sechele & Others*.[283] The plaintiff, a senior High Court judge, instituted the action against the defendants, a reporter, and the editor of a newspaper, for damages for defamation arising out of the publication of a report in the defendant's weekly paper which alleged that the plaintiff, who had previously been an attorney, had taken money from a client and had not appropriated it for its proper purpose. The defendants admitted that the article was defamatory of the plaintiff but failed to make an apology until after the pleadings had closed and when they published it, did so on page 3 of the newspaper. The defendants alleged that they believed the report to be true and had not been able to get the plaintiff's version of the events. It emerged from the evidence however that at the time the client paid the amount to the attorneys, the plaintiff had been a judge for more than two years and the defendants could easily have ascertained this. The newspaper was a serious weekly newspaper which had a wide circulation in Botswana and the article had been published on the Internet as well. It was held, first that the fact that the plaintiff was a High Court judge and thus a public figure had a strong bearing on the quantum of damages. The only way of impressing upon all that such unfounded attacks were not to be made was by awarding exemplary damages; the more so in the present case where the attacks bore the hallmark of being not only exaggerated but also smacked of a high degree of wantonness, which was exacerbated by dishonest persistence in a futile endeavour to persist in an unwarranted belief in the truth of the allegations. Second, any damages awarded to the plaintiff had to reflect the delicate balance between the competing interests of the defamed person's right to enjoy a reputation which he deserves and the defendant's right of freedom of speech. The only real factor of mitigation which merited consideration was the apology which was tendered by the defendants through the newspaper as well as the regrets expressed by the plaintiff's witnesses in court. The apologies, when given, were honestly given but there could be no doubt that their mitigatory effect was toned down substantially by the cavalier manner in which the defendants handled the case, especially after the letter of demand was sent. The sum of BWP 5 million claimed by the plaintiff was considered way out of line with any comparable claims in Botswana or elsewhere and an award in the region of BWP 300,000 would be more appropriate but this had to be scaled down to BWP 250,000 to give effect to the fact that an apology was made. Although the first impression is that this case illustrates the extent to which an apology can influence the amount of damages that are awarded, it is submitted that this is not a very good example that needs to be emulated. It is difficult to see the justification for reducing the award by 16% to take into account a belated and half-hearted apology. There is no justification for not considering the very serious nature of the allegations and the fact that these were recklessly made against a sitting judge as aggravating factors which should certainly have counted against whatever mitigatory effects the apology could have

283. [2001] BLR 588.

merited. The judge might have been too sensitive to the fact that this was a case brought by his fellow judge and wanted as much as possible to avoid any semblance of bias.

§3. Privacy

I. Definition and Nature of the Right to Privacy

145. The right to privacy is recognized as an independent personality right within the concept of *dignitas*.[284] The various definitions of the legal concept of privacy revolve around the ideas of 'withdrawal', 'seclusion', 'being let alone', 'solitude, intimacy, anonymity and reserve', and 'minimum interference with one's own life'.[285] An injury to privacy therefore involves any intentional and wrongful interference with a person's private and secluded existence. This entitles the plaintiff to sue for sentimental damages under the *actio injuriarum*. To succeed, the plaintiff must prove the existence of the essential requirements of the *actio injuriarum* viz.:

- that the act was intentional;
- that it was wrongful; and
- that it impaired his personality.

II. The Scope of Liability

146. The possible scope of the modern action for invasion of privacy in the law of delict can be brought within Prosser's four categories:

(1) unreasonable intrusion into private sphere;
(2) public disclosure of private facts;
(3) appropriation of name or likeness; and
(4) false light.[286]

There is considerable room for some overlap because the categorization is neither rigid nor is it exhaustive.

Under the first category, the intrusion into the private sphere will become actionable only if the intrusion was substantial and of a kind that a reasonable person of normal sensitivity would regard as offensive and intolerable. There are countless ways in which a person's privacy could be invaded. These include the planting of listening devices in a person's home, peeping at a woman while she is undressing – the

284. *See generally*, N. MacCormick, *A Note upon Privacy*, 89 L. Q. Rev. 23 (1973); B.S. Markesinis, *The Right to Be Let Alone Versus Freedom of Speech*, 67 Pub. L. 67 (1986); D.J. McQuoid-Mason, *The Law of Privacy in South Africa* (Juta & Co. Ltd 1978); B. Neil, *The Protection of Privacy*, 25 Modern L. Rev. 393 (1962).
285. McQuoid-Mason, *The Law of Privacy in South Africa* 99.
286. W.L. Prosser & G.W. Keeton, *Prosser and Keeton on Torts* (5th edn., West Publishing 1984).

so-called peeping Tom cases, and photography by investigators using telephoto lenses without permission.

The second category raises one of the most controversial issues in the whole field of privacy, namely, balancing the protection against unwanted publicity, against the public's 'right to know'. Public facts, however embarrassing, provided they are true, may be aired. A typical example is where the plaintiff has become the involuntary object of public attention because he is the victim of a crime or a natural disaster. But where it relates to private facts, the public generally has no legitimate right to know. Instances from South African case law where the right to privacy was considered to have been invaded include: the publication of a woman's photograph as part of an advertisement without her consent;[287] the publication of photographs of nurses in a newspaper without their consent;[288] the publication of facts concerning an alleged romance between the plaintiff and a singer;[289] the publication of facts relating to the petitioner's secret abduction of children who were placed under the custody of their former spouses;[290] and the publication of facts concerning the relationship between a well-known rugby player and his mistress, and the child he allegedly fathered with her.[291] A recent local example is *Maje v. Botswana Life Insurance Ltd & Another*.[292] The plaintiff instituted an action for damages claiming BWP 50,000 from the defendants for injuries arising from the unlawful publication by the defendants of her photograph in their newsletter under the heading, 'So you're HIV positive, where do you go from here?' In an exception to the plaintiff's particulars of claim, the excipient contended that the respondent failed to aver that the excipient had acted *animus injuriandi* in publishing her photographs and failed to plead facts to show that an association with HIV was injurious or to avert any secondary or adverse meaning deriving from the context of the article. It was held that whether or not the publication constituted an aggression on the plaintiff's *dignitas* depended on the particular circumstances of the case and on the context of the publication. The publication of a person's photograph without the person's consent in circumstances where the publication caused offence or humiliation to that person was an actionable wrong for which the remedy lay in the *actio injuriarum.Animus injuriandi* did not need to be specifically pleaded; it was sufficient to plead the facts which disclosed such an *animus*, in whatever form. It was also sufficient for the plaintiff to plead that her privacy had been wrongly invaded and that she was aggrieved thereby. As in the case of other communicable diseases, unguarded or unjustified references in relation to such maladies were capable of causing hurt or offence to the persons referred to whether or not they suffered from such diseases. The court therefore concluded that whether such hurt or offence was actually suffered or should have been suffered in the present case would be determined at the trial and hence the exception was dismissed.

The third group, the unauthorized use of a person's name or likeness, usually in aid of advertising or other commercial purposes may also constitute other wrongs such

287. *O'Keeffe v. Argus Printing and Publishing Co. Ltd* [1954] 3 SA 244 (C).
288. *Kidson v. SA Associated Newspapers Ltd* [1957] 3 SA 461 (W).
289. *Mhlongo v. Bailey* [1958] 1 SA 370 (W).
290. *Rhodesian Printing and Publishing Co. Ltd v. Duggan* [1975] 1 SA 590 (RA).
291. *National Media Ltd v. Jooste* [1996] 3 SA 262 (A).
292. [2001] 2 BLR 626.

as defamation, passing off and breach of copyright, patent or trade mark. In *O'Keeffe v. Argus Printing & Publishing Co. Ltd*[293] the plaintiff, a well-known radio personality consented to herself being photographed at a pistol range to illustrate a news story. The photograph was subsequently published in an advertisement for firearms without her consent. This was held to constitute an aggression upon the plaintiff's *dignitas*.

The false light category arises where a person is exposed to publicity that places him in a false light. In most such cases, the defendant may also be sued for defamation. The facts of *Kidson v. SA Associated Newspapers Ltd*[294] could have given rise to an action for invasion of privacy but was disposed of on other rather questionable grounds.[295] In the case itself, the plaintiffs were nurses, one of whom was married and two others engaged. They had consented to their photographs being taken to illustrate a nursing journal. They subsequently discovered that the photograph had been captioned 'off duty: lonely and nowhere to go', and had been used to illustrate a report in a Sunday newspaper headed '97 lonely nurses want boyfriends'. By so doing, the plaintiffs' private lives had been falsely exposed to the public eye.

III. Defences

147. Generally, the defences to an action for defamation are also available to the defendant in an action for invasion of privacy. The main difference is that since invasions of privacy often involves the publication of truthful information that deals with the private life of the plaintiff, the defendant can only defend himself by pleading 'public benefit' or 'public interest' rather than 'truth for the public benefit'. Besides this, the only other defences that merit a brief examination here are consent, necessity, and statutory defence.

148. The defence of public benefit may be relied upon either because a person is a public figure or disclosures concerning him are in the public interest. Prosser defines as public figure 'a person who, by his accomplishments, fame, or mode of living, or by adopting a profession or calling which gives the public a legitimate interest in his doings, his affairs and his character, has become a "public personage"'.[296] Unlike private individuals, the publication of facts concerning the private lives of such public figures is considered to be in the public interest. Such individuals, who include actors, entertainers, sports celebrities and politicians are considered to have forfeited to a certain extent, their right to privacy. The extent of this will depend not only on the particular circumstances but also the status of the public figure in question. Courts have said that when a person moves into communal relations and activities such as business and social interaction, the scope of personal space shrinks accordingly.[297]

Disclosures concerning a person may still be in the public interest although such a person is not a public figure. This can occur when a person is suddenly thrust into the limelight involuntarily as a result of, for example, being the innocent victim of a

293. [1954] 3 SA 244 (C).
294. [1957] 3 SA 461 (W).
295. McQuoid-Mason, *The Law of Privacy in South Africa* 89.
296. *Prosser and Keeton on Torts* 859–860.
297. *Bernstein v. Bester* 1996 2 SA 451.

natural catastrophe or even a criminal attack such as rape or indecent assault. There must be limits to the public's right to know certain intimate details about these public figures, especially those involuntarily catapulted into the public eye.

149. There are several factors that a court will take into account in determining whether a defence of public benefit should be upheld. Some of these factors from decided cases include:

(1) Whether one is a public figure or not, i.e., a person who by virtue of their status, office, occupation or conduct grant the public a legitimate interest in information regarding not only their public activities, but also to some extent, their private lives.[298]
(2) Whether the person is involved in newsworthy event, that is, an event in which the public have a legitimate interest in the information.[299]
(3) The extent of the violating conduct.[300]
(4) The motive with which the defendant acted.[301]
(5) The fact that private facts were obtained wrongfully, either by intrusion or in breach of a confidential relationship.

150. Consent, whether express or implied, may negate liability, provided this was given voluntarily. Implied consent may be inferred from the plaintiff voluntarily accepting to be part of a group photograph which he knows will be published. If the form of publication does not comply with the plaintiff's consent, then the defence of consent will not avail the defendant. Thus in *O'Keeffe v. Argus Printing & Publishing Co. Ltd*[302] the plaintiff had consented to her photograph being used to illustrate a news item but not an advertisement. In *Kidson v. SA Associated Newspapers Ltd*,[303] the plaintiffs were also considered to have consented to their photographs being used to illustrate a nursing journal, but not a nationwide appeal for funds in a popular Sunday newspaper. Consent, especially where it is implied, requires knowledge and a full appreciation of all the circumstances. It is also possible to infer that a person voluntarily assumed the risk of his privacy being invaded.

151. Necessity may be a good defence to an action for invasion of privacy where the defendant proves that he acted to prevent a threat of greater harm to himself personally or his property or that of another, arising from a force of nature or some conduct unconnected with himself. There must be clear proof of an urgent situation of imminent peril; lest necessity becomes simply a mask for anarchy. Some examples of this are: entering another's home to shelter from a storm, searching through letters and other personal documents of an unconscious man to ascertain his identity or address and entering into the home of a critically ill person to render assistance.

152. Finally, the defendant could plead statutory authority when he is able to cite a statute which justifies the invasion of the privacy of the plaintiff. An example

298. *Tshabalala-Msimang and Another v. Makhanya and Others* 2008 6 SA 102.
299. *Prinsloo v. RCP Media* 2003 2 SA 456.
300. *Ibid.*
301. *MEC for Health, Mpumalanga v. M-net* 2002 6 SA 714.
302. [1954] 3 SA 244 (C).
303. [1957] 3 SA 461 (W).

of this is the right that is given to the police sometimes to intercept postal communications and telephone communications. The defence will fail if the statutory authority is abused.

Chapter 4. Right to Reply

153. Many countries, especially in Europe, now have right-to-reply laws on their statute books. With perhaps the exception of Mozambique, such legislation hardly exists in many African countries.[304] The Media Practitioners Act 2008, for the first time introduced a statutory right-to-reply in Botswana. Before that, the Media Code of Ethics produced by the Press Council of Botswana contained a clause dealing with the right to reply.

The right-to-reply legislation usually presents two main problems – the first, being its constitutionality, since a requirement that the press must publish the reply of another source could be harmful to the freedom of the press to decide what to publish. The second, is the practical issue of the scope of such a right to reply.

154. Opponents of a statutory right to reply usually cite the US case of *Miami Herald v. Tomillo*[305] as authority for the view that such legislation is unconstitutional. The US Supreme Court unanimously invalidated a Florida statute providing a mandatory right of reply to election candidates whose character was attacked by a newspaper. One rationale for the decision was that the statute intruded into the function of the editors to determine the contents of the paper and the treatment of public issues, compelling them to publish a reply whether they thought it appropriate or not. The language of the court's opinion was so sweeping in its condemnation of the idea of the government telling a newspaper to print something it might not want to that Justices William Brennan and William Rehnquist felt moved to add, in a one-sentence concurrence, their understanding that the decision did not invalidate statutes which compel publication of a retraction as a remedy in cases where the plaintiff has proven defamation in court.[306]

The main objection voiced by the court that compelling communicators to utter words or publish material which they may not wish to publish is not convincing. They are not compelled to publish such material and have a choice to retract the statements, disseminate a reply or face an action for defamation. The editor's constitutional right is infringed only where he is compelled to say or write something he does not want to say or write. This is certainly not the case because the right-to-reply law makes it clear that the views published are those of the complainant and not those of the editor.[307]

155. Two arguments are raised to justify this right to reply. First, it is said that it offers a more efficient tool to restore a person's dignity. The Supreme Court of Argentina has held that the right to reply offers protection to a person's dignity, honour, feelings, and privacy by offering the aggrieved individual an opportunity to challenge

304. C. Bussiek & H. Bussiek, *The Media: Making Democracy Work* 41 (Friedrich-Ebert-Stiftung 2004).

305. 418 US 241 (1974).

306. For an elaborate discussion of the arguments for and against a right-to-reply legislation, *see* Haiman, *Speech and Law in a Free Society* 48–51.

307. Barendt, *Freedom of Speech* 95.

untruthful information disseminated about them.[308] The second argument is that the right to reply ensures diversity of opinions relating to matters of general interest.[309] The right ensures that the public has a chance to gain knowledge of the true facts and the opinion of the person affected by the untruthful publication of facts by a media outlet.

156. The right-to-reply legislation raises a number of problems and questions of a practical nature that relate to the definition and scope of such right: does the right apply only to facts or to opinions or both?[310] Should the reply be published contemporaneously with the article or after? If after, how soon after the publication of the article? Should the reply be published exactly as it is received or it could be edited? Should there be an additional right to reply beyond the first reply?

Right-to-reply laws come in several varieties. In order to better understand and appreciate the system adopted by the Media Practitioners Act, it is worthwhile briefly mentioning what obtains elsewhere:

- In Austria, the Press Act of 1922 as amended by the Media Act of 1981 grants a right of reply to incorrect statements. If the media refuses to publish it, then the complainant can sue for compensation.
- Denmark through its Media Liability Act gives a right to reply on matters of factual inaccuracy within four weeks of the publication.
- In France, the Freedom of the Press Act gives a right to reply to an article whether or not it is inaccurate or defamatory with alternative speedy remedies if the editor refuses to comply with the request.
- In Germany, each state within the federation has a press law which obliges the press to publish replies from people affected by assertions of fact in an article failing which the complainant can resort to the civil courts.

157. One way in which an attempt is made to strike a balance between media freedom and the exercise of the right of reply is to limit the application of the latter to information of a factual nature. This is the approach adopted by the Inter-American Court of Human Rights, the European Court of Human Rights and a number of mature democracies such as Denmark and Germany.[311] An absolute application of the right of reply may result in an unjustifiable invasion of third-party rights and the public interest, news media should therefore be allowed to decline publishing replies that would violate third-party rights or the public interest. The Council of Europe's Recommendation on the Right of Reply in the New Media Environment for example, provides that news media may refuse to publish a reply in the following cases:

---

308. *Ekmeksdjian v. Sofovich,* SC, decision of 7 Jul. 1992, cited in Art. 19, *The Article 19 Freedom of Expression Handbook: International and Comparative Law, Standards and Procedures* (Art. 19, 2003) p. 166.

309. *See Meinychuk v. Ukraine,* App. No. 28743/03, European Court of Human Rights, 6–7 (judgment of 5 Jul. 2005).

310. L. Eithan & L. Yehiel, *The 'Right to Reply' in Journalistic Ethics: The Case Study of the Ruling by the Israel Press Council,* www.allacademic.com//met/p_mla_research_citation/ 0/9/0/9/6/ pages9096.

311. *Ibid.*

- Where the length of reply exceeds what is necessary to correct the contested information;
- If the reply is not limited to correction of the facts challenged;
- If the publication of the reply would involve a punishable Act, or render the media outlet liable to civil law proceedings or would transgress standards of public decency;
- Where the reply would be contrary to the legally protected interests of a third party;
- If the individual concerned cannot show the existence of a legitimate interest; and
- Where the contested information is part of a truthful report on public sessions of the public authorities or the courts.[312]

158. As stated above, until the Media Practitioners Act, the right to reply was regulated by the Media Code of Ethics. Clause 4 states as follows:

> Where a person or organisation believes that a media report contains inaccurate information or has unfairly criticised the person or organisation, the media institution concerned must give the person or organisation a fair opportunity to reply.

It is not clear what is meant by 'a fair opportunity to reply'. Be that as it may, this voluntary regime has now been replaced by a statutory right to reply contained in the Media Practitioners Act. Section 10 in this Act states:

(1) Without prejudice to anything contained in sections 11 to 14, a publisher who publishes a statement about or against a person shall when requested to do so by the person in respect of whom the publication is made, publish a reply from him or her.

(2) A reply published by a publisher, after a request is made under subsection (1), shall be published –

(a) in not later than two subsequent editions of the publication; and
(b) with the same prominence as the original statement published.

(3) Where a person in respect of whom a publication is made feels aggrieved by an act or omission of a publisher under this section, he or she may lodge a complaint before the Council under section 12.

This manifestly sloppily drafted piece of legislation may not pass the constitutionality test for at least for two reasons:

312. Recommendation Rec (2004) 16 of the Committee of Ministers to Member States on the right of reply in the new media environment, para. 5, (adopted by the Committee of Ministers on 15 Dec. 2004 at the 909th meeting of the Ministers' Deputies).

First, the basis on which a person may exercise the right of reply is couched in very vague and obscure language namely, the publication of 'a statement about or against a person'. One of the reasons why the US Supreme Court stroke down the statute in the Miami Herald case was because it felt that it was too broad and went beyond defamation to include any potential political attacks.[313] Section 10(1) of the Media Practitioners Act is even broader: it appears to give a right to reply to any person against whom a statement is made whether the statement is true or false, and whether it is factual or just an opinion.[314]

Second, the fact that under section 10(3), a complainant who feels aggrieved by 'an act or omission of a publisher', whatever this means, is given the right to lodge a complaint before the Media Council, is an element of compulsion which appears to suggest that the publisher is under an obligation to publish a response submitted in pursuance of a right of reply under this Act.[315] As explained above, the 'Miami Herald' case principle applies only where it is clear, as is the case under this legislation, that the publisher is under an obligation to publish the complainant's response.

It is not clear whether the intention of section 10 is to ensure that the publisher publishes any response it receives no matter its merits. This could leave the newspapers to be full of nothing but replies. A carefully worded right-to-reply legislation will certainly enhance freedom of speech. As an alternative to time-consuming and expensive defamation actions, it would potentially benefit both sides. It makes sure that members of the public get their version of facts published, if need be, and thus safe newspapers having to pay damages, fines or even incurring jail sentences in the case of criminal defamation. The right-to-reply legislation in the Media Practitioners Act is not only practically defective but legally suspect from the point of view of its conformity to the constitution.

---

313. *See* Haiman, *Speech and Law in a Free Society* 49.
314. B.T. Balule, *The Media Practitioners Act 2008: Does It Preserve Media Freedom or Is It a Case of Taming the Beast?*, 12 *U. Bots. L. J.* 3–21 (2011).
315. A series of sanctions are provided for in ss 14 and 15 of the Act.

Chapter 5. Press Council

159. In order for the media to serve the public properly, it must be free from the distorting pressure usually exerted by economic and political forces. To obtain, keep and increase their freedom, the media needs to be trusted and protected by the general public. To gain that support, the media needs to inform readers, listeners, and viewers properly as well as listen to and render account to them. Such media accountability may come through a voluntary body established by the media industry itself or through a statutory body created by the legislature. The media in Botswana is arguably regulated by both the Press Council and the statutory Media Council.

The Press Council of Botswana, was set up under a Notarial Deed of Trust of 12 August 2004. Membership of the Council is voluntary and it adopted a Media Code of Ethics which regulates media content by adopting an imperative regulatory approach through the imposition of requirements and prohibitions on media content. The Council established a Complaints Committee under clause 17.1 of the Notarial Deed of Trust that enforces the Media Code of Ethics.

Initially, the Press Council experienced a good response and support from the public. The Complaints Committee adjudicated a number of high-profile cases and succeeded in considerably reducing the number of defamation and invasion of privacy cases that have gone before the courts since it became operational.[316] In recent times however, the Press Council has become dormant. The dormancy of the Press Council is attributed to two main reasons:

(1) Critical shortage of resources to effectively carry out its mandate.
(2) Lack of commitment by the media to the Press Council, manifesting in failure to pay annual fees and some media houses simply refusing to be members of the Council.

316. *See* MISA & Friedrich Ebert Stiftung, *African Media Barometer: Botswana 2007* 47.

Chapter 6. Media Council

160. Section 3(1) of the Media Practitioners Act provides for the establishment of a Media Council having, according to its long title, 'the purpose of preserving the maintenance of high professional standards within the media and to provide for matters related there to'. The rest of the Act is concerned with defining its composition, modus operandi, and other ancillary bodies that will assist it to discharge its functions.[317]

§1. Establishment and Membership of the Media Council and the Executive Committee of the Council

161. The Media Council is established as a body corporate with perpetual succession, capable of suing and being sued in its own name. It is funded from four possible sources:

(1) members' voluntary contributions, bequests, and subscription fees;
(2) fees and other monies paid for services rendered by the Council;
(3) monies from the rental or sale of any property of the Council; and
(4) grants, gifts or donations from lawful organizations or sources.[318]

162. The governing body of the Council is the Executive Committee which consists of a chairperson, vice-chairperson, treasurer, and six additional members. The members of this Committee are to be elected at an ordinary general meeting or a special meeting of the Council. The Committee is charged with implementing the objects of the Council as defined in section 5 of the Act and shall have such powers and may perform such duties as it may consider necessary or expedient to do so. The Committee is required to appoint a full-time chief executive to the Council who shall act as the administrative head of the Council and work under the general supervision and direction of the Council. The chief executive shall be subject to the directions of the chairperson and will be responsible for the management and administration of the Council. The Executive Committee is also expected to appoint a secretary who will thereby become an ex officio but non-voting member of Council charged with responsibility for keeping minutes and such other documentation as may be required. A member of the National Assembly or a local authority or an employee or official of any political party or similar organization is disqualified from becoming a member of the Executive Committee or must resign from the Committee if they subsequently attain these positions. Any allowances that are paid to members of the Committee must come from funds generated by the Council.

The Executive Committee has responsibility for making binding regulations subject to approval by a special resolution of Council, on all matters for which regulations are required and more specifically the following:

317. Unless stated or the context indicates otherwise, all the information on which this section is based is obtained from the Media Practitioners Act.

318. Section 32(1) of the Media Practitioners Act.

(a) the regulation of powers exercisable by the Council and of committees appointed by the Council;
(b) the delegation of functions of the Council under section 23;
(c) the manner of applying for registration and accreditation of resident media practitioners under section 6(2);
(d) the manner of convening meetings of the Council and of committees appointed by the Council, voting procedures and other procedures thereof;
(e) the manner of application or membership of the Council and termination of such membership; and
(f) such other matters as may be deemed by the Council to be necessary for the promotion of the functions and the regulation of the affairs of the Council.[319]

It would ordinarily be reassuring to note that the regulations dealing with registration and accreditation of resident media practitioners will be drawn by the media practitioners themselves through the Executive Committee. There are however two causes for serious concern – the potential powers of the minister to control this Committee or even override what it does. First, under section 35, the minister has been given the powers to dissolve the Executive Committee on the flimsy reasons that it has failed to submit its annual report in accordance with section 34(2). There is no justification for the requirement in section 34 of the Act that the Executive Committee should 'submit to the Minister an annual report indicating the activities and operations of the Council in respect of that financial year'. Any supervisory powers that need to be exercised, should be exercised by the body which elected this Committee and to which it is accountable. It is not exactly clear what the minister is supposed to do with this annual report or even why its non-submission should result in such a drastic measure as dissolving the Executive Committee. The apparent ability of the Executive Committee to perform the duties that the members of the general meeting elected it to do is subject to the rather sweeping powers of interference and intervention by the minister under section 38. According to it, the minister may, by statutory instrument, make regulations:

(a) directing that the Executive Committee be dissolved and that the Council elects a new Executive Committee;
(b) relating to any other matter intended to safeguard the interests of the public and promote professional standards in the media;
(c) giving effect to the Code of Ethics issued by the Council;
(d) relating to the registration and accreditation of non-resident media practitioners; and
(e) prescribing anything to be prescribed by the minister under this Act.

The effect of section 38 of the Media Practitioners Act is practically to give the minister absolute powers to control the mass media. Any regulations that the media industry may introduce through its own representatives in the Council and in the Executive Committee can simply be overridden by any statutory instrument that the minister introduces.

319. Section 37(1) of the Media Practitioners Act.

§2. Aims and Objects of the Media Council

163. The objects of the Council as spelt out in section 5 are as follows:

(a) to preserve media freedom;
(b) to uphold standards of professional conduct and promote good ethical standards and discipline amongst media practitioners;
(c) to promote the observance of media ethics in accordance with the Code of Ethics issued by the Council under section 9(1);
(d) to promote public awareness of the rights and responsibilities of media practitioners, through such outreach programmes as may be established;
(e) to establish links with similar organizations within and outside Botswana;
(f) to monitor the activities of media practitioners;
(g) to receive complaints directed against media practitioners;
(h) to bring together media practitioners and other media stakeholders in Botswana, with a view to exchanging information, sharing ideas and dealing with any challenges facing the development of the media industry;
(i) to register and accredit resident media practitioners; (j) to issue accredited resident media practitioners with identity cards;
(j) to maintain a media register;
(k) to seek financial and other assistance for the operations of the Council;
(l) to sponsor training in media work and advise on matters pertaining to the education and training of media practitioners; and
(m) to undertake such research into the performance of the media as may be consistent with the furtherance of the Council's objectives.

In spite of the obscure wording of section 6 of the Act, it seems clear that all media practitioners resident in Botswana, whether national or non-nationals must be registered and accredited by the Executive Committee of the Media Council. Meanwhile, according to section 7(1) and (2) of the Act, membership of Council is reserved to 'all publishers of news and information, whether or not in the private or public sector', who must however, apply for such membership to the Executive Committee. 'Associate membership' is reserved, according to section 7(3) to 'any person in Botswana having a legitimate interest in the development of the media industry', who 'may' apply for such associate membership to the Executive Committee. Section 7(5) is very interesting: it states:

> A person who contravenes the provisions of this section commits an offence and is liable to a fine not exceeding P 5,000 or to imprisonment for a term not exceeding three years, or to both.

There are a number of points regarding the meaning and scope of section 7 which need to be clarified especially since the punishment for its violation is unusually severe. First, those who appear to qualify for compulsory membership of the Council in Botswana are 'publishers of news and information'. Section 2 defines a 'publisher' as '*a media institution or a person* who is responsible for the production of a publication'.[320]

320. The emphasis is added.

The words 'a' and 'or' suggests that the intention is to have one person to represent each publication and this could be either the manager or proprietor of the 'media institution' or the editor acting as 'the person responsible for the production of the publication'. But then, strangely, 'associate membership' is open to all and sundry provided the person can satisfy the vague criteria that he qualifies to be considered 'a person ... having a *legitimate interest* in the development of the local media industry'.[321] However, since membership is not automatic and the Act expressly gives the Executive Council the powers to make regulations dealing with this, further clarification will certainly be made on this issue.[322] But what is puzzling about the issue of membership is that the Act makes membership of the Council compulsory to an ill-defined group without any guarantees that the Executive Committee is under an obligation to accept all applications submitted to it and provides harsh penalties for those who fail to apply and possibly those whose applications are turned down because they are unable to fulfil the terms that the Executive Committee might have laid down for membership. It is rather unsatisfactory to insist on pain of severe penalties that certain 'media practitioners' should belong to a statutory body on terms that will be determined by that body alone. The potential chilling effect of this provision on freedom of speech cannot be underestimated because the media practitioner faces twin uncertainties with respect to the scope of application of this provision and the possibility of prosecution and imprisonment under it.

164. In carrying out its functions and exercising its powers under the Act, the Council is required to 'take into account' the following:

(a) whether the conditions for effective competition exist in the market;
(b) whether any act by a publisher is likely to cause the lessening of competition in the market; and
(c) whether any act by a publisher is in contravention of the applicable laws relating to competition issues.[323]

The Council is required to refer any issues relating to competition that arise in the course of the discharge of its functions to the appropriate authority established to deal with competition issues.

§3. Conduct of Media Practitioners

165. The Media Practitioners Act contemplates the drawing up of a new Code of Ethics to replace the present Media Code of Ethics that has been in force since 2004. The anticipated Code of Ethics is required, under section 9(3) of the Act to contain the following:

321. The emphasis is added.
322. Section 8(2) of the Media Practitioners Act, although it is worth pointing out that this subsection appears to limit the regulations only to applications for membership and termination of membership.
323. Section 29(1) of the Media Practitioners Act.

(a) provisions relating to the duties and obligations of media practitioners;
(b) provisions relating to the protection of minors;
(c) provisions relating to the protection of persons suffering from physical or mental disability;
(d) provisions relating to advertising content;
(e) provisions allowing for fair competition in the media industry;
(f) provisions relating to the protection of the privacy of individuals, as guaranteed in the constitution of Botswana;
(g) provisions relating to the unlawful publication of defamatory matter in accordance with the provisions of the Penal Code.

Any media practitioner who will violate any of the provisions of the Code of Ethics will be brought before the Complaints Committee of the Media Council.

Section 10 allows anybody aggrieved by a published 'statement' to request a reply from the publisher. Since under section 10(1), the exercise of this right to request a reply is 'without prejudice' to lodging a complaint under sections 11–14, the additional right given under section 10(3) to lodge a complaint is superfluous.

§4. Lodging Complaints with the Complaints Committee

166. Any person aggrieved by an Act or omission of a media practitioner in respect of a publication may lodge a complaint before the Council against the practitioner. The Council is required to refer the complaint within fourteen days to a Complaints Council, which shall make an investigation. The Complaints Council itself is surprisingly not a body derived from the Council but one appointed by the minister and consists, according to section 11(1) of:

(1) a chairperson, who shall be a member of the public; and
(2) eight representatives of the public who –

i) have a serious interest in the furtherance of the communicative value of the media;

ii) do not have a financial interest in the media; and

iii) are not in the employ of the media.

The Committee shall appoint a secretary who shall be a non-voting ex officio member with responsibility for keeping minutes of the Committee and such other documentation as may be required.

The composition of this important Committee is curious: none of the three criteria indicated as a guide to the minister has anything to do with the functions of this Committee. Far from ensuring that the minister appoints people who have experience, expertise, and the requisite knowledge to deal with the main issue that the Committee will be dealing with, that is media complaints, the only criteria that comes close to being relevant to what they have to do is that the person should 'have a serious interest in the furtherance of the communicative value of the media'. It is not exactly clear what this means. The composition of the Committee also fails to reflect the legitimate interests of the media and the public in dealing with such matters, as is the case with similar bodies in other countries.[324] Nevertheless, section 11 constitutes a regressive step in the development of media law in Botswana. For one thing, there seems to be no reason why an important Committee like this, dealing with something as sensitive as complaints relating to the media should be composed of government appointees. Perhaps more worrying is the fact that no safeguards have been built into the appointment criteria to ensure that those appointments are based on ability to contribute constructively to the Committee discharging its functions rather than political affiliations. It is all the more surprising because the provisions in the Notarial Deed of Trust of the Press Council dealing with the composition of its Complaints Committee had ensured that the Committee was independent and balanced in terms of expertise. It would have been more rewarding if this clause in the Notarial Deed of Trust had been adopted.[325] Although section 17(1) states that 'a member of the Complaints Committee or Appeals Committee shall not be a member of the National Assembly or a local authority, or an employee or official of any political party or similar organisation', this, it is submitted, will not prevent politicians, who at the best of times, are suspicious of the media, from ensuring that those who are appointed are sympathetic towards them rather than towards the media. Furthermore, the fact that any allowances paid to members of both the Complaints Committee and the Appeals Committee comes from money appropriated by the National Assembly for that purpose, but based on what the 'Minister may, in writing, determine', provides yet another indirect avenue for political interference and influence. If there has to be some public funds to be used, this should not depend on the whims and caprices of the minister who may use the absolute discretion given to determine the amount, to increase or reduce the allowances, depending on his subjective appreciation of the performance of this Committee.

Be that as it may, once a complaint is referred to the Complaints Committee, it is required to provide in writing and giving 'full reasons' any or a combination of the following rulings:

(a) dismiss the complaint;
(b) record criticism of the conduct of the media practitioner in relation to the complaint, where such criticism is in view warranted;
(c) direct that a correction or an apology be published by the offending party in such manner as may be determined by it;
(d) direct disciplinary action; or
(e) make supplementary or ancillary rulings as may be considered necessary for putting into effect any previous rulings made in terms of this section.[326]

324. Simon Gallant & Jennifer Epworth, *Media Law. A Practical Guide to Managing Publications Risks* 249 (Sweet & Maxwell 2001).
325. Clause 17.6 of the Notarial Deed of Trust of the Press Council of Botswana.
326. Section 14(1) of the Media Practitioners Act.

The disciplinary action which it may take under section 14(1)(d) above may include any or a combination of the following:

(a) warning or reprimanding a media practitioner;
(b) imposing a fine on a media practitioner;
(c) suspending a media practitioner's registration by the Council for a specified period; or
(d) removing a media practitioner's name from the register.

§5. Appeals from the Complaints Committee

167. A person aggrieved with any ruling of the Complaints Committee may within fourteen days of such ruling lodge an appeal to an Appeals Committee. The Appeals Committee is also composed of the following persons appointed by the minister:

(a) a legal practitioner, admitted to practise in the courts of Botswana and recommended by the Law Society of Botswana, who shall be the chairperson of the Committee;
(b) a member of the public; and
(c) a representative of the media recommended by the Council.[327]

The prospects for having a better balance in this Committee are very good because it will be possible to ensure that the members are knowledgeable in media issues and there is very limited scope given to the minister to make appointments dictated by political considerations.

A person aggrieved with the decision of the Appeals Committee may within thirty days of the decision appeal to the High Court, which may confirm, vary, or set aside the decision, or remit the matter to the Complaints Committee for further consideration.[328]

In the final analysis, the Media Practitioners Act does not appear to have delivered an entirely satisfactory legal framework for regulating the print media. This perhaps explains why, nine years after the promulgation of the law, the provisions have still not been implemented. The law has been gathering dust and there does not seem to be any political will on the part of the government to implement the law.

327. Section 15(1) of the Media Practitioners Act.
328. Section 15(7), *ibid.*

Part III. Regulation of Audiovisual Media (Broadcasting)

168. Although, as we have seen,[329] neither section 3 nor section 12(1) of the constitution, which recognize and protect freedom of speech in Botswana, expressly refer to the broadcast media, there is no doubt that this method of expression is covered by these constitutional provisions. Nevertheless, broadcasters in Botswana, as broadcasters all over the world continue to be subjected to a significantly special regime of stricter regulations than those of the print media. A number of reasons have been advanced in justification of this stricter regulation of the broadcast media.

The first and probably the most important historical justification of these differences in treatment of the broadcast media, the scarcity of frequencies argument, has been rendered redundant by the tremendous advances in information and technology that have seen the introduction of cable, satellite, and digital broadcasting. Another argument is that the broadcast media is so uniquely pervasive and powerful that it needs to be specially regulated to protect viewers such as children from unsuitable programmes such as pornography, violent films, and other socially unsuitable programmes. As Eric Barendt points out, it cannot be consistent with general free speech principles to impose greater restrictions on a mode of speech merely because it is thought to be more effective than other media of communication.[330] Perhaps the only sustainable argument generally, but particularly true in Africa as a whole today, is the fact that the broadcast media has for long been controlled and dominated by the state. In fact, historically, the broadcast media in Africa, especially the radio, was often exploited first by the colonial powers, and later by the corrupt and incompetent leaders who succeeded them, to ruthlessly shut out dissent and perpetuate themselves in power. The radio still remains the most powerful and most widely accessible means of communication available to the public and African governments have been very reluctant to relinquish their stranglehold over it.

169. The advent of the so-called third wave of democratization in the 1990s has raised the level of political and civil rights consciousness, especially freedom of speech and this has combined with the monumental advances in communications technology to make 'democratization' and 'liberalization' of the broadcast media not only necessary but imperative. In fact, with the availability of cable, satellite, and digital systems, total state control of the broadcast media has become very difficult to justify and anomalous.

State monopoly of the broadcast media in Botswana ended in 1999 when the government granted licences to two private radio stations. The legal framework for regulating the broadcast media was, for the first time, laid down in the Broadcasting

329. *See* para. 56 *supra* .

330. Barendt, *Freedom of Speech* 446.

Act, 1998. This Act provided a framework for the establishment and functioning of a NBB which was given powers to issue broadcasting licences. The Act provided for three types of broadcasting: public service broadcasting, private broadcasting service, and community broadcasting service. The Broadcasting Act, 1998 was repealed in 2011[331] and replaced by the Communications Regulatory Authority Act, 2012.[332] The latter Act provides for the creation of an independent regulatory authority, the Botswana Regulatory Authority (BOCRA), which is responsible for regulating the communications sector comprising of telecommunications, Internet, broadcasting, information technologies, radio communications, and postal services. At the time that the government was proposing to enact the Communications Regulatory Authority Act, 2012, it justified the new law on the basis that it was going to create a converged communications regulatory authority 'to bring about efficiencies in the tele-communications sector by removing duplicate agencies and housing their regulation and licensing under one roof'.[333] The rationale for the new law, on the face of it, was innocuous given the worldwide trend towards merging telecommunications and broadcasting regulators due to the convergence of the two sectors. There was no indication at all that the new law would make major changes to the regulation of broadcasting. However, when the government published the Communications Regulatory Authority Bill, the public were surprised to note that, not only did it merge the broadcast and telecommunications regulators, but it also made significant changes to the regulation of the broadcast sector by derecognizing public service broadcasting, and community broadcasters. The Communications Regulatory Authority Act, 2012, unlike the Broadcasting Act, 1998, only provides for two types of broadcasters: state and commercial broadcasting services.

The Communications Regulatory Authority Act, 2012 is supplemented by the Broadcasting Regulations, 2004 in the regulation of the broadcast media. The Broadcasting Regulations, 2004 are for the time being, in force as per section 96(a) of the Act which provides that all subsidiary legislation under the repealed Broadcasting Act, 1998 shall remain in force in so far as they are not inconsistent with the new law. This means the Broadcasting Regulations, 2004, in so far as they apply to commercial broadcasters, will remain in force. The draft Communications Regulations, 2015, will eventually replace the Broadcasting Regulations, 2004. Under the section on broadcasting, the draft regulations retain most of the provisions relating to commercial broadcasting under the Broadcasting Regulations, 2004.

170. The Broadcasting Act was supposed to have been complemented by a national broadcasting policy. As we have seen,[334] in spite of several years of consultation, the draft national broadcasting policy that was tabled before Parliament in 2006 could not be adopted because of disagreements over the issue of the public service broadcasting and community services broadcasting. Nevertheless, the discussion that follows will make occasional references to the 2006 version of the draft national broadcasting policy.

---

331. Broadcasting (Repeal) Act 2011.

332. Act No. 19 of 2012.

333. Frank Ramsden, then Minister of Transport and Communications' Keynote address at the 2nd National ICT Stakeholders Consultative Forum held in Gaborone on 1 Sept. 2011, http://www.gov.bw. (Accessed on 4 Apr. 2013).

334. *See* para. 21 *supra* .

Chapter 1. Public Service Broadcasting

§1. The Concept and Mission of Public Service Broadcasting

171. A large proportion of the world's media, especially radio and television, is owned and operated by the state usually through public service bodies.[335] In spite of this, the meaning of the concept of 'public service' has probably remained one of the most elusive and amorphous in media studies. In fact, Trine Syvertsen, after a study of more than thirty different definitions concludes that not only did the definitive criteria differ in each of them but also many were in fact directly contradictory.[336] There is apparently no common understanding of the term although it can be said to have several closely related meanings, varying with the extreme diversity of public service statutes around the world. From a semantic analysis of the concept, Syvertsen is able to discern three main meanings that are worthy of note.[337]

The first of this involves the use of 'public service' in the sense of 'public utility', or 'public good'. In this technical-economic sense, it refers to the kind of services that governments usually provide, such as, postal services, roads, and public security. She argues that John Reith, the BBC's first Director-General used the term in this sense when he developed his paternalistic ideology of radio as an agent of public enlightenment and a vehicle for the distribution of culture.[338] It is a pure public good in the sense that its cost of production is largely independent of the number of people who consume it, very much like public roads and public security. The second meaning arises from the assumption that the word 'public' in 'public service' can be taken to refer to the 'public sphere' or the 'commons'. In this sense, the public sphere represents institutions in which members of the public take part as citizens and collectively make decisions for the common good. To Habermas, the PSM must be capable of feeding into and nourishing this 'public sphere' that 'mediates between society and the state, in which the public organizes itself as bearers of public opinion'.[339] This conceptualization requires a guarantee that all members of the public have access to the information and knowledge that they need in order to properly discharge their civic duties as good citizens. Finally, the third definition takes as its starting point, the equation of 'public' with 'audience' and takes public service to mean a service whose prime purpose is to satisfy the needs of all citizens.

335. There are basically two regulatory philosophies that have emerged influenced by the initial responses of the governments of the United Kingdom and the United States. The PSM model is usually associated with the United Kingdom while what may be referred to as the 'commercial model', is the United States approach. Trine Syvertsen, *The Many Uses of the 'Public Service' Concept*, 20 Nordicom Rev. 5–12 (1999).

336. Syvertsen, *The Many Uses of the 'Public Service' Concept.*

337. *Ibid.*, 6–7.

338. *Ibid.*

339. J. Habermas, *The Public Sphere*, in *Communication and Class Struggle: Vol. 1. Capitalism and Imperialism* 198 (A. Mattelart & S. Seigelaub eds, International General 1979).

172. However, these different definitions in reality reflect the trends in perception of the concept over the years dictated by political, social, economic, and technological factors. The concept has fluctuated between conceptions based on paternalism, elitism, and consumerism, with the current trend being towards the latter.[340] The development of digital technology and the convergence of telephonic, information, and media services may well stretch the concept into new directions. Even if this were to happen, a review of the current activities of the PSM in those countries where it has worked well around the world reveals a remarkable unanimity of purpose.[341] From these six defined features or general principles, largely derived from the guarantee of freedom of speech, have come to be associated with the PSM.[342]

The first feature, general availability, is a direct consequence of the public nature of the service. This sees the PSM as a national service that should be made available, if not to everyone throughout the country, then, to as many people as is possible. On the basis of this principle, it is argued that it would not be fair to offer a public service to only part of the population; for example, those living in cities, although all the regions do not necessarily have to receive identical programmes. Underlying this is the principle of equality that requires that access to a public service must be made available to everyone and rules out discrimination from the standpoint of either rights or costs. Eric Barendt in arguing this point maintains that it would be constitutionally suspect for a country to provide a basic publicly funded service on a subscription basis, which would effectively discriminate against the poorer members of the community.[343]

The second public service feature, which requires concern for promoting national identity and culture, is sometimes considered as controversial because it impinges on editorial freedom and might lead to some chauvinism as well as provide an excuse for the government to interfere and require the showing of programmes sympathetic to its policies. To this extent, it may run counter to the third feature, which requires some immunity from control by the government or vested commercial interests. However, conceptualization of this national identity and cultural mission may take different forms, not all of which are controversial. This may require broadcasters on the PSM to regard themselves as having a special cultural mission of disseminating the country's linguistic, spiritual, aesthetic, and ethnic wealth. Thus, the BBC was for many years styled 'the national instrument of broadcasting'; while in French, presidents have termed the national radio and television service as the 'voice of France'.[344]

The third feature, independence from both state and commercial interests, is really a crucial aspect of freedom of expression on the PSM. The greatest threat to

340. *See* Thomas Gibbons, *Regulating the Media* 58 (2nd edn., Sweet & Maxwell 1998).

341. *See* Robin Foster, *Public Broadcasters. Accountability and Efficiency* (Edinburgh University, 1992).

342. *See generally*, Eric Barendt, *Broadcasting Law. A Comparative Study* 51–59 (Clarendon Press 1993); and Toby Mendel, *Public Service Broadcasting. A Comparative Survey*, www.unesco.org/webworld/publications/Mendel/features.html; and Gibbons, *Regulating the Media*, at 56 and R.C. Smith, *Broadcasting Law and Fundamental Right* 5 (Clarendon Press 1997).

343. Barendt, *Broadcasting Law* 53.

344. *See* Jay G. Blumler, *Public Service Broadcasting Before the Commercial Deluge*, in *Television and the Public Interest. Vulnerable Values in West European Broadcasting* 13 (Jay G. Blumler ed., Sage Publications 1992).

this usually comes from attempts by the state to control these publicly funded facilities to achieve their own ends. As creatures ultimately of the state, the PSM institutions have been highly politicized, even in those societies where safeguards for their editorial independence have been carefully crafted. Nevertheless, it is generally unfair for the government of the day or a branch of the state to control the PSM in such a way that it acts as its mouthpiece to the detriment of the public interest and the right of citizens to receive a diverse range of information. On the contrary, independence from commercial interests implies that the PSM should not compete for funds in the same way as the private media will do. Commercial dependency may lead them into subjecting programme production and scheduling to profit-oriented and advertisement-driven popularity tests, rather than the dictates of public interests. Although independence from commercial interests have always been one of the important justifications for the existence of the PSM, it is now recognized and accepted that a blend of public and commercial funding will not necessarily compromise it or distract it from promoting pluralism and other public service goals.

The fourth feature, promoting impartiality, is closely linked to the previous point. Impartiality is usually considered as one of the fundamental features of the public service and requires a dispassionate presentation of information and an even-handed treatment of all opinions. This makes it wrong for a PSM, financed by all citizens, to take sides on political or social controversies or to be seen to promote or support a particular political party.

As a fifth feature, the PSM is required to provide a wide range and variety of programmes. This involves a varied menu of programmes that combine news bulletins and documentaries with light entertainment, films, drama, and sports. The ultimate goal of such diversity is to ensure that the public has access to, if not all, then as much of the information they need to live comfortably, perform their civic duties and live as good citizens. This means that the programme outputs must be such that all significant sectors of the community, divided by interests, values, and identities will still be able to have their concerns reflected in a tolerably authentic way.[345]

Finally, there is the issue of funding of the PSM. There are many who feel that it should be by a general charge on all users. This should reinforce the point that commercial interests should not dominate the PSM. Generally, the PSM are usually funded by one of three possible means; a licence fee, paid by television viewers, as is the case in Britain, funds directly voted by Parliament or, by commercial advertisement. The licence fee approach, although often difficult and costly to administer, has the advantage of being more stable and less susceptible to government interference. A general charge voted for by Parliament may lead the PSM to compete for ratings with commercial stations in order to justify the general charge, rather than concentrate on promoting quality and diversity. The third option of funding through advertisements carries the risk of programme schedules and type being influenced by the advertising agencies. Today, however, a mixture of a general charge and advertising revenue finances most European PSM. This has the advantage that it reduces the risk of dependence on any particular source.

These six features or principles reflect certain values and ideals that appear to have worked reasonably well in Europe where the PSM model originated. Despite

345. *Ibid.*, at 10.

many constitutional, linguistic, cultural, and political differences amongst the European countries, it was, until the early 1980s, these six features that distinguished the PSM model from the more market-oriented approach of the United States. Variants of the PSM, particularly the British and French models, were transported to Africa during the colonial period and used more or less as a medium for propaganda than anything else. After independence, postcolonial governments continued in the same tradition.

§2. The Organization of Public Service Broadcasting

173. Historically, because of the close colonial links between Botswana and South Africa at the early stages of the development of its broadcasting, the Botswana authorities were caught between two competing models – the BBC model of a semi-public corporation and the South African model of direct government control through a responsible minister.[346] As a result, unlike many former British colonies that began life at independence with a BBC model and gradually moved towards greater direct government control, the Botswana government followed the South African approach. Under this model, the state-owned radio was housed within the government Department of Information and Broadcasting (DIB) first, under the Ministry of Home Affairs, and later, moved to the then Ministry of Presidential Affairs and Public Administration, and then back to the Office of the President. Today, all state media are controlled by the Media Division in the Office of the President.

174. The exact nature of the role of the state-owned public media in Botswana as a public service facility has never been defined. Zaffiro, in his study of the establishment and evolution of RB cites two consultancy reports that were supposed to lay down policy guidelines. The first, a 1968 *Report on the Information Functions of Government*, recommended that RB workers should be subject to the 'duty to promote politically determined policies', and were not to be allowed to consider themselves as 'an independent body operating on public service corporation lines'.[347] It also recommended that they were to function as part of the 'government's publicity machinery'. The report made it clear that RB was not to be considered as a public service corporation like the BBC but rather a government department that was under no circumstances to be used to embarrass, frustrate or oppose the government. It was on the basis of one of its recommendations that control over radio broadcasting was taken from the Ministry of Home Affairs and placed within the Office of the President. The 1968 Report became the 'guidepost for the next twenty years', until it was modified by a second consultancy report, in 1978.[348] The second report amongst other things criticized what it perceived as the unsatisfactory coverage of ministerial tours and speeches and the alleged unfair coverage of opposition parties and leaders.[349] Many of the recommendations in these reports were adopted as government policy and had the net effect of increasing government control over RB. In 1989, the minister with responsibility for information

346. *See generally*, James J. Zaffiro, *From Police Network to Station of the Nation* 13–27.
347. *See* A.J. Hughes, *Report on the Information Functions of Government* 11–17 (Government Printer 1968).
348. James J. Zaffiro, *From Police Network to Station of the Nation* 39–40.
349. *Ibid.*

and broadcasting warned government journalists that, 'Radio Botswana and the *Daily News* cannot operate like the private media', since they were vehicles through which the government of the day communicates with the people that brought it to power.[350] Government interference with the editorial independence of state media has led to a perception that these media outlets are mouthpieces of government and do not disseminate balanced information.

§3. STATE BROADCASTING

175. The Communications Regulatory Authority Act, 2012 provides for state broadcasting, which is defined as a government department designated as a provider of broadcasting services. The department charged with the responsibility of providing state broadcasting services is the Department of Broadcasting Services (DBS). The Department currently offers two national radio stations, RB 1 and RB 2, and a national television service, Btv.

A state broadcaster is owned by the state or government which directly controls its programming. The main difference between a state broadcaster and public broadcaster, both which are public media, is that the programming of a state broadcaster is driven by political interests while that of a public service broadcaster (PSB) is driven by the public interest.[351]

176. In general, the government's position has throughout been that the state media purveys official information; therefore, civil servants who work for it are controlled by civil service conventions. They are free to report anything they want as long as they toe the official line.[352] Although the Botswana public media is considerably freer than most in the region, it shares a number of important characteristics with most of them. These include, an emphasis in coverage and news selection upon official speeches, on the comings and goings, and the images of top national political leaders, particularly the president; heavy and often conflicting demands to serve national development goals as well as to inform, educate and entertain; and a structure that ensures a top-down communications flow with a susceptibility to monopolization and political manipulation at the top.

177. The government of Botswana should amend the regulatory framework of the broadcast media to provide for an independent PSB that will serve the public interest. Such a move will be in line with the position taken by the African Commission on Human and Peoples' Rights that state- and government-controlled media should be transformed into PSB.[353]

The exclusion of community broadcasting in the Communications Regulatory Authority Act, 2012 is also regrettable considering the potential that this medium has in contributing to the dissemination of a wide range of content, catering to the needs

350. *Ibid.*, at 88.

351. T. Mendel, *Public Service Broadcasting: A Comparative Legal Survey* 3 (UNESCO 2011).

352. *See* M. Leepile, *An Overview of the Press in Botswana*, Paper presented at the International Seminar on the 'Feasibility of the Ombudsman Institution in Botswana', at the University of Botswana, 2–3 Nov. 1993.

353. Declaration of Principles on Freedom of Expression in Africa, Principle VI.

of different audiences. Community media help the development of different sectors of a territorial, ethno-linguistic, and other communities.[354] They strive to improve the quality of life of their communities and contribute to the well-being of its members by sharing a community's interests, challenges, and concerns.

354. *See* Report of the United Nations Special Rapporteur on the promotion and protection of the right to freedom of opinion and expression, 20 Apr. 2010, A/HRC/14/23, para. 68.

Chapter 2. Commercial Broadcasting Service

§1. Commercial Broadacsting

178. The Communications Regulatory Authority Act, 2012 defines commercial broadcasting as a broadcasting service operating for profit and available free of charge or through subscription. This definition covers all private entities that provide free-to-air and subscription broadcasting services.

§2. Licensing Requirements

179. One of the major issues addressed by the repealed Broadcasting Act 1998 and now in the Communications Regulatory Authority Act, 2012 is that of providing clear procedures as well as the conditions for the issue of a broadcasting licence. Before the enactment of the Broadcasting Act, 1998, the power to issue broadcasting licences had been vested in the BTC but due to uncertainties in the procedure, the BTC used to forward all licence applications to the Office of the President for clearance, which the latter never did.[355] Responsibility for issuing licences is now conferred on BOCRA.

Section 31(1) of the Communications Regulatory Authority Act, 2012 makes it clear that 'a person shall not carry out any broadcasting or re-broadcasting activities' in Botswana without obtaining a licence issued in accordance with the Act. A state broadcaster however does not require a licence to operate.[356] An application for a broadcasting or rebroadcasting licence, according to section 31(2) of the Act must be addressed to BOCRA and must be in the prescribed manner. BOCRA may invite applications for broadcasting licences through a tendering process or in any other competitive process.

Section 31(1) states that regulations may provide for:

(a) the payment of annual or other fees for broadcasting or rebroadcasting licences;
(b) the frequencies that may be used in the operation of a station, the power of limitations in respect of a station and any other technical specifications;
(c) the location of a transmitter station and the geographical area to which the broadcast or rebroadcast may be made;
(d) the classification of broadcasting licences, subscription management service licences, and the applicable conditions thereto.

On receipt of an application for broadcasting or rebroadcasting licence, BOCRA, if satisfied that the applicant has fulfilled all the requirements for a grant of a licence, and subject to the availability of frequencies, issue licence to the applicant subject to such conditions and restrictions, including geographical restrictions, as it considers

355. *See* Balule, *Enhancing the Media's Democratic Role* 124–135.
356. Section 31(2).

necessary. It is not exactly clear why section 32(1) of the Act subjects the issue of a broadcast or rebroadcast licence to 'the availability of frequencies', when, as we noted earlier,[357] the introduction of other forms of signal delivery, notably cable, satellite, and microwave transmitters have undermined the scarcity principle. In addition, in considering whether to grant a licence, BOCRA is required to promote quality and a variety of services to consumers and ensure competition in the market.[358]

Whenever the name of any broadcasting or rebroadcasting service licensed under the Act is changed or any person acquires the proprietorship or any interest in the proprietorship of any broadcasting or rebroadcasting service or the director, producer or proprietor of any such broadcasting or rebroadcasting service is changed, notice of such change and approval of the change must be obtained from BOCRA.

All licensees are required to keep and store sound and video recordings of all programmes broadcast or rebroadcast for a minimum period of three months after the date of transmission of the broadcast or rebroadcast, or for such further period as may be directed by BOCRA. The licensee should be ready to produce all such material when demanded to do so by BOCRA.

It is also worth noting that Regulation 27 of the Broadcasting Regulations allow the NBB, after consultation with a licensee to amend any licence conditions to such extent as may be necessary by virtue of an international agreement or convention to which Botswana is a party or where the amendment does not cause substantial prejudice to the licensee. Under Regulation 28, where it is the licensee who applies to BOCRA to amend its licence conditions, BOCRA may invite other licensees to make representations on the applicant's proposed amendment or indicate to BOCRA in writing whether the proposed amendment may be prejudicial to their interests. BOCRA may consult the applicant before making a final decision on the proposed amendment and there is no reason to think that an applicant aggrieved by the decision refer the matter to the High Court for review.

357. *See* para. 169 *supra* .

358. Section 6(2), Communications Regulatory Authority Act, 2012.

Chapter 3. Programme Standards

180. Programme standards are designed to ensure that viewers and listeners are protected from being harmed or offended by the content of material that is broadcast. These standards are designed to promote impartiality in programmes, cultural diversity, protect minors as well as protect human dignity in general. The standards are laid down in the Broadcasting Regulations, 2004 and form the basis of a Broadcasting Code of Conduct for all licensed broadcasters and is part of their licences.

Programme standards in Botswana are laid down in Regulation 11 of the Broadcasting Regulations which states:

> A licensee, or any employee thereof, shall not broadcast any matter which, measured by contemporary community standards –
>
> a) offends against good taste or decency;
>
> b) contains the frequent use of offensive language, including blasphemy;
>
> c) presents sexual matters in an explicit and offensive manner;
>
> d) glorifies violence or depicts violence in an offensive manner; or
>
> e) is likely to incite or perpetuate hatred or vilify any person or section of the community on account of the race, ethnicity, nationality, gender, sexual preference, age, disability, religion or culture of that person or section of the community.

The Broadcasting Regulations, 2004 contain certain specific standards which are required of the licensed broadcast services in different situations.

§1. Impartiality

181. A number of provisions in the Broadcasting Regulations, 2004 are specifically designed to promote 'impartial reporting' and state as follows:

(1) A licensee, its employees or agents shall report news and information accurately, fairly, and impartially.
(2) A licensee shall ensure that news and information are broadcast and presented in a balanced manner, without any intentional or negligent departure from any facts

through distortion, exaggeration, misrepresentation, material omissions or through excessive summarizing or editing.

(3) A licensee, its employees or agents shall broadcast a fact fairly, having regard to its context and importance.

This requirement of impartiality is further buttressed by Regulation 14 dealing with the broadcast of unconfirmed reports. It states:

(1) A licensee shall not broadcast any report that is not based on a fact or that is founded on an opinion, supposition, rumour or allegation unless the broadcast is carried out in a manner that indicates these circumstances clearly.
(2) Where any doubt exists as to the accuracy of a report, and verification is not possible, this fact shall be mentioned in the report.
(3) A licensee shall not broadcast any report where there exists sufficient reason to doubt the accuracy thereof and it is possible to verify accuracy of the report before it is broadcast.

Where a factual error occurs, Regulation 15 imposes on the licensee a duty to broadcast the correction of the factual error first, without reservation as soon as is reasonably possible after the error has been committed and second, with such degree of prominence and timing as may be adequate and fair so as to easily attract attention and, where appropriate, include an apology. Regulation 16 provides a special procedure to be followed in reporting controversial issues. It provides:

(1) A licensee shall ensure that, when reporting on controversial issues, a wide range of views and opinions is reported, either within a single programme or within a series of programmes, which shall be broadcast as soon as is reasonably possible.
(2) A licensee shall endeavour to ensure that when broadcasting controversial issues of political, industrial or public importance during phone-in programmes, a wide range of views and opinions is represented.
(3) A person or organization whose views have been criticized on any controversial issues of political, industrial or public importance during a programme, and who makes any representations, within a reasonable time, to the licensee responsible for the programme, that he or she or the organization is aggrieved, shall be offered an opportunity by the licensee to reply to such criticism.
(4) A reply to a criticism under sub-regulation (3) shall be given a similar degree of prominence to the original criticism during its broadcast, and shall be broadcast during a similar timeslot to the original criticism, as soon as is reasonably possible after the original criticism.
(5) For the purposes of this regulation 'programme' includes news bulletins, current affairs programmes, informative programmes, interviews, panel discussions, and phone-in discussions.

The regulations also try to ensure that there is impartiality in the conduct of interviews. In this regard, Regulation 17 requires that the person to be interviewed by a licensee is advised of the subject of the interview and informed before the interview takes place as to whether the interview is to be recorded or broadcast live. Before conducting an interview with a minor, the licensee must request permission from the parents or guardian. A licensee is also required to exercise sensitivity in conducting interviews with bereaved persons, survivors of traumatic incidents or witnesses thereof.

§2. Cultural Diversity

182. The Botswana constitution of 1966 does not expressly say anything about cultural or linguistic rights. There is no reason to assume that these rights are not thereby recognized or protected although it would have been better for this to be expressly stated as is the case in most post-1990 African Constitutions. It can be argued that section 3(b) of the constitution which recognizes the right to freedom of association protects the freedom of 'every person freely to associate with others, which would encompass the right to participate in the cultural life of one's choice'.[359] Similarly, a combination of sections 3 and 15 of the constitution which guarantee equality and prohibit discrimination can be interpreted as also protecting both individual and group interests in cultural integrity and linguistic rights.

The issue of diversity figures very prominently in the draft broadcasting policy of 2006. In dealing with the issue of Botswana content, it states:

There is a need for especially the public broadcaster to reflect the reality that people find themselves in, to have its own recognizable flavour and identity. The use of local content on radio and TV will instil a common sense of pride in the achievements of the country and its people. On a practical level, it will further develop the quality of local production. Increased production and broadcasting of local content will create local employment and a viable local production industry and thus contribute to citizen empowerment.

The desire to promote cultural diversity finds expression in rule 10 of the Broadcasting Regulations which provides:

(1) Except otherwise stated as a specific licence condition, a licensee shall broadcast programmes with a minimum local content of 20% of all programmes for television broadcasts, and a minimum local content of 40% of all programmes for radio broadcasts.
(2) The provisions of sub-regulation (1) shall not apply to news broadcasts.
(3) Except as otherwise stated as a specific license condition, local news shall constitute the majority of a licensee's news broadcast content.

The African Media Barometer Botswana 2007 report indicates that the two state-owned radio stations offer diverse programmes that cater for various interests but there is no language diversity as broadcasts are only in either English or Setswana. Local content on Btv has increased tremendously since the station started operating in 2000, especially with respect to music. There are however still too few local productions with respect to popular programmes such as dramas and talk shows.[360] With regard to commercial

359. *See* Burns, *Communications Law* 97.
360. *See* MISA & Friedrich Ebert Stiftung, *African Media Barometer, Botswana 2007* 34–35.

broadcasters, Duma FM was the only licensee that met the local content quota in 2016 at 41%. Gabz FM was at 36%, Yarona FM at 15% and e-Botswana, the only private television station, at 7%.[361] The broadcasters attribute their failure to meet the set quotas to unavailability of local content that meet their respective programming standards.[362]

§3. Protection of Minors

183. The prime purpose of protection of minors in programme content is the desire to protect them from material which would, or could damage them morally, psychologically or physically. A typical example of this is the protection against pornography. The fear is that early exposure of a child to sexually explicit material might endanger the upbringing of the child because at that tender age, he is unable to place what he is seeing in perspective and may be tempted to regard this as a normal portrayal of sexual relations.[363] Section 37 of the Communications Regulatory Authority Act, 2012 states simply that, 'without prejudice to the provisions of section 178 of the Penal Code (relating to obscene publications) a licensee shall, where a programme to be broadcast or re-broadcast is not suitable to be exhibited to children, advise or warn members of the public accordingly'. There are a number of provisions in the Broadcasting Regulations, 2004 that are specifically designed to protect minors.

First, there is Regulation 12 on 'protection of children', which states:

(1) A licensee shall ensure that due care is exercised in order to avoid content which may disturb or be harmful to children when the licensee broadcasts programmes at times where a large number of children may be expected to be watching or listening to radio or television programmes.
(2) A licensee shall, when determining whether a large number of children are watching or listening to any programme, take into account any available audience research carried out, as well as the times that programmes are broadcast.
(3) The content of programmes which may disturb or be harmful to children includes offensive language, explicit sexual or violent material, music containing sexually explicit lyrics or music containing lyrics which depict violence.

Second, there is Regulation 21(2) dealing with sexual offences, which provides that 'a licensee, its employees or agents shall not disclose, in a broadcast, the identity of a minor where such minor is a victim of a sexual offence'. It is also worth recalling Regulation 17(2) which provides that before conducting interviews with children, permission must be obtained from his parents or guardians.

Banning the broadcast of all material which may be harmful to children is probably the best way of protecting children but such an extreme measure is socially and politically unacceptable. While the law tries to protect children against harmful broadcast, it is impossible for it to guarantee that no child will be watching material

361. *See* BOCRA Annual Report 2016 at p. 38 www.bocra.org.bw accessed 3 Aug. 2017.
362. *Ibid.*
363. *See* Barendt, *Freedom of Speech* 374.

that is unsuitable to children. Where state responsibility stops, parental responsibility takes over. With the duty on broadcasters to warn about unsuitable material and the so-called watershed period, generally from 10 p.m. when progressively adult material is being shown on television, it is the duty of parents to ensure that their children heed the warning and do not view inappropriate or potentially harmful material.

§4. Human Dignity

184. Human dignity is what gives a person their intrinsic worth as a human being, a sense of self-worth and self-respect.[364] The courts in Botswana have repeatedly made it clear that respect for human dignity lies at the very heart of the constitution.[365] Although it is concerned with physical and psychological integrity, the right to respect one's human dignity is broader than the Roman-Dutch concept of *dignitas*. As the decided cases show, it is closely linked with the other rights such as the right to life, liberty, security of the person and the protection of the law as well as the right to equality. Nevertheless, dignity, like the concept of equality, is a complex moral and political concept whose exact scope is difficult to determine. However, it will always require a careful balancing of freedom of speech and dignity in the light of the particular facts in any given situation. For example, while free speech will require that the media report on ghastly accidents, there can be no justification for showing close-up photographs of a dead or seriously wounded victim of such an accident.

§5. Right of Reply

185. The Broadcasting Regulations, 2004 provide a right of reply where a broadcaster has broadcast a programme on controversial issues. Regulation 16 (3–5) provides:

(3) A person or organization whose views have been criticised on any controversial issues of a political, industrial or public importance during a programme, and who makes any representations, within a reasonable time, to the licensee responsible for the programme, that he or she or the organization is aggrieved, shall be offered an opportunity by the licensee to reply to such criticism.

(4) A reply to criticism under sub-regulation (3) shall be given a similar degree of prominence to the original criticism during its broadcast, and shall be during a similar time-slot to the original criticism, as soon as is reasonably possible after the original criticism.

---

364. *See* Dingake J in *Diau v. Botswana Building Society* [2003] 2 BLR 409 at 434; and again in *Lemo v. Northern Air Maintenance (Pty) Ltd* [2004] 2 BLR 317 at 329.

365. Some of the important cases where this point has been reiterated include, *Petrus & Another v. The State* 1984 BLR 14; *Attorney-General v. Dow* [1992] BLR 119; *Mabote v. Mabote* [1999] 1BLR 386; *Attorney-General v. Otlhomile* [2004] 1 BLR 21; and *Sesana & Others v. Attorney-General* [2006] 2 BLR 633.

(5) For the purpose of this regulation 'programme' includes news bulletins, current affairs programmes, informative programmes, interviews, panel discussions and phone-in discussions.

The right of reply provided in the above regulations is designed to ensure that a person who has been criticized is given an opportunity to defend himself. The right of reply protects a person's dignity and at the same time, promote diversity of views on programmes on controversial issues.

§6. Complaints Procedure

186. An elaborate procedure is provided in the regulations for dealing with complaints. Regulation 34 states in this respect:

1) A licensee shall establish procedures to investigate and deal with complaints levelled against it by members of the public.

2) A licensee shall submit to the Board –

a) before such licensee begins its operation, the procedures established under sub-regulation (1) and the names and addresses of the persons designated to handle complaints; or

b) where there is a change in the procedures previously submitted to the Board, the change in those procedures, within 7 days of the change being made.

3) A licensee shall broadcast information on the procedure for lodging complaints at least 3 times per week, during prime-time.

4) Where a complaint is made to a licensee, the licensee shall advise the complainant that the complainant has the right to refer the complaint to the Board if the complainant is dissatisfied with the licensee's response to the complaint.

5) Where a complaint is referred to the Board under sub-regulation (4), a licensee shall –

a) submit, on request any recordings or documentation required by the Board;

b) respond to queries from the Board relating to allegations of non-compliance with the Act or with licence conditions;

c) submit, on request by the Board, written reports or written responses to allegations of non-compliance with the Act or with licence conditions; and

d) appear, when requested, before the Board during the adjudication of any complaint or investigation into any alleged non-compliance with the Act or with license conditions.

6) The Board shall invite a licensee to make written or oral representations within such period as may be specified by the Board, where it intends to investigate –

a) any alleged non-compliance with the Act or with licence conditions; or

b) any complaint relating to the licensee's failure or refusal to deal with any complaint, or the unsatisfactory handling of any complaint, by a member of the public.

7) Where the Board finds that a licensee has failed to comply with any provisions of the Act or has breached any of its licence conditions, the Board may make such order as it considers appropriate: Provided that where the Board imposes a fine, such fine shall not exceed P 500.

8) Where an order is made by the Board under these Regulations, the Board may, where necessary, order a licensee to broadcast an apology, correction or retraction, in such terms as the Board may specify.

Chapter 4. Political Broadcasting

187. Elections usually raise lots of problems between politicians and the media, particularly the broadcast media. Many countries have drafted codes of conduct to deal with some of the frequent problems that arise with political broadcasting in general and broadcasting during elections. The Code of Practice for broadcasters which is part of the licence has provisions that address political broadcasting. The Code prohibits party-political broadcasts except during an election period. Party-political broadcasts during an election period are subject to the following rules:

(1) A licensee shall air contesting party-political broadcasts and afford all contesting political parties similar opportunities.
(2) If, during an election period, the programming of any licensee extends to the elections, political parties and issues relevant thereto, the licensee shall provide reasonable opportunities for the discussion of conflicting views and shall treat all political parties equitably.
(3) In the event of any criticism against a political party being levelled in a particular programme of any licensee without such party having been afforded an opportunity to respond thereto in the same programme or without the view of such political party being reflected therein, the licensee concerned shall afford such party a reasonable opportunity to reply to the criticism.
(4) If, within 48 hours before the commencement of the polling period, a licensee intends broadcasting a programme in which a particular political party is criticized, the licensee shall afford the political party a reasonable opportunity to reply thereto in the same programme, or as soon as is reasonably practicable before polling day.
(5) The opportunity to reply referred to in sub-regulations (3) and (4) shall be broadcast with the same degree of prominence and, where applicable, in substantially the same timeslot as the initial criticism.

The provision in the Code of Practice dealing with party-political broadcasts is aimed at ensuring that the broadcast media affords all contesting political parties and candidates access to the media and promote fair and equitable treatment. The media play a critical role in promoting free and fair elections as they promote a participatory process where the electorate can engage in public debate. This can only be achieved if the broadcast media is fair and impartial in their dealing with political parties and candidates. Unfortunately, since state broadcasters are exempted from licensing requirements, this means the regulation only applies to commercial broadcasters.

§1. Rules on Political Independence of Broadcasters

188. Neither the Botswana constitution nor any particular piece of legislation specifically contains rules which recognize and protect the political independence of broadcasters generally and the public media in particular. There are several reasons why it is argued that the continuous monopolization of the public media by the Botswana government at this delicate period of democratic consolidation is in many respects, contrary to the long-term political, economic, and social development of the country.

First, because the public media has come to be associated with a government service offered by a government department and therefore under the control and directives of politicians, it has been reduced to a government rather than the public service that it should be. With the considerable wealth of information now available via satellite, cables, Internet, and other forms of digital communication, it is difficult to justify the huge sums of tax payers' money that is spent on a service that many people perceive merely as an actual or potential government propaganda institution and whose services they no longer see as serving their needs.

Second, the public media at this stage of Botswana's development is too important not only in terms of its actual reach but also its accessibility for it to be controlled by the government. Neither the abundant satellite television channels that are now available nor the legalization of commercial broadcasting is sufficient to guarantee either access or even a plurality of voices on the airwaves. Only a few elites in the population can afford the satellite services. Even if commercial alternatives were available, the small size of the population and the low population density do not make commercial television or radio operation over the whole national territory a viable proposition. Besides, the extent of rural poverty is such that the profit-driven private media operators will usually concentrate only on the heavily populated areas of the country in order to increase their appeals to advertisers and will ignore rural areas. It is therefore no surprise that the only private commercial television station that operates, e-Botswana, transmits from the capital Gaborone and covers only a radius of 60 km. Even then, the e-Botswana faces tough competition because studies show that Batswana prefer to watch South African television channels.[366] Therefore, the availability of commercial television and radio services in Botswana, will not promote as much plurality or diversity on the media as can be expected from the public media.

Third, the effect of citizens preferring to watch or listen to politically neutral foreign television channels and radio stations as noted above can have serious negative repercussions not only on the country's cultural but also its political development. In the words of Cohen, state control of the PSM is the road to 'deadening government controls … with the result that both the cultural and political publics are seriously deformed'.[367] In this respect, it can be argued that the PSM can today be regarded as one of the strongest defences that are available against the negative effects of the deregulatory and globalizing impulses that the digital revolution has unleashed. In fact, the driving force behind the introduction of the Btv in 2000 was to counter South African influence on the airwaves, or what has been referred to as 'cultural pollution',[368] and win back Batswana viewers who had taken to watching South African television channels. On the contrary, privatizing the services offered by the PSM, even if that were financially feasible, may only bring in profit-driven commercial operators who usually take a short-term view and tend to concentrate on importing cheap foreign

366. Sechele, *Deepening Democracy or Creeping Authoritarian Rule?* 108–109.
367. J.L. Cohen, *The Public Sphere, the Media and Civil Society*, in *Rights of Access to the Media* 48 (A. Sajo & M. Price ed., Kluwer Law International 1996).
368. Sechele, *Deepening Democracy or Creeping Authoritarian Rule?* 93.

entertainment programmes rather than the education or cultural programmes that promote national culture and stimulate creativity and innovation through the production of local programmes. In fact, the very nature, logic and trajectory of the commercial media system, with its emphasis on profits and the high risk of concentrated ownership may not promote the diversity, pluralism, and high quality information that goes with freedom of expression.

It is also quite obvious that a partisan public media is undesirable and likely to be counterproductive in the long-term. An ideal PSM should ensure a free market of ideas. This can only be achieved by the institutionalization of freedom of expression through carefully crafted constitutional and statutory provisions, which should provide such checks that the PSM, whether state, government or public controlled or, whether controlled by a government department, parastatal or a trust, can be protected from political manipulation. It may well be argued that constitutional considerations have played no part in the development of, for example, British Broadcasting Law, which is nevertheless similar in many respects to the law in France and Germany, where constitutional provisions expressly protect this right. It would however, be wrong to conclude that constitutions and Bills of Rights or legislation with provisions protecting freedom of expression on the public media in them are unnecessary.[369] Unlike in France and Germany, broadcasting in Britain, because it depends on weak conventions that can be easily disregarded by a confident or arrogant government, has left broadcasters, particularly at the BBC, vulnerable to political pressure. They cannot rely on the law, as their colleagues in France and Germany can do, to protect their independence.[370] The British situation is very similar to what obtains in Botswana, but with perhaps one major difference; besides the weak conventions, there is a strong sense of media justice built around a long history and a solid democratic foundation that ensures fair play in the British public media. For example, the most common source of complaints of bias in the BBC's coverage of politics have been from the British governments themselves, both Labour and Conservative,[371] and not from the opposition as is usually the case in Botswana. On the other hand, Botswana, with its weak and tenuous one-party dominated democracy, needs provisions guaranteeing freedom of expression in both the public and private media to be clearly spelt out in such a way as to prevent political bias.

It is contended that Botswana needs a fairly comprehensive well-thought out PSM Act that will provide for a more accessible, accountable, credible, and independent public media fully equipped to meet the information needs of the whole nation. Such legislation should incorporate the fundamental ideals of the PSM concept which are, by and large, still relevant in the digital age, if not more so, because of the insidious dangers of media globalization. Such legislation must however be adjusted and adapted to reflect the realities of today. For any revised PSM model to legitimate itself, it is submitted that it must be constructed and enshrine at the very least, the following five fundamental principles:

---

369. *See* Barendt, *Freedom of Speech* v.
370. *Ibid.*, 32–60.
371. R. Gunther & A. Mughan (eds), *Democracy and the Media. A Comparative Perspective* (Cambridge University Press 2000).

(1) guarantees of freedom from control, interference or domination by the state;
(2) guarantees of pluralism, diversity, fairness, and impartiality;
(3) clear rules on elections and political broadcasting;
(4) clear rules on funding;
(5) rules on the creation of an independent statutory body to control and supervise the PSM.

§2. News and Current Affairs Programmes

189. No particular piece of legislation in Botswana specifically addresses the issue of news and current affairs programming. Nevertheless, Regulation 32(4) (a) in the Broadcasting Regulations, 2004 indirectly touch on aspects of this. It allows commercial broadcasters to interrupt their programmes to broadcast a public service announcement.

§3. Political Advertising

190. The Broadcasting Code of Practice does not permit party-political advertising under any circumstances. The position taken here is similar to that adopted in other countries such as England where political advertising on television and radio is prohibited even at elections times.

Chapter 5. Advertising Rules

191. For a long time it was doubted whether advertising or what is often referred to as commercial speech is protected by the freedom of speech provisions in the constitution.[372] Since the US Supreme Court held unequivocally in *Virginia State Board of Pharmacy v. Virginia Citizens Consumer Council*[373] that pure commercial advertising, at least when it provides accurate information about a product or service, is covered by freedom of speech, this position is now generally accepted in most jurisdictions and also accepted by most writers on the topic. Two of the reasons given by Blackmun J for this conclusion in the *Virginia State* case are worth mentioning. According to the learned judge, the first reason is the interest of consumers in the free flow of commercial information which he argues may be 'as keen, if not keener by far, than his interest in the day's most urgent political debate'.[374] The second reason is that society has a strong interest in the unimpeded flow of commercial information, partly because that information may have a public interest component, but more generally because the flow is important in enabling consumers to make informed choices, which cumulatively are essential to the working of a free-enterprise economy.[375]

192. The media, particularly the private media, are owned by commercial enterprises whose primary objective is to make profits through advertising. Left unchecked, this right to make profits through advertising could be abused. There are therefore a number of restraints, mainly of a legal nature, but some through voluntary self-regulation by the media industry itself, which apply. We shall *inter alia*, examine the various forms of commercial communications that apply in Botswana, the restrictions that are imposed on content and other restrictions based on time and frequency.

§1. Various Forms of Commercial Communications

193. Before examining the various forms of advertising that are provided for in the present legislation, it is worth referring to the policy position espoused in the 2006 draft Botswana Broadcasting Policy. It starts by noting that the high costs of quality broadcasting, limited public resources, and the need to keep fees affordable has caused many public broadcasters in the world today to increasingly rely on advertisements and sponsorships. It points out that to allow a level playing field with the private sector, advertising time on services partly funded by public resources must be limited. These limitations could be in the form of restrictions on minutes per hour or prohibition of advertising for certain periods and further that the public broadcaster should not be allowed to offer rates which give it an unfair advantage over other broadcasters. It also suggests that the amount and nature of advertising and sponsorship on public broadcasting should be limited to ensure fair competition and viability of all the three tiers of broadcasting. However, because this draft policy has never been

372. For a full discussion of this, *see* Barendt, *Freedom of Speech* 392–416.
373. 425 US 748 (1976).
374. *Ibid.*, 763.
375. *Ibid.*, 764–765.

accepted, the public media, especially the public print media has been accused of unfair advertising practices.[376] Be that as it may be, the only piece of legislation dealing with advertisements is the Broadcasting Regulations, 2004.

194. Regulation 2 of the Broadcasting Regulations, 2004 defines 'advertising' to mean:

> … the broadcasting of any item in return for payment or other valuable consideration to a broadcaster with the intention of –

(a) selling to a viewer or listener, any product;
(b) convincing a viewer or listener of a belief or course of action; or
(c) promoting a product, service, belief, course of action, person or organisation.

An advertisement as defined above is distinguished from 'infomercial' which is also defined in the same part of the regulations as:

any advertising broadcast in visual or audio form, lasting for more than 2 minutes, which may contain demonstrations of the use of the product or service advertised, entailing direct offers to the public in return for payment, and which results in the broadcaster receiving payment in monetary terms or otherwise.

The third form of advertisement is by way of a 'sponsored programme' which is defined as a 'programme that has all or part of its costs paid by a sponsor, with a view to promoting that sponsor's, or another sponsor's name, product or service'.

Finally, the regulations also provide for 'special event broadcast' programme, which means broadcasting licence issued for an event that does not last for more than seven days and which is broadcast either outside a licensee's coverage area or in partnership with a foreign broadcasters.[377]

§2. Restrictions on Content

195. There are usually a number of restrictions which are imposed on advertising for a variety of reasons mainly on public policy, health or moral grounds. For example, there may be a ban or restriction on the advertisement of certain products such as cigarettes and tobacco on health grounds or restrictions on certain advertisements to children, and so on. Regulation 5 of the Broadcasting Regulations, 2004 deal with 'fairness in advertising' and states:

> 1) A licensee shall ensure that any advertisements that are broadcast by him or her are –

(1) lawful;
(2) honest;

376. *See* para. 20 *supra* .
377. This is mentioned here possibly as a form of advertising because Regulation 24(2) in dealing with this special event broadcast licence makes a distinction between 'a profit-making applicant', and 'a non-profit making applicant'.

(3) decent; and
(4) in conformity with the principles of fair competition in business.

2) A licensee shall ensure that any advertisements that are broadcast by him or her –

a) do not contain any descriptions, claims or other material which may, directly or by implication, mislead members of the public in relation to the product or service advertised, or about its suitability for the purpose recommended; and

b) do not unfairly attack or discredit, directly or by implication, any other advertisers, products or advertisements.

3) A licensee shall, before broadcasting an advertisement, ensure that any descriptions or claims in the advertisement have been adequately substantiated by the advertiser thereof.

4) A licensee shall not unreasonably discriminate against or in favour of any advertiser.

As regards infomercials, whether broadcast in visual or audio form, Regulation 8(2) requires that the licensee must ensure that they must be distinguishable from any programme material being broadcast. In addition to this, the licensee must ensure that the infomercials broadcast are lawful, honest, decent, and are in conformity with the principles of fair competition in business.

Although Regulation 36 provides that any person who contravenes a provision of these regulations for which no specific penalty is prescribed shall be guilty of an offence and liable to a fine not exceeding BWP 500, this does not prevent the victim from bringing a civil action claiming damages. When the regulations provide that advertisements and infomercials should be lawful, it simply means that they must comply with all other laws especially consumer protection legislation. Thus, advertisements must comply with any special rules that apply in the sale of the particular article, for example the rules governing the sale of alcohol, cigarettes and tobacco, and gambling. Besides the Broadcasting Regulations, 2004 the following are some of the pieces of legislation which an illegal advertisement or infomercial could violate:

- The Consumer Protection Act Cap. 42:07.
- The Control of Goods, Prices and Charges Act, Cap. 43:08.
- The Copyright and Neighbouring Rights Act, Cap. 68:02.
- The Industrial Property Act, Cap. 68:03.
- The Lotteries and Betting Act, Cap. 19:02.
- The Penal Code, Cap. 08:01.

In addition to this, there are a number of common law principles which illegal advertising could violate and give rise to actions for unfair competition such as passing off and injurious falsehood.[378] Honesty in advertising means that the broadcast content should be fair. It is particularly important that advertisements should be decent because unlike programmes where viewers and listeners have a choice, advertisements come unannounced without prior warning as to their content. They should therefore be careful in ensuring that there is nothing that will offend viewers or listeners, especially children. Finally the principles of fair competition in business require that advertisements should be truthful and not misleading.

§3. Time and Frequency Restrictions

196. It is of the utmost importance that the viewers and listeners should be able to clearly distinguish between a normal programme and an advertisement. The Broadcasting Regulations, 2004 attempt to make sure not only that there is a clear separation between formal advertising and normal programmes but also that they try to regulate the frequency of the former.

Thus, Regulation 6 dealing with 'scheduling advertisements' states:

> 1) A licensee shall exercise responsible judgment when scheduling advertisements which may be unsuitable for children during periods when large numbers of children may be expected to be watching and listening.
>
> 2) A licensee shall ensure that any advertising breaks are clearly distinguishable from broadcast programmes.
>
> 3) A licensee shall ensure that its presenters, when reading advertisements, make a clear distinction between programming material and the advertisements they deliver.

Regulation 32 which provides more details on the timing and frequency of advertisements states:

> 1) A licensee who engages in commercial broadcasting shall ensure that advertise ments are broadcast in the allotted breaks in a programme and in the interval between the end of one programme and the beginning of another.

378. *See for example*, *Capital Estate and General Agencies (Pty) Ltd v. Holiday Inns Inc.* [1977] S SA 916 (A); *Pasquali Cigarette Co. Ltd v. Diaconicolas & Capsopolus* 1905 TS 472; *Tie Rack Plc v. Tie Rack Stores (Pty) Ltd* [1989] 4 SA 427 (T); and *Williams t/a Jenifer Williams & Associates v. Life Line Southern Transvaal* [1996] 3 408 (A).

2) There shall be no more than four advertising breaks per hour in the case of television broadcasts.

3) The advertising content of any programme shall not exceed –

a) thirty seconds, in a programme lasting five minutes;

b) two minutes, in a programme lasting ten minutes;

c) three minutes, in a programme lasting fifteen minutes; and

d) five minutes, in a programme lasting thirty-five minutes.

4) In a period of programming lasting for sixty consecutive minutes, an advertisement shall last for not more than twelve minutes, except where –

a) a licensee broadcasts the programme as a public service; or

b) there is a national broadcast which interrupts a scheduled programme and results in the loss of advertising time.

5) A licensee shall be entitled to compensate for any loss caused by the broadcast under sub-regulation (4), over a period of seven days following the day on which the interruption occurred, by increasing the time specified under sub-regulation (4) to not more than fourteen minutes.

As regards infomercials, Regulation 8 specifies that this shall not be broadcast:

(1) for a period exceeding three hours of the performance period in any day;
(2) during prime-time; or
(3) during any break in the transmission of a children's programme.

197. Generally, BOCRA is given the powers, under section 32(2) of the Communications Regulations Act, 2012 and subject to the availability of frequencies to issue licences to broadcasters 'subject to such conditions and restrictions, including geographical restrictions, as the Board may consider necessary'. Regulation 9 provides that 'a licensee who operates a broadcasting station by transmitting on an assigned frequency in the broadcasting service band shall not cause harmful interference to any broadcasting service provided by another station'. Although broadcasters are required to operate strictly within the frequencies they have been allocated by BOCRA, they are allowed to apply to have these and any other conditions specified in the broadcasting licence to be amended as the need arises.

§4. Sponsorship

198. Although the regulations defined what is meant by a sponsorship, this definition does not clearly distinguish it from advertising. Generally, sponsorship involves a commercial arrangement through which a company or other business concern purchases an association with a programme and attaches its brand and branding message to it. It is distinguished from advertising by ensuring that no strictly advertising messages are included in the sponsor credit. It is of critical importance for sponsored programmes to maintain their editorial integrity, in other words, the broadcaster and not the sponsor should have final editorial control over the content of the programme. With respect to the content of sponsorship programmes, Regulation 7 states:

1) A licensee shall not accept sponsorship of news broadcasts.

2) A licensee may accept sponsorship of weather broadcasts, financial broadcasts or traffic reports.

3) A licensee shall ensure that sponsorship of an informative programme does not compromise the accuracy and impartiality of the programme's content.

4) A licensee shall not unreasonably discriminate against or in favour of any particular sponsor.

5) A licensee shall not broadcast any programme which has been sponsored by a political party.

6) The sponsorship of a programme shall clearly be acknowledged by a licensee immediately before and after the programme is broadcast, and any link between the programme's subject matter and the sponsor's commercial activities must be made clear.

199. Product placement, or what in some jurisdictions is referred to as 'surreptitious advertising' or 'undue prominence', is the surreptitious promotion of a product or service in a manner which is not transparent to the viewer or listener and is indirectly frowned upon by the regulations. Examples of this are the requirement in Regulation 5(d) that advertisements should conform with the principles of fair competition in business, Regulation 6(3) which requires a clear distinction being made between programming material and advertisements and Regulation 7(6) which states that any links between a programme's subject matter and the sponsor's commercial activities must be made clear.

Chapter 6. Right to Information

200. Freedom of speech as a means of exercise of the popular sovereignty is an empty vessel without access to the information necessary for intelligent decision-making.[379] As James Madison once said:

> A popular government without popular information, or the means of acquiring it, is but a prologue to a farce or a tragedy; or, perhaps both. Knowledge will forever govern ignorance: And a people who mean to be their own governors, must arm themselves with the power which knowledge gives.[380]

Most of the information which the public needs to know is in the hands of the government officials and agencies who often try to prevent the people having access to this information, often on grounds of national security. Despite the explosion in freedom of information statutes all over the world in the last decade, Africa has largely remained absent.

201. Freedom of information or the right to know is now regarded as a multidimensional human right that can make a huge difference to both people and their governments, backed by international legal instruments. Botswana is a party to numerous international and regional human rights instruments which recognize freedom of information as a fundamental human right and a touchstone of all other human rights such as the UDHR, the ICCPR, the ACHPR, and the African Charter on Democracy, Elections and Governance. In 2002, during the 32nd Ordinary Session of the African Commission on Human and Peoples' Rights in Banjul, African countries adopted a Declaration of Principles on Freedom of Expression in Africa, which recognized the fact that public bodies hold information not for themselves but as custodians of the public good and that everyone has a right to access this information, subject only to clearly defined rules established by laws. It stated that the right to information shall be guaranteed by law in accordance with principles set in the Declaration, which include the following:

> Everyone has the right to access information held by public bodies, everyone has the right to access information held by private bodies which is necessary for the exercise or protection of any right; any refusal to disclose information shall be subject to appeal to an independent body and/or the courts; public bodies shall be required, even in the absence of a request, actively to publish important information of significant public interest; no one shall be subject to any sanction for releasing in good faith information on wrongdoing, or that which disclose a serious threat to health, safety or the environment save where the imposition of sanctions serves a legitimate interest and is necessary in a democratic society; and secrecy laws shall be amended as necessary to comply with freedom of information principles.

379. Haiman, *Speech and Law in a Free Society* 368.
380. Cited *ibid.*

A number of countries, such as South Africa, Malawi, Mozambique, the Democratic Republic of Congo, and Tanzania have enacted legislation which expressly guarantees the right to information within their constitutional framework.

In Botswana, section 12(1) of the constitution provides for the right to 'hold opinions without interference, freedom to receive ideas and information without interference, freedom to communicate ideas and information without interference (whether the communication be to the public generally or to any person or class of persons) and freedom from interference with his correspondence'. The provision, unlike the provisions in the UDHR and ICCPR, does not make express reference to the right to 'seek' information. The critical question is whether the absence of an express textual guarantee to right to seek information in the constitution precludes the protection of an active right of access to information. It is worth noting that section 12(1) of the constitution is modelled on Article 10(1) of the European Convention on Human Rights which also does not make any express reference to the right to seek information. In *Leander v. Sweden,*[381] a case that was later to become the jurisprudential position on the scope of the right to information guaranteed under the European Convention on Human Rights, the European Court of Human Rights held that the right basically prohibits a government from restricting a person from receiving information that others may be willing to impart to him or her. Some commentators, such as Eric Barendt, have also argued that in the absence of a constitutional provision or specific legislation sanctioning this, it is not to be assumed that the right of access to information is necessarily an integral part of freedom of speech.[382] Due to the influence of decisions of the European Court of Human Rights, the dominant view in Botswana appears to be that the constitution only guarantees a passive right to information because of the absence of an express textual reference to the to seek information in section 12(1).

202. Recent developments in the jurisprudence of the European Court of Human Rights on the scope of the right of access to information protected under the European Convention on Human Rights call for further reflection on the scope of the right of access to information guaranteed under the constitution of Botswana. In a majority decision, the Grand Chamber of the European Court of Human Rights in the case of *Magyar Helsinki Bizottsag v. Hungary*[383] observed that in interpreting and applying the provisions of the Convention, they must be applied in a manner which renders rights practical and effective and not theoretical and illusory.[384] The court noted that the Convention cannot be interpreted in a vacuum, but should, as far as possible, be interpreted in harmony with other rules of international law of which it forms part.[385] The court further noted that the existence of a right of access to information is now recognized under the UN, African and Inter-American systems of human protection, and also that in about thirty-one contracting states to the European Convention on Human Rights, a statutory right of access to information was recognized. These developments persuaded the court to conclude that, under certain conditions, a right to freedom of information is an inherent element of the freedom to receive and impart

381. ECtHR (26 Mar. 198, Application No. 9248/81, Series A No. 116).
382. Barendt, *Freedom of Speech* 108.
383. ECtHR 8 Nov. 2016, No. 18030/11.
384. *Ibid.*, at paras 119–121.
385. *Ibid.*, para. 123.

information enshrined in Article 10.[386] The court based its conclusion on the premise that, to hold that the right of access to information may under no circumstances fall within the ambit of Article 10 would lead to situations where freedom to receive and impart information is impaired in such a manner and to such a degree that it would strike at the very substance of freedom of expression.[387] The court concluded that where access to information is instrumental for the exercise of the applicant's right to receive and impart information, its denial may constitute an interference with that right. Whether access to state-held information is instrumental for an individual's exercise of freedom of expression is to be assessed on a case-by-case basis. The European Court of Human Rights went a step further to set the threshold criteria for assessing whether the right of access to state-held information is necessary for the exercise of the right of freedom of expression. The criteria involves four critical factors, which are:

(1) The purpose of the person requesting access to state-held information must be necessary for the exercise of freedom of expression. It would appear that this criteria will be satisfied where the gathering of information is a relevant preparatory step in journalistic activities or in other activities creating a forum for, or constituting an essential element of public debate.
(2) The nature of the information to which access is sought must generally meet a public interest test. This will be met where disclosure provides transparency on the manner of conduct of public affairs and on matters of public interest for society as a whole and allow participation in public governance by the public at large.
(3) The role of the seeker of the information. The court gives special recognition to journalists, social watchdog organizations whose activities are relevant to matters of public interest.
(4) And the fact that the information requested is ready and available will weigh in favour of disclosure.

203. The Court of Appeal of Botswana has said that when interpreting the provisions of the constitution, a court must adopt a generous and purposive approach in order to breathe life into the constitution in the light of its liberal democratic values.[388] A purposive interpretation of the provisions of the constitution requires that courts should not whittle down any rights and freedoms unless such interpretation is warranted by the very clear and unambiguous wordings of the statute..[389] Furthermore, the court has also said a constitution is not a static document, but a living instrument that must be interpreted to reflect the mores and norms of the time.[390] There is nothing in the wording of section 12(1) of the constitution of Botswana to suggest that the protection of an active right of access to information is specifically excluded its ambit. The

386. *Ibid.*, para. 151.
387. *Ibid.*, para. 155.
388. *Ramantele v. Mmusi and Others*, CACGB-104-12 (unreported judgment of On 3 Oct. 2013) at para. 69.
389. *Dow v. Attorney-General, supra* paras 37, 42-43.
390. *Law Society of Botswana and Another v. The President of Botswana and Others*, CACGB-031-16 (unreported judgment delivered on 17 Apr. 2017) at para. 32.

protection of the right of access to information is now generally considered under international law to be inherent in the protection of freedom of expression. A purposive interpretation of section 12(1) must embrace this development.

204. In the 1997 Vision 2016: Long Term Vision for Botswana,[391] it is clearly stated that, 'Botswana must introduce a freedom of information Act to protect the rights of citizens to obtain and use information', but the government on numerous occasions ignored strong calls from the opposition and civil society organizations including media groups to introduce a Freedom of Information Act.[392] In fact, in 2011 the government used its majority in the National Assembly to reject a private member's Freedom of Information Bill that was tabled by the then Leader of the Opposition. What is more worrying is that the government is on record that an access to information law was not a priority.

205. The absence of a Freedom of Information Act has led the government, in the opinion of many analysts to develop and refine the art of secrecy which ensures that the media and the public in general knows as little as is possible of what goes on in government. All these have been reinforced with a number of punitive media unfriendly laws, such as the National Security Act, the Intelligence and Security Services Act, the Corruption and Economic Crime Act, and a whole host of others that were discussed in an earlier part of this work.[393] A Member of Parliament in highlighting the absurdity of government secrecy pointed out how during a constituency meeting he asked for information about the number of destitute persons so that he could donate some blankets to them and was told by the social worker that she needed to get permission from her superiors to divulge such information.[394] The most serious indictment of the government's failure to introduce the Freedom of Information legislation that many have clamoured for, comes from a surprising quarter, the Ombudsman. In his 2006/2007 report, he regretted that there is a growing tendency by public servants to withhold information. The report states that:

> Information is generally perceived as power and there is an unfortunate belief here that the right of access to public information is vested in the authority concerned or its employees. On the contrary, the reverse is true. Public servants have custody of the information on behalf of members of the public for use by the latter as and when they need to do so.

After decrying the lack of legislation to enforce the right to information, it points out that:

> it is not enough that as a policy, our institutions are open to any inquiry pertaining to any matter which is non-confidential and to which people are entitled. The

391. *Vision 2016, Long Term Vision for Botswana*, at 69.
392. *See* ''Rakhudu to Table Freedom of Information Motion' <www.mmegi.bw/index.php?sid=1&aid=42&dir=2008/July/Friday18>.
393. *See* paras 59–82 *supra.*
394. 'Rakhudu To table Freedom of Information Motion', *supra* no. 392.

> full enjoyment of rights needs to be guaranteed by legislation, because then enforcement is more predictable, hence guaranteed through relevant instruments.[395]

Research has found that 'the lack of a Freedom of Information Act means Botswana's citizens are unable to participate fully and pro-actively in the development and democracy of the country'.[396] Lack of access to public information is felt keenly by the media outside urban areas because local papers find it impossible to get any facts or news from civil servants who will usually refer them to the head office in Gaborone.

206. The lack of a freedom of information legislation is one of the important missing cornerstones to Botswana's widely acclaimed liberal democracy. Access to information is restricted and official secrecy laws have ensured that the media and the public in general know as little as possible of what goes on in government. There have been numerous commentaries on the extensive secrecy not only of what goes on in government[397] but also how 'the press is kicked out of public meetings of critical public interest, like party congresses and other forums, all-party conferences, council proceedings, conferences of the Botswana Confederation of Commerce, Industry and Manpower, and so forth'.[398]

Perhaps what is worrying for southern Africa's oldest democracy is the number of laws that actually reinforce governmental secrecy. In many respects, almost all the laws that limit the freedom of speech discussed earlier,[399] contain provisions that restrict access to governmental information. A few examples of provisions in some of these laws that inhibit public access to information will suffice. Section 23 of the Education Act, which gives the Minister of Education powers to proscribe publications, can be used to prevent schools from gaining access to government documents. Section 44 of the Corruption and Economic Crime Act also prohibits the disclosure of information concerning the details of any investigations being carried out by the DCEC. Section 138 of the Prisons Act prohibits anybody who, without the authority of the Commissioner of the Prison, takes a photograph or makes a sketch of any prisoner, or takes a photograph or makes a sketch, plan or other representation of a prison or any part of a prison or any object within the precincts of a prison. The Public Service Act[400] constraints public officers from freely responding to requests from members of the public for information. It states in section 21 under the heading, 'publications interviews and use of official information', the following:

395. E. Keoreng, *Botswana: Batswana Have a Right to Know – Ombudsman*, www.mmegi.bw/index.php?sid=1&aid=12&dir=2009/April/Friday17.
396. Media Sustainability Index 2006–2007, www.irex.org/programs/MSI_Africa/2007/MSI07_Botswana.pdf, 19.
397. *See* MISA & Friedrich Ebert Stiftung, *African Media Barometer: Botswana 2007* 11–12; Konrad Adenauer Stiftung, *A Comparative Overview of Media Law and Practice in Botswana, Swaziland & Zambia* 16 (Konrad Adenauer Foundation 2004); Sechele, *Deepening Democracy or Creeping Authoritarian Rule?* 119–145; and Sechele, *The Role of the Press in Independent Botswana*.
398. Sechele, *The Role of the Press in Independent Botswana* 419.
399. *See* paras 59–83.
400. Cap. 26:01.

Subject to the provisions of any other written law, every public officer shall comply with the following rules of conduct –

(a) he shall not, without the express permission of the Permanent Secretary to the president, act as the editor of a newspaper (not being a publication of the Government), nor take part directly or indirectly in the management thereof, nor publish in any manner anything which may be reasonably regarded as of a political or administrative nature, but he may publish in his own name other matter relating to subjects of general interest;
(b) whether on duty or on leave of absence, he shall not (except with due authority) allow himself to be interviewed on questions of or connected with any matter affecting or relating to the public policy, defence, military or economic interests or resources of Botswana;
(c) he shall not directly or indirectly reveal, or use for private purposes, any information coming to his knowledge or acquired by him of the nature or the contents of any document communicated to him either in the course of his duties or in his capacity, as an officer, otherwise than in the proper discharge of his duties as authorized by law or competent authority.

One commentary concludes that because of this Act, 'there is a lot of arrogance within the civil service whose members regard themselves as gate-keepers'. Another commentator says:

> The conditions are sometimes lacking in Botswana where overzealous government officials still make access to information difficult because 'they have not been authorised'. They also refuse access under all manner of interpretations of the civil service's General Orders, the Education Act and other stringent regulations governing conditions of service.

There is also section 4 of the National Security Act, dealing with 'wrongful communication of certain information', which states:

(1) Any person who, having in his possession, or control, any secret official codes, password, sketch, plan, model, note, document, article or information that relates to or is used in a prohibited place or anything in such a place, or that has been made or obtained in contravention of this Act, or that has been entrusted in confidence to him by any person holding office under the Government, or owing to his position as a person who holds or has held office under the Government, or as a person who is or was party to a contract with the Government or a contract the performance of which in whole or in part is carried out in a prohibited place, or as a person who is or has been employed by or under a person who holds or has held such an office or is or was a party to such a contract –

  (a) uses the information in his possession for the benefit of any foreign power or in any other manner or for any purpose prejudicial to the safety or interests of Botswana;

(b) communicates the codes, password, sketch, plan, model, article, note, document or information to any person other than a person to whom he is authorized to communicate with, or to a person to whom it is in the interest of Botswana his duty to communicate it;
(c) fails to take reasonable care of, or so conducts himself as to endanger the safety of, the sketch, plan, model, article, note, document, secret official codes, password or information; or
(d) retains the sketch, plan, model, note, document or article in his possession or control when he has no right to retain it or when it is contrary to his duty to retain it, or fails to comply with any lawful directions issued with regard to the return or disposal thereof, shall be guilty of an offence and liable on conviction to imprisonment for a term not exceeding 30 years.

(2) Any person who, having in his possession or control any sketch, plan, model, note, document, article or information that relates to munitions of war communicates it directly or indirectly to any person in any manner for any purpose prejudicial to the safety or interests of Botswana shall be guilty of an offence and liable on conviction to imprisonment for a term not exceeding 30 years.
(3) Any person who receives any secret official codes, password, sketch, plan, model, note, document, article or information, knowing or having reasonable grounds to believe, at the time when he receives it, that the codes, password, sketch, plan, model, article, note, document or information is communicated to him in contravention of the provisions of this Act shall, unless he proves that the communication to him of the codes, password, sketch, plan, model, article, note, document or information was against his wish, be guilty of an offence and liable on conviction to imprisonment for a term not exceeding 30 years.
(4) Any person who communicates any information relating to the defence or security of Botswana to any person, other than a person to whom he is authorized by an authorized officer to communicate it or to whom it is in the interests of Botswana his duty to communicate it shall be guilty of an offence and liable on conviction to imprisonment for a term not exceeding 25 years.

Section 5 of this Act deals with the protection of classified information and provides that:

(1) Any person who communicates any classified matter to any person other than a person to whom he is authorized to communicate it or to whom it is in the interests of Botswana his duty to communicate it shall be guilty of an offence and liable on conviction to imprisonment for a term not exceeding 25 years.
(2) In a prosecution for a contravention of subsection (1) it shall be no defence for the accused person to prove that when he communicated the matter he did not know and could not reasonably have known that it was a classified matter.

As several commentators have observed, the mere existence of these laws, particularly the National Security Act and its threatened use in many instances has had a chilling effect on the free flow of information in Botswana. This chilling effect has been bolstered by the newly enacted Intelligence and Security Services Act.[401] Section 20(1) of this Act prohibits the disclosure by an officer or support staff working in the intelligence services, without the authority of the Director-General of the Directorate of Intelligence and Security. Perhaps more sweeping is section 20(2) of this Act which states:

> No officer or support staff shall be required to produce, before *any public body other than a Parliamentary Committee* established under the Standing Orders of the National Assembly, any document or other evidence where –

(1) it is certified by the Director-General –

> i) that the document or other evidence belongs to a class of documents or evidence, the production of which is injurious to public interest; or
>
> ii) that disclosure of the evidence or of the contents of the document will be injurious to public interests; or

(2) the Central Intelligence Committee certifies –

> i) that the document or other evidence belongs to a class the production of which is prejudicial to national security; or
>
> ii) that the disclosure of the evidence or of the contents of the document will be prejudicial to national security (emphasis added).

However, the fact that any party aggrieved by the decision of the Director-General or Central Intelligence Committee certifying that the production of a document or any other evidence could be injurious to public interest or prejudicial to national security may apply to the High Court for a final determination of the matter will ensure that this law is not abused to prevent the public being informed about how this important but sensitive arm of the government is operating.

§1. Access to Major Events

207. Before the 2008 Media Practitioners Act, there was no special formality to comply with for any journalist who wanted to attend a function: all he had to do was to be in possession of a press card and to present this when asked to identify himself. One of the controversial provisions which never made its way into the 2008 Act would have required all journalists to apply for and obtain a press card before attending any official event in Botswana. The Media Practitioners Act in section 6

401. *See* many instances of this discussed in Sechele, *Deepening Democracy or Creeping Authoritarian Rule?* 119–145; and *id.*, 'The Role of the Press in Independent Botswana'.

simply states that media practitioners will be required to be registered and accredited in accordance with regulations made by the Executive Committee of the Media Council. It is unlikely that the Council will make regulations which will give the government the discretion to pick and choose those media practitioners that it wants to attend media events.

§2. Short News Reporting

208. Short news reporting usually arises where a primary broadcaster holds exclusive rights to broadcast an event. Short reporting means the brief sound and picture sequences about such an event to enable the viewers of a secondary broadcaster wishing to provide information on the event, to provide a sufficient overview of the essential aspects of the event only. There is at present no legislative provision dealing with this in Botswana. It does apply in practice but this is based on mutual agreements reached between the broadcasters.

Chapter 7. Access to Networks

§1. Must Carry Rules

209. The Broadcasting Regulations, 2004 contain a number of 'must carry' regulations for commercial cable broadcasters which are aimed at ensuring that their broadcasting meets certain important national needs. Regulation 30 provides as follows:

(1) A cable owner shall re-transmit the television terrestrial broadcasts of a local public television which is licensed in Botswana.
(2) A television terrestrial broadcast which is re-transmitted under sub-regulation (1) shall have the use of at least one channel of a cable network.
(3) Any programme that is subject to obligatory re-transmission shall be transmitted via channels that are available to every subscriber to a cable network.
(4) Where a cable network utilises three or less channels, the broadcasts of the Btv shall be subject to obligatory transmission.
(5) A cable owner shall identify the broadcasts that its subscribers wish to have re-transmitted via the cable network, and shall broadcast its subscribers' choices.
(6) Where there are unutilised channels in a cable network, after the cable owner has broadcast its subscribers' choice of broadcasts under sub-regulation
(7) the cable owner may utilise the channels to broadcast any programmes:
(8) Provided that the cable owner notifies its subscribers of its intentions regarding such use at least two months before the commencement of broadcasting.
(9) Where a majority of a cable owner's subscribers oppose the cable owner's intention to utilise channels to broadcast any programmes under sub-regulation
(10) the cable owner may utilise such channels if it ensures that shielding is provided, at no extra cost, to the subscribers who do not wish to receive the broadcasts.

§2. Other Access Obligations for Networks

210. There are not any other special access obligations for networks in Botswana that are contemplated in any of the existing pieces of legislation.

Part IV. Cross-Ownership Regulation

211. A diverse, pluralistic, independent and vibrant media cannot be achieved by leaving the development of the media industry to market forces alone. Generally, limits are imposed on cross-ownership between the print and broadcast media to avoid monopolies over the 'opinion market'. The collective right of the people to be informed by a diverse media is crucial for a healthy democracy to grow and thrive.

There are no specific regulations on cross-media ownership in Botswana. Cross-media ownership can however be addressed through competition law. Competition matters in the economy of Botswana fall under the mandate of the Competition Authority (CA) which was established in 2009. The main function of the CA is the prevention of, and redress for anticompetitive practices in the economy and the removal of constraints on the free play of competition in the market.[402] The jurisdiction of the CA extends to all economic activities within or having effect within the country, including the media.[403] The CA has enacted regulations that, amongst others, determine what will amount to a dominant position in the economy.[404] In terms of Regulation 4, the CA may consider an enterprise to be in a dominant position if it supplies or acquires at least 25% of the goods or services in the market; or three or fewer enterprises supply or acquire at least 50% of the goods or services in the market.

212. There is however a general scepticism on the ability of competition law to promote pluralism of ownership and control of the media. It is argued that competition law is concerned with securing economic objectives and not designed to deliver pluralism in the media.[405] Competition law is primarily concerned with the operation of economic markets and not with the distinctive wider needs of public policy in relation to the media. There seems to be some credence to this scepticism as there is already evidence of some market dominance in the country by one company which has interests in both print and broadcast media. Mmegi Investment Holdings (Pty) Ltd (MIH) is the holding company to two subsidiaries which own four newspapers between them whose combined circulation figures account for 35% of the total circulation figure of local private papers. In terms of the threshold set by the CA, MIH is in a prima facie dominant position in the sector. In addition, MIH also has under its stable Dikgang Publishing Company (Pty), a wholly owned subsidiary, which publishes newspapers and is currently publishing over half of the local papers. MIH also has a 60% shareholding in Bonesa (Pty) Ltd, a newspaper distribution company that is responsible for the distribution of a number of local papers. Furthermore, MIH holds 20% of the shares in Your Friend (Pty) Ltd, which owns one of the three commercial

402. Section 5 (1), Competition Act, No. 17 of 2009, Laws of Botswana.
403. Competition Act, No. 17 of 2009, s. 3(1).
404. Competition Regulations, 2011.
405. Department for Culture, Media and Sport, *Consultation on Media Ownership Rules (2001)* para. 1.10.

radio stations in the country. While it appears that MIH is a dominant player in the media market, the CA has so far failed to investigate the affairs of the company to determine whether or not its position affects media pluralism. The CA has however in recent case rejected to approve an acquisition of 28.73% shares in MIH by Universal House (Pty) Ltd.[406] One of the majority shareholders in the latter company also owns about 45% of the shares in a company that owns one of the three commercial radio stations. The acquisition would have resulted in Universal House (Pty) Ltd having significant interests in both the print and broadcast media.

There is a need to put in place clear regulations on cross-media ownership in Botswana. In South Africa, for example, no person who controls a newspaper may acquire or retain financial control of a commercial broadcasting service in both television and sound broadcasting services.[407] A 20% shareholding in a commercial broadcasting service licence is deemed to constitute control.[408] Botswana's media sector is small compared to South Africa's. The fact that MIH controls newspapers that account for over 35% of the newspaper circulation figures in the country and also owns a 20% stake in a commercial radio broadcasting service, makes it a dominant player. This demonstrates that Botswana's legal framework for limiting cross-media ownership is wanting.

406. Merger Decision No. 10:27 – *Decicion on the Merger between Mmegi Investment Holdings (Pty) Ltd and Universal House (Pty) Ltd*, 17 Feb. 2017.
407. *See* s. 66(2), Electronic Communications Act, 2005, Act No. 36 of 2005.
408. *Ibid.*, s. 66(5).

Part V. Supervision: Media Regulator

213. For an independent broadcasting industry to develop and provide the variety of sources of information and opinion that are needed by the population to make informed decisions during elections, there must be in place an independent regulatory system to license broadcasters and generally oversee the industry. As we have seen, for far too long, African governments, including the Government of Botswana, have controlled the broadcast media.[409] The primary purpose of the Communications Regulatory Authority Act, 2012 is to set up a telecommunications regulatory authority for Botswana. According to the long title to the Act it is an Act 'to provide for the creation of an independent authority for the regulation of the communications sector in Botswana, comprising of telecommunications, Internet, and information and communication technologies, radio communications, broadcasting, postal services and related matters'. The next three sections will look at the organization of the Board, its functions and its sanctioning powers.

409. *See* paras 160–163.

214. A key to the success of any broadcast regulatory body is that the manner in which its members are appointed and their tenure, must be such that it will safeguard their independence. The African Commission on Human and Peoples' Rights recommend that the appointment process for members of public authorities that regulate broadcasting should be open and transparent, involve the participation of civil society, and should not be controlled by any particular political party.[410] Members of BOCRA as noted above are appointed by a government Minister exercising his or her sole discretion. The Act does not prescribe any procedure that must be followed in the appointment of the members to ensure that the process is open and democratic. This leaves the regulator vulnerable to political interference. The Act also does not guarantee the administrative independence of BOCRA. The omission is a serious indictment on the independence of the regulator. Further support for the view that the BOCRA is not an independent body is the fact that section 6(2)(h) of the Act requires that prior to the issuance of any broadcasting licence, the regulator must first notify the minister. This requirement suggests that the issuance of broadcasting licences must first have the approval of the minister, which means the regulator does not have exclusive jurisdiction on licensing matters. The minister is further given the power under section 91 to rescind a decision of BOCRA, which in the minister's opinion, may adversely affect the security of the country or relations with a foreign government. These are very wide discretionary powers given to the minister that may be easily abused to frustrate the BOCRA in the performance of its mandate. The BOCRA can therefore not be said to an independent regulator from the government.

Members of the BOCRA hold office for a period not exceeding three years and are eligible at the expiry of their first term for reappointment for one further term.[411] Once appointed, members enjoy security of tenure and can only be removed from office by the appointing authority on grounds set out in the Act. The grounds upon which a member of the BOCRA may be removed from office broadly include: bankruptcy, conflict of interest – real or perceived, conviction of a criminal offence, and appointment to a political office.[412]

BOCRA is accountable to a government Minister through submission of annual reports that cover its operations.[413] The reports are available to members of the public upon payment of a prescribed fee. In addition, BOCRA is obliged to make its decisions in an open, transparent, and accountable manner.[414] These obligations are aimed at ensuring that BOCRA is accountable to the public for its activities. It is, however, objectionable that BOCRA is made accountable to a government Minister and not to a multiparty body. It would have been ideal to have BOCRA account to the National Assembly as it does for financial accountability, where it is required to submit its annual audited reports to the National Assembly.

410. Declaration of Principles on Freedom of Expression in Africa, Principle VII.

411. Section 9, Communications Regulatory Authority Act, 2012.

412. Section 10.

413. Section 28.

414. Section 6(2)(w).

BOCRA is funded from different sources, which include fees levied in respect of licensing, annual fees paid by regulated suppliers and loans granted by Parliament.[415] The funding model for BOCRA is sufficiently open and transparent and would arguably insulate it from threats of the executive branch to use budget cuts to undermine its mandate. The funding model of the Authority is also commendable as it should be able to allow it to raise enough funds to enable it to carry out its functions without undue pressure from both the executive branch and private industry.

415. Section 28.

Chapter 2. Tasks

215. The functions of BOCRA are specified as follows in section 5(1) of the Communications Regulatory Authority Act, 2012:

(1) To be responsible for the effective regulation of the regulated sectors.
(2) To promote and ensure universal access with respect to provision of communication services.
(3) To impose, a universal access and services levy on identified operators for the purpose of funding universal access in the communications sector.
(4) To promote and ensure enhanced performance in the communications sector.

In addition to the above, BOCRA is mandated to:

i. process applications for and issue, licences, permits, permissions, concessions and authorities for regulated sectors as may be prescribed;

ii. protect and promote the interests of consumers in respect of, among others, ensuring availability of quality and varied services; and

iii. monitor availability, quantity and standards of services and competition.[416]

416. *See* s. 6.

Chapter 3. Sanctioning Powers

216. Any regulatory body can only be effective if it is given the powers to sanction violations of its decisions. There are three main instances when BOCRA is given the powers to impose sanctions for non-compliance with its decisions. The first of this is provided for under section 86 of the Communications Regulatory Act, 2012. This provision gives the authority the power to revoke the licence of any licensee who fails to comply with any lawful direction or requirement of the authority under the provisions of the Act, or where the authority is satisfied that the conditions of any licence are not being adhered to. Such sanctions may only be imposed after the authority has given the licensee a reasonable opportunity to be heard.

The second instance is provided for under Regulation 34 of the Broadcasting Regulations. This regulation provides a detail procedure for a licensee to investigate and deal with any complaints levelled against him by members of the public. A licensee is required to broadcast information on the procedure for lodging complaints against it at least three times per week, during prime time. Where a complaint is made against it, the licensee is required to advise the complainant that he has a right to refer the matter to the Board if he is dissatisfied with the licensee's response to the complaint. Regulation 34(5)–(8) then specify in detail what procedure the Board is required to follow in dealing with the matter and the sanctions that it may impose. This states as follows:

> 5) Where a complaint is referred to the Board under sub-regulation (4), a licensee shall –
>
> a) submit, on request, any recordings or documentation required by the Board;
>
> b) respond to queries from the Board relating to allegations of non-compliance with the Act or with licence conditions;
>
> c) submit, on request by the Board, written reports or written responses to allegations of non-compliance with the Act or with licence conditions; and
>
> d) appear, when requested, before the Board during the adjudication of any complaint or investigation into any alleged non-compliance with the Act or with licence conditions.
>
> 6) The Board shall invite a licensee to make written or oral representations within such period as may be specified by the Board, where it intends to investigate –

a) any alleged non-compliance with the Act or with licence conditions; or

b) any complaint relating to the licensee's failure or refusal to deal with any complaint, or the unsatisfactory handling of any complaint, by a member of the public.

7) Where the Board finds that a licensee has failed to comply with any provisions of the Act or has breached any of its licence conditions, the Board may make such order as it considers appropriate:

Provided that where the Board imposes a fine, such fine shall not exceed P 500.

8) Where an order is made by the Board under these Regulations, the Board may, where necessary, order a licensee to broadcast an apology, correction or retraction, in such terms as the Board may specify.

Finally, Regulation 35 also provides an elaborate procedure for settling any dispute that may arise between a licensee and another licensee, or between a licensee and any other party. The Board may order that the parties engage in mediation before it accepts a referral of a matter for dispute resolution. Where the Board accepts a matter referred to it, it may appoint a person to assist in the resolution of the dispute or proceed to render a decision. Any agreement reached by the parties to a dispute after the dispute resolution process shall be in writing and must be signed by all the parties to the dispute. Where however no agreement is reached by the parties after the dispute resolution process, the person appointed by the Board to mediate shall submit a report to the Board concerning the unresolved matters pertaining to the dispute. The Board may, after accepting the referral of a matter for dispute resolution, render a decision concerning any unresolved matters between the parties to the dispute. Although both Regulations 34 and 35 do not expressly state so, there is no reason to think that any decisions arrived at by the Board cannot be submitted for review by the High Court, especially where the rules of natural justice may have been violated.

Selected Bibliography

Articles

Balule, B.T. 'Diversity and Pluralism Compromised: From the Botswana Brodcasting Act 1998 to the Communications Regulatory Authority Act 2012'. *Statute Law Review* 34 (2013) 189–206.

Balule, B.T. '*Good v. The Attorney-General (2)*: Some Reflections on the National Security Dilemma in Botswana'. *University of Botswana Law Journal* 7 (2008): 153–172.

Balule, B.T. 'Striking a Balance Between Media Freedom and Protection of Reputation: The Defence of Reasonable Publication in Botswana'. *The Comparative and International Law Journal of Southern Africa* 46 (2013): 1–18.

Balule, B.T. 'The Botswana Media Practitioners Act, 2008: Does It Preserve Media freedom or Is It a Case of Taming the Beast?'. *University of Botswana Law Journal* 12 (2011): 2–21.

Dockray, M. 'Courts on Television'. *Modern Law Review* 51 (1988): 593–604.

Emerson, T. 'Towards a General Theory of the First Amendment'. *Yale Law Journal* 72 (1963): 877–885.

Fombad, C.M. 'Curbing Corruption in Africa: Some Lessons from Botswana's Experience'. *International Social Science Journal* 160 (1999): 241–254.

Fombad, C.M. 'Media Reform in Southern Africa: Challenges and Prospects'. *Openspace* 5 (2006): 49–52.

Fombad, C.M. 'The Enhancement of Good Governance in Botswana: A Critical Assessment of the Ombudsman Act 1995'. *Journal of Southern African Studies* 27 (2001): 57–77.

Good, K. 'Corruption and Mismanagement in Botswana: A Best-Case Example?'. *Journal of Modern African Studies* 32, no. 3 (1994): 499–521.

Koltay, A. 'The Concept of Media Freedom Today: New Media Editors and the Traditional Approach of the Law'. *Journal of Media Law* 7 (2015): 36–64.

MacCormick, N. 'A Note upon Privacy'. *Law Quarterly Review* 89 (1973): 89–102.

Markesinis, B.S. 'The Right to Be Let Alone Versus Freedom of Speech'. *PublicLaw* 67 (1986): 83–104.

Mutula, S.M. 'Making Botswana an Information Society: Current Developments'. *Electronic Library* 22, no. 2 (2004): 145–147.

Neil, B. 'The Protection of Privacy'. *Modern Law Review* 25 (1962): 393–405.

Otlhogile, B. 'Defamation by a Judge: A Note on *Idah Ngope v. James AidenO'Brien-Quinn*'. *Lesotho Law Journal* 7, no. 1 (1991): 107–133.

Pain, J.H. 'The Reception of English and Roman-Dutch Law in Africa with Reference to Botswana, Lesotho and Swaziland'. *CILSA* 11 (1978): 163.

Sanders, A.J.G.M. 'Legal Dualism in Lesotho, Botswana, Swaziland – A General Survey'. *Lesotho Law Journal* 1 (1985): 47–67.

Sangwa, P. 'Zambia'. *Media Law and Practice in Southern Africa* 7 (1998): 8–15.

Syvertsen, T. 'The Many Uses of the "Public Service" Concept'. *Nordicom Review* 20 (1999): 5–12.

Thompson, E. 'Does the Open Justice Principle Require Cameras to Be Permitted in the Courtroom and the Broadcasting of Legal Proceedings?'. *Journal of Media Law* 3 (2011): 211–236.

Tshosa, O. 'Giving Effect to Treaties in Domestic Law of Botswana: Modern Judicial Practice'. *Lesotho Law Journal* 10 (1997): 205.

Waldock, H. 'Human Rights in Contemporary International Law and the Significance of the European Convention'. *International and Comparative Law Quarterly* 11 (1965): 15.

Williams, K. 'Defaming Politicians: The Not So Common Law'. *Modern Law Review* 63 (2000): 748.

Books

Allot, A. *New Essays in African Law*. London: Butterworths, 1970.

Balule, B.T. 'An Overview of the Regulatory Framework of the Media in Botswana'. In *Essays on the Law of Botswana*, edited by C.M. Fombad. Cape Town: Juta & Co. Ltd, 2007.

Balule, B.T., K. Kandjii & R. Louw. *Undue Restriction. Laws Impacting on MediaFreedom in the SADC*. Windhoek: MISA, 2004.

Barendt, E. *Broadcasting Law. A Comparative Study*. Oxford: Clarendon Press, 1993.

Barendt, E. *Freedom of Speech*. Oxford: Clarendon Press, 1987.

Bennett, L. & W. Serrin. 'The Watchdog Role'. In *The Press*, edited by G. Overholser & K. Jamieson. Oxford: Oxford University Press, 2005.

Blumler, J.G. 'Public Service Broadcasting Before the Commercial Deluge'. In *Television and the Public Interest. Vulnerable Values in West European Broadcasting*, edited by J.G. Blumler. London: Sage Publications, 1992.

Selected Bibliography

Bricoe, A. & H.C.L. Hermans. *Combating Corruption in Botswana: A Review of the Relevant Policies, Law and Institutional Capacity to Combat Corruption in Botswana.* Gaborone: Friedrich-Ebert-Stiftung, 2001.

Brownlie, I. *Principles of Public International Law*. Oxford: Oxford University Press, 2003.

Burchell, J. *The Law of Defamation in South Africa*. Cape Town: Juta & Co. Ltd, 1985.

Burns, Y. *Communications Law*. Durban: Butterworths, 2001.

Bussiek, C. & H. Bussiek. *The Media: Making Democracy Work*. Windhoek: Friedrich-Ebert-Stiftung, 2004.

Butler, D. & S. Rodrick. *Australian Media Law*. Pymont: Lawbook Co., 2004.

Campbell, T. 'Rationales for Freedom of Communication'. In *Freedom of Communication*, edited by T. Campbell & W. Sadurski. Aldershot: Dartmouth Publishing Co., 1994.

Clapham, A. 'The European Convention on Human Rights in the British Courts: Problems Associated with the Incorporation of International Human Rights'. In *Promoting Human Rights Through Bills of Rights: Comparative Perspectives*, edited by P. Alston. Oxford: Oxford University Press, 1999.

Cohen, J.L. 'The Public Sphere, the Media and Civil Society'. In *Rights of Access to the Media*, edited by A. Sajo & M. Price. The Hague: Kluwer Law International, 1996.

Dugard, J. *International Law. A South African Perspective*. Lansdowne: Juta & Co., 2005.

Edwards, A.B. *The History of South African Law. An Outline*. Durban: Butterworths, 1996.

Emerson, T. *The System of Freedom of Expression*. New York: Vintage Books, 1970.

Fleming, J.G. *The Law of Torts*. 7th edn. Sydney: The Law Book Co. Ltd, 1987.

Fombad, C. & E.K. Quansah. *The Botswana Legal System*. Durban: LexisNexis Butterworths, 2006.

Fombad, C.M. & D. Sebudubu. 'The Framework for Curbing Corruption, Enhancing Accountability and Promoting Good Governance in Botswana'. In *Essays on the Law of Botswana*, edited by C.M. Fombad. Cape Town: Juta & Co. Ltd, 2007, 82–126.

Fombad, C.M. 'The Protection of Human Rights in Botswana: An Overview of the Regulatory Framework'. In *Essays on the Law of Botswana*, edited by C.M. Fombad. Cape Town: Juta & Co., 2007, 8–15.

Forsyth, C. 'The Protection of Political Discourse: Pragmatism or Incoherence?'. In *Freedom of Expression and Freedom of Information: Essays in Honour of Sir David Williams*, edited by J. Beatson & Y. Cripps. Oxford: Oxford University Press, 2000.

Foster, R. *Public Broadcasters. Accountability and Efficiency*. Edinburgh: Edinburgh University, 1992.

Gallant, S. & J. Epworth. *Media Law. A Practical Guide to Managing Publications Risks*. London: Sweet & Maxwell, 2001.

Gibbons, T. *Regulating the Media*. 2nd edn. London: Sweet & Maxwell, 1998.

Glasser, T. & M. Gunther. 'The Legacy of Autonomy in American Journalism'. In *The Press*, edited by G. Overholser & K. Jamieson. Oxford: Oxford University Press, 2005.

Gunther, R. & A. Mughan (eds). *Democracy and the Media. A Comparative Perspective*. Cambridge: Cambridge University Press, 2000.

Habermas, J. 'The Public Sphere'. In *Communication and Class Struggle: Vol. 1. Capitalism and Imperialism*, edited by A. Mattelart & S. Seigelaub. New York: International General, 1979.

Haiman, F.S. *Speech and Law in a Free Society*. Chicago: University of Chicago, 1981.

Hughes, A.J. *Report on the Information Functions of Government*. Gaborone: Government Printer, 1968.Jayawickrama, N. 'Hong Kong and the International Protection of Human Rights'. In *Human Rights in Hong Kong*, edited by R. Wacks. Oxford: Oxford University Press, 1992.

Konrad Adenauer Foundation. *SADC Media Law: A Handbook for Media Practitioners*. Johannesburg: Konrad Adenauer Foundation, 2004.

Malanczuk, P. *Akehurt's Modern Introduction to International Law*. London: Routledge, 1997.

Mckerron, R.J. *The Law of Delict*. 7th edn. Cape Town: Juta & Co., 1971.

McQuoid-Mason, D.J. *The Law of Privacy in South Africa*. Cape Town: Juta & Co. Ltd, 1978.

Meiklejohn, A. *Political Freedom: The Constitutional Powers of the People*. New York: Oxford University Press, 1965.

Middleton, K.R., W.E. Lee & B.F. Chamberlin. *The Law of Public Communications*. Boston: Pearson Education Inc., 2003.

MISA & Friedrich Ebert Stiftung. *African Media Barometer. Botswana 2007*. Gaborone: MISA & Friedrich-Ebert-Stiftung, 2007.

MISA. *So This Is Democracy? Report on the State of Media Freedom and Freedom of Expression in Southern Africa*. Gaborone: MISA, 2007.

Neethling, J., J.M. Potgieter & P.J. Visser. *Law of Delict*. 3rd edn. Durban: Butterworths, 1999.

Otlhogile, B. *A Casebook on Defamation*. Mimeo: University of Botswana, 1995.

Prosser, W.L. & G.W. Keeton. *Prosser and Keeton on Torts*. 5th edn. St Paul: West Publishing, 1984.

Robertson, G. & A. Nicol. *Media Law. The Rights of Journalists and Broadcasters*. London: Oyez Longman, 1984.

Rogers, W.V.H. *Winfield & Jolowicz on Tort*. 15th edn. London: Sweet & Maxwell, 1998.

Schauer, F. *Free Speech: A Philosophical Enquiry*. Cambridge: Cambridge University Press, 1982.

Selected Bibliography

Sechele, S.T. 'The Role of the Press in Independent Botswana'. In *Botswana Politics and Society*, edited by W.A. Edge & M.H. Lekorwe. Pretoria: J.L. van Schaik, 1998.

Sechele, S.T. *Deepening Democracy or Creeping Authoritarian Rule?: Media/ Government Relations in Botswana in Historical Perspective*. Unpublished Dissertation: University of Botswana, 2000.

Smith, R.C. *Broadcasting Law and Fundamental Right*. Oxford: Clarendon Press, 1997.

Spitz, D. (ed.). *On Liberty*. New York: W.W. Norton, 1975.

Suffolk, J.C. (ed.). *Areopagitica*. London: University Tutorial Press, 1968.

Tshosa, O. 'The Status and Role of International Law in the National Law of Botswana'. In *Essays on the Law of Botswana*, edited by C.M. Fombad. Cape Town: Juta & Co., 2007, 229–246.

Zaffiro, J.J. *From Police Network to Station of the Nation. A Political History of Broadcasting in Botswana*. Gaborone: Botswana Society, 1991.

Zimbabwe Lawyers for Human Rights. *Under Siege? Freedom of Expression in Zimbabwe. 'The ANZ Saga'*. Harare: Zimbabwe Lawyers for Human Rights, n.d.

Zimmermann, R. 'Roman Law in a Mixed Legal System – The South African Experience'. In *The Civil Law Tradition in Scotland*, edited by R. Evans-Jones. Edinburgh: The Stair Society, 1995.

Others Including Electronic Sources

Balule, B.T. *Enhancing the Media's Democratic Role: A Comparative Study of the Legal Environment of the Media in Botswana and South Africa*. Unpublished PhD thesis submitted to the University of Edinburgh, 2003.

Carver, R. 'A Formula for Allocating Direct Access Slots – South Africa'. www.aceproject.org/main/english/me/mey11.htm.

Dube, C. 'Privatisation Initiative in Botswana: Any Bearing on Competition?'. *CUTSC-CIER Policy Brief*, No. 1/2008, www.cuts-ccier.org/7up3/pdf/PolicyBrief6.pdf.

Eithan L. & L. Yehiel. 'The "Right to Reply" in Journalistic Ethics: The Case Study of the Ruling by the Israel Press Council'. www.allacademic.com//met/p_mla_research_citation/0/9/0/9/6/pages9096.

Good, K. & I. Taylor. 'Presidential Succession in Botswana: No Model for Africa' (Unpublished).

Hall, R. & D. Lewin. 'Recommendations on Further Liberalisation of the Telecommunications Industry of Botswana. A Final Report to the Botswana Telecommunications Authority'. February 2005 www.bta.org.bw/pubs/Liberalisation%20Consult2.pdf.

Keoreng, E. 'Botswana: Batswana Have a Right to Know – Ombudsman'. www.mmegi.bw/index.php?sid=1&aid=12&dir=2009/April/Friday17.

Leepile, M. 'An Overview of the Press in Botswana'. Paper presented at the International Seminar on the 'Feasibility of the Ombudsman Institution in Botswana', at the University of Botswana, 2–3 November 1993.

Media Sustainability Index 2006–2007. www.irex.org/programs/MSI_Africa/2007/MSI07_Botswana.pdf.

Mendel, T. 'Public Service Broadcasting. A Comparative Survey'. www.unesco. org/webworld/publications/Mendel/features.html.

Odubeng, M. 'Mixed Feelings on Draft Code of Conduct'. *Mmegi*, Friday, 7 October 2005. www.mmegi.bw/2005/October/Friday7/8604789511836.htm.

Presidential Task Group. *Vision 2016. Long Term Vision for Botswana*. Gaborone: Government of Botswana, 1997.

Report of the Special Rapporteur. UN Economic and Social Council Doc. No. E/CN. 4/20000/63/Add.3 of 11/2/2000.

Thapisa, A.P.N. & E. Megwa. *Situation Analysis and Profile of Mass Communications in Botswana*. A Consultancy Report Prepared for the Ministry of Finance and Development Planning, 1998.

Table of Cases

The numbers here refer to the paragraph numbers.

Botswana Cases

Attorney-General v. Dow [1992] BLR 119, 37, 42, 43, 57, 184

Attorney-General v. Otlhomile [2004] 1 BLR 21, 184

Attorney-General v. Ghanzi Hotel [1986] BLR 178, 116, 120, 121, 124

Bojang v. The State [1994] BLR 146, 38

Botswana Motor Vehicle Insurance Fund v. Marobela [1999] 1 BLR 21, 45

Collins Newman & Co and Others v. Genuispoint Investment (Pty) Ltd and Others, UAHGB-000085-16 (Unreported), 111

Diau v. Botswana Building Society [2003] 2 BLR 409, 184

Dibotelo v. Sechele & Others [2001] BLR 588, 144

Ghanzi Hotel (Pty) Ltd v. A-G (No. 2) [1985] BLR 452, 121

Gobudilwe & another v. Shaobuye & another [1993] BLR 56, 116

Good v. The Attorney-General (2) [2005] 2 BLR 337, 85

Graham v. Ker [1984] BLR 138, 125

Kamanakao & Another v. Attorney-General [2001] BLR 654, 43

Karim v. Weterings [1974] 2 BLR 34, 115, 116, 121

Kgafela v. Maoto [1992] BLR 256, 116

Law Society of Botswana and Another v. The President of Botswana and Others, CACGB-031-16 (Unreported), 203

Lemo v. Northern Air Maintenance (Pty) Ltd [2004] 2 BLR 317, 184

Maauwe & Another v. Attorney-General [1999] 1 BLR 275, 45

Mabote v. Mabote [1999] 1 BLR 386, 184

Maje v. Botswana Life Insurance Ltd & Another [2001] 2 BLR 626, 146

Masieman v. Maswabi [1976–1978] BLR 92, 116

Masipa v. Leshope [1991] BLR 133, 116, 131

Media Publishing (Pty) Ltd v. Attorney-General [2001] 2 BLR 485, 21, 48, 57, 58, 99

Monyamane v. Anderson [1987] BLR 270, 116

Monyena v. Gambule [2004] 1 BLR 102, 142

Muir v. January C T 860/88, 116

Mulwa v. Mosienyane [1984] BLR 138, 116, 118, 125, 144

MultiChoice (Botswana) Pty v. National Broadcasting Board Civil Appeal 022/07 (Unreported), 47

Ngope v. O'Brien Quinn [1987] BLR 398, [1988] BLR 121, 131, 134,

Ntuane v. Your Friends (Pty) Ltd t/a GABS FM 96.2 [2003] 1 BLR 49, 47

Patrick Motlhwa v. The State CR APP 175/82, 121

Outsa Mokone v. Attorney General and Others, UAHGB-000153-14 (Unreported), 72

Petrus & Another v. The State [1984] BLR 14, 184

Ramantele v. Mmusi and Others, CACGB-104-12 (Unreported), 203

Sesana v. Attorney-General [2006] 2 BLR 633, 16

Students' Representative Council of Molepolole College of Education v. Attorney-General [1995] BLR 178, 43

Tsodilo Services (Pty) Ltd t/a Sunday Standard and others v. Tibone [2011] 2 BLR 494, 140, 142

Your Friend (Pty) Ltd t/a Gabz FM v. Law Society of Botswana and Others, CACGB-130-15 (Unreported), 111, 112

Cases from Other Jurisdictions

A (Respondent) v. British Broadcasting Corporation (Appellant) (Scotland) [2014] UKSC 25, 111

Abrams v. US 250 US 616, 630–631 (1919), 53

Application for Review of Judgment No. 333 of the United Nations Administrative Tribunal Case ICJ Reports 1987, 38

Application of Cojuangco (No. 2) (Unreported, New South Wales Supreme Court, 6 January 1989, 106

Argus Printing and Publishing Co. Ltd v. Inkatha Freedom Party [1992] 3 SA 579 (A), 120

Ashworth Security Hospital v. MGN Ltd [2002] UKHL 29, 106

Association of Independent Journalists & Others v. The Minister of State for Information and Publicity & Others SC 136/02, 87

Attorney-General v. Leveller Magazine Ltd [1979] AC 440, 450, 111

Table of Cases

Table of Cases

Index

The numbers here refer to the paragraph numbers.

Index

Index

Made in the USA
Monee, IL
13 September 2026

62974264R00109